Mr. Wrong

Mr.  Wrong

Real-Life Stories About the Men We Used to Love

Edited by Harriet Brown

Ballantine Books   New York

Published in the United States by Ballantine Books,
an imprint of The Random House Publishing Group,
a division of Random House, Inc., New York.

BALLANTINE and colophon are registered trademarks
of Random House, Inc.

The essay entitled "My First Husband's Girlfriend and Me"
by Caroline Leavitt was originally published on Salon.com
in February 2000.

ISBN 978-0-345-49021-6

Library of Congress Cataloging-in-Publication Data
Mr. Wrong : real-life stories about the men we used to
    love / edited by Harriet Brown.
        p. cm.
    ISBN 978-0-345-49021-6
        1. Mate selection—Anecdotes. 2. Man-woman
    relationships—Anecdotes. I. Brown, Harriet.

    HQ801.M793 2007
    306.82—dc22

                                            2006049859

Printed in the United States of America on acid-free paper

www.ballantinebooks.com

9 8 7 6 5 4 3 2 1

First Edition

Text design by Laurie Jewell

Contents

Introduction

Harriet Brown

*M*r. Wrong is the tug behind your navel, the guy who lights you up like a Roman candle, the danger you can't resist. At some point in her life, just about every woman encounters one—or many.

He's the fellow who lives on a houseboat (seasick sex, anyone?), the guy who can't sweat. The one who's thrown out of a restaurant because of the hideous orange coat that makes him look homeless or deranged (or both). The med student who says, at least once a day, "My body is my temple." The banker who insists on eating kimchi before making love. The classical guitarist with inch-long fingernails on one hand. The guy with the banana-shaped penis (it hurts!). The man who thinks bathing once a week is enough (it's not). The one who can't get it up and the one who won't go down. The married man who's been having affairs for twenty-five years and says his wife doesn't know. Right.

And those were just the ones *I'd* run into.

I don't think I've had especially bad luck when it comes to men (although I will never, ever eat kimchi again). What I do think is that to date men is to experience the full range of male behaviors, from harmless to charming and, occasionally, on to revolting and offensive. I'm sure there's a similar statement to be made about dating women, but that's another book.

So why, I wondered, do so many beautiful, charming, intelligent, sexy women (and men) get tangled up with tacky, untrustworthy men? Why do we race around and around the gerbil wheel of a dead-end love affair? As I began talking to other people about their Mr. Wrongs, I realized that no matter how freakishly idiosyncratic these guys were, they all had one thing in common: they fulfilled some need of ours. They were the other half of the broken locket, the key to the locked door, the last piece of the puzzle. They clicked with us on a primal level that went beyond words, intellect, or sense. They triggered all-too-familiar feelings of loss and abandonment and shame. Like parasites, they had an uncanny ability to burrow to the heart and stay there.

We tend to go for what's familiar, even if it's unpleasantly so—the devil you know and all that. And then there's the incandescent sex: Say what you will about their other qualities (or lack thereof), many Mr. Wrongs make a career out of pleasing women in bed. Well, they have to have *something* going for them.

As the veteran of more crappy relationships than I like to admit, I have come to understand that while Mr. Wrongs *can* be sadistic, mind-fucking, manipulative, lying, cheating dirtbags, sometimes the trouble isn't with them at all. It's with us. It's with our habit of projecting our own insecurities, our fears of failure and success, commitment and love, loneliness and loss, onto the seemingly blank screen of another person. True, sometimes a guy is just a guy, and a bad romance is just a bad romance. But most of us see it coming and still don't get out of the way. We see the red flags and we say to ourselves, *Gee, this seems like a bad idea.* And then we do it anyway.

Every bad relationship that lasts more than a week or two does so because it triggers some of our deepest, darkest, most uncomfortable feelings. I still squirm at the memory of one of mine, one that I knew practically from the first moment was doomed for all sorts of reasons. I was a fish twisting on the hook, and he was reeling me in for the sheer sport of it. Or at least that's how it felt.

Then one night I dreamed he was walking across my living room floor when—poof!—his head popped off and my father's head appeared on his body. I woke up laughing: Of course, why didn't I see it before? No wonder I couldn't extricate myself. And embarrassed: what a Freudian cliché! And crying: Why did this man, this *kind* of man, still hold so much power in my life?

You can learn a lot about yourself from a truly soul-sucking relationship.

Of course, it works both ways: we, too, are Ms. (and Mr.) Wrongs, the stars of other people's bad-relationship stories. We, too, fail to be kind enough, sexy enough, loving enough. Sometimes we're just not that into *them,* either.

Which, maybe, explains in part why true stories about Mr. Wrong can have the appeal of romance novels. The plot may stay the same—boy meets girl, girl falls hard, boy proves spectacularly unsatisfactory—and we know how the story will turn out. But it's still deliciously cathartic to hear how others have succumbed and overcome.

The real-life stories in this collection run the emotional gamut, from jealousy and despair to revenge and redemption. In Whitney Otto's eminently satisfying essay, for instance, one Mr. Wrong gets his comeuppance in an unexpected way. Robin Westen's steamy account of her relationship with an oversexed Zen master embodies the ultimate power trip. Jane Smiley writes about the intersection of romance and socialism in the 1960s. Jackie Mitchard describes a relationship that was absolutely perfect—except for one little thing (and I *do* mean little).

Sometimes—maybe most of the time—we blame ourselves when romance unravels. Caroline Leavitt writes movingly about how it took a series of phone calls from her ex-husband's next lover to help her understand and let go of a failed marriage. Roxana Robinson's essay about going to senior prom with a boy she barely knew evokes the self-consciousness, longing, and confusion of adolescence—and beyond. Raphael Kadushin's account of love at first French kiss sets the stage for the loss of his youthful innocence, while Ethel Smith's wry riff on cyberdating after forty is a convincing argument for friendships of the nonsexual kind.

Some of these essays are laugh-out-loud funny, like Sara Ekks's rueful "I Married a Wanker!" and Marion Winik's "The Ten Most Wanted." Some, like Joyce Maynard's "Your Friend Always" and Catherine Texier's "Russian Lessons," take us to the dark side of love and longing. And some speak to our own longings, like Susan Jane Gilman's essay "I'm Still Waiting . . ." and Audrey Niffenegger's beautifully written "The Composite Boyfriend." All of them, I hope, will both entertain you and give you something to think about.

For every Prince Charming there are a million frogs. If you've ever trusted a man you couldn't trust, turn the page, dear reader, and see if you recognize yourself in any of these true tales of love gone wrong.

Mr. Wrong, that is.

The Guru

Robin Westen

If anyone peeked at the hand I was dealt they would see all aces. In the mid-nineties I had a glamorous job writing for television with an Emmy Award to prove it, a handsome British boyfriend, Zeke, a spacious downtown loft, a purse packed with credit cards, perfectly manicured nails, and plenty of shiny baubles. I spent lunch hours at designer boutiques and evenings ordering martinis in New York's high-profile restaurants.

But behind my *Sex-and-the-City*-Dream-Life-come-true, I was feeling like a clam ripped of her pearl, empty and searching for what I'd lost. I wondered from a place deep in my core: "Is this *all*? Is this *IT*?"

I was probably propelled toward introspection because despite the glitz, these were tough times. My mother was battling breast cancer, my relationship with the cool Brit often left me longing for fire, and my television work felt flimsy and meaningless. The glittering veil was flapping.

During my period of cosmic questioning, out of the blue a photographer showed up at my office door. Expecting to give his book no more than a cursory glance, I ended up lingering over each image, *stunned*. The pictures felt oddly alive, shimmering with translucent color.

"It's called Kirlian photography," he said in a hush. "As you can see, there's an aura or life force that surrounds each living thing. These colors"—his fingers fluttered like bird wings above the picture—"are the physical manifestation of this energy."

Then the searing look: "Of course, most of us *can't* see this stuff with our naked eyes."

Okay, I was at a particularly vulnerable moment in my life, and perhaps susceptible to spiritual hype, but I was no fool. This sounded like hooey.

"I'm pretty busy," I said, snapping his book shut and feeling uncomfortable, bristling as my defenses spiked.

Before leaving, he handed over a card with a downtown address written on it. I tossed it on top of a pile of papers, expecting never to give it a second glance.

But I was dead wrong.

There's a Buddhist adage: "When you're ready, your teacher will find you." It didn't take long. The very next day, the mysterious photographer reappeared at my office door; this time he wasn't alone. Beside him stood a stocky Asian man with a shaved head and a rock-steady gaze. He wore a midnight-blue velvet shirt over his round-as-the-globe belly, jean shorts, and flip-flops. It was the dead of winter.

Our encounter was so shockingly out of place within the context of my daily office routine that I was suddenly struck dumb. Like a mime I beckoned the odd pair inside my office, shutting the door behind us.

The photographer gave a few directions. "Just sit across from Master Eknath and look into his eyes. No talking."

It didn't occur to me to question why they were here or whether this was a good idea; suddenly I had no thoughts. Simply, it was clear that I should do just as suggested, and I seated myself as instructed. I let my gaze settle on the master's eyes and within minutes—or an eternity—everything turned into a flickering grid of light.

Oddly, the light show seemed perfectly normal. More striking was the sudden infusion of love pouring into me like smooth cream from a pitcher. This was love at first sight, the unsentimental version. After about five minutes of relentless eyes-to-eyes gazing, Master Eknath stood up abruptly and said, "We'll see you soon." Then the odd couple turned around and walked out of my office. Just like that.

What transpired on that day is still in many ways a mystery to me, but what I can tell you is that some kind of psychic door or channel opened and everything around me shifted. I suddenly felt simpatico with my colleagues—even those who only hours before had scratched like needles against my skin. The script I wrote that afternoon breezed along as if I had a direct line to the muse. And I was happy. Happier than I had felt in months.

It seemed only natural to follow the yellow brick road. I reached for the card tossed aside the day before and called Zeke to cancel our evening plans.

After work, I went straight to Eknath's martial arts studio, which was off a busy New York cross street. When I walked in, I scanned the room and saw Eknath sitting on a round cushion at the head of the studio, posture erect, eyes lowered, looking impressive and serene, like an overstuffed pasha. Several dozen lithe and attractive men and women dressed in ghostly white moved silently in front of him in a series of slow tai chi movements.

I stood by the door, shy and uncomfortable and thinking I had made a ridiculous mistake. Just as I was about to turn and walk out, Eknath's boom-box voice bellowed, *"Come! Here!"* He beckoned me with a patting gesture to sit on the floor beside him. I remember feeling terribly self-conscious, but I obeyed, folding my legs and sitting as still as I could for almost an hour. There I was, the Queen to King Tut. And once again bathed in a feeling of all-is-well-with-the-world. Simply, I felt *golden.*

Let me admit right here: Even before rooting around my inner life of awareness, I knew this much about myself. It wasn't looks or money that grabbed my heart (my recent handsome boyfriend the exception); it was power and dominance. Thus, my romantic history included falling for—and bedding—my college professors, a couple of bosses, a well-known broadcasting mogul, an aging pop artist, a renowned opera impresario who was old enough to be my grandfather, and a narcissistic politician. Many of these men were married. Yet even with this eclectic repertoire, it never occurred to me that a short, fat, middle-aged, manipulative, and conniving cult leader could ever be added to the list.

But I should have known better. Love *is* blind, or, more likely, as Bruce Springsteen put it: "I was blinded by the light."

If Jim Jones could get 913 followers to commit mass suicide, wasn't it possible for a charismatic Zen master to gaze into my eyes and convince me to leave my boyfriend, no longer fraternize with friends and colleagues, and give up the glamorous life of restaurant-hopping and designer shopping in exchange for twelve hours a day of meditation, manual labor on the cult's rustic estate, unquestioned obedience, and the willingness—no, *eagerness*—to hand over several thousand dollars as well as sex on demand?

Experts who study cults say it's usually the best and the brightest at a vulnerable moment in their lives who are most susceptible to falling for unscrupulous gurus. Eknath's Zen cult was no exception. His glassy-eyed followers, who forked over thousands of dollars monthly, were attractive and accomplished, among them a lawyer, an architect, a computer software executive, the owner of an advertising agency, a renowned artist and pop singer, a couple of Connecticut socialites, a published author and journalist, and several university graduate students studying everything from molecular chemistry to social work. Red flags, flashing lights, screeching sirens should have been going off in my head, and they were. But I turned away and opened the window instead.

After I had gone through a month of tai chi classes, meditated with the group three times weekly, and paid five thousand dollars for a series of *energizings* to help clear my system of "bad vibes," Master Eknath was waiting outside the ABC studios in his black Mazda Miata to whisk me away for an energizing session—free of charge. "What an honor," I thought, innocently enough.

A CD of Louis Armstrong's *What a Wonderful World* was playing as he sped along the West Side Highway en route to a park underneath the George Washington Bridge. I sat bolt upright in the leather seat (trying to hold my meditation posture), staring unabashedly at my driver, utterly mesmerized by Eknath's huge stomach, the way his stubby fingers grabbed the gear shift, the snapping clack of his chewing gum. *Everything* about him felt irresistible, and by the time we reached the park, innocence had gone on a hike; my body was aching for the master's touch.

I didn't have to wait long. As Master Eknath led me along a steep path, he suddenly stopped and pulled me so close I could feel his breath against my neck. "You'll come deep and hard for the *Universe*," he whispered into my ear as his fingers deftly lifted my Prada shift. A few minutes later the Universe was vibrating. Eknath, it turned out, was also a master of clitoral massage, and my orgasm sprang from so deep inside me and traveled with such velocity through my body that it was as if a switch, one I never knew existed, had been flipped on: sexually charged—one thousand watts and burning.

For the past few months I had been futilely trying to ignite sparks under my coolly British Zeke. This was instantaneous combustion. Within a month of my first rendezvous with the Zen master, Zeke and I were splitting our joint possessions down the middle and I was leaving our spacious loft for a ground-floor hovel in the West Village.

Precious real estate—2,000 square feet of New York City rent-controlled loft—forfeited. But I was dazed by my sudden sexual connection to the Universe, as well as the spiritual practice at the tai chi studio where I attended classes now *every* night after work, and my devotion to the powerful Eknath and his ability to make me shudder and come with fingers, tongue, and his surprisingly puny but adept penis. I considered a lost loft worth the sacrifice.

Most women can recall at least one man who so meshed with their body's needs that sex became like a drug. But my connection with Eknath leapt to another dimension. Sex with him was exactly as Shelley Duvall described to Woody Allen in the classic film *Annie Hall*. It was *transcendental*. Yet this was no Hollywood yarn. It was real-life consumption.

We met each evening on the sly after the tai chi classes, unbeknownst to his other students. Sometimes Eknath came to the apartment where I lived sparingly with only a desk, two straight-backed chairs, a bureau, a bed, a meditation cushion, dinner service for two (guess who?), and a wok to stir-fry meals for Eknath.

But more often we went to his penthouse apartment for a five-star seduction. There Eknath would slowly pull off my clothes and then lower me into a sudsy warm bath. After caressing my body with a soft sponge, he would help me out of the water, tenderly wrap my relaxed-as-a-lemming body in a fluffy towel, oil me down with jasmine, and slide me between his silk sheets. Then he would slowly, very slowly, work to arouse me to such heights, I eventually, and quite literally, left my body. As crazy as this might sound, without the use of drugs, alcohol, or staged special effects, when Eknath was inside me I saw the constellations: stars and planets and lights whipping around like a strobe.

In a few months, I was as utterly lost to him as a dog devoted to her master. Eknath knew it. In fact, I was convinced he knew *everything*. He would often tell me where I went for lunch and what I ordered on those afternoons we *hadn't* met. Sometimes he read my thoughts and would repeat them aloud as though he had a direct line into my mind. He predicted news events before they happened, catastrophes years in advance (one time when we were walking through the World Trade Center he said, "These buildings are temporary"). He once bought me the very dress I had tried on during a lunch hour. And he was never, ever wrong about how to keep me yearning for his practiced touch.

As the months wore on, my life revolved around Eknath in smaller and tighter circles. No longer did I share any personal news with colleagues or get together with old friends. I spoke with other cult members only on the condition that gossip or negative talk was off-limits. Weekends were spent at the Westchester Zendo, a several-million-dollar estate-in-progress forty-five minutes north of the city.

Soon Eknath was extracting a price for his attention. He made demands.

"The only underwear you can wear is this," he said one night, handing over a tight black leather thong with a silver clamp by the crotch. "Now try it on and show me how it looks."

Self-consciously I changed out of my comfortable Fruit of the Loom into the groin-killing leather bondage panties and modeled them in front of him, my head hanging, shamed. Eknath grinned, then reached out and pulled them up by the thong straps until I felt bruising from the clamp. "You'll get used to this. But don't *ever* come here unless they're on you," he said, eyes glinting.

Eknath wasn't kidding. One time I showed up at his penthouse without underwear, thinking this would be a real turn-on. He opened the door, pulled up my skirt, and pushed me away, slamming the door in my face. I wept all the way home. Feeling lost, abandoned, unloved, and hopeless, I was near suicidal. What had become of the independent, career-driven woman, the one who dangled New York City hotshots like beads on a necklace?

As time moved along, Eknath's demands became harsher and more sinister. If he was in the mood, I had to feed him while I sat on my knees. Other times he humiliated me in front of the group by announcing, "No one talk to her. She has a bad vibe." Once, he stopped his car abruptly, reached over, opened the door, and pushed me out because I had worn a scent other than jasmine.

Our lovemaking, which I continued to crave, was now mixed with smarting smacks and contorted positions. I couldn't tell the pain from the pleasure. But the light show explosions were massive. When I left his place, I walked home like a zombie in a state of arousal and misery. I was Patty Hearst without the family bucks.

Who knows how long this might have gone on and where it would have led? But almost as easily as I'd slipped into the underbelly of Eknath's manipulative world, I snapped out of it when he commanded me to carry out a particularly heinous plan.

Eknath had told me to convince a cult member's father—an extremely wealthy elderly man with a somewhat public image as a successful financier—that his daughter had written an inflammatory book claiming he had sexually molested her. I was to call the father and set up a meeting at a restaurant under the pretense that I was writing a profile of him for a magazine. Once there, I was to tell him about the book and insist it was about to be published—that is, unless he paid for the manuscript with a hefty sum.

It was a convoluted plot that only someone who was comfortable with extortion would have thought up—or arranged. I was not that person.

I got as far as the restaurant meeting. But once there, I pretended to interview the man, and never mentioned his daughter's supposed book—or that I knew her.

At the tai chi studio the next evening, I told Eknath I hadn't gone through with it. He was enraged. I watched his face turn crimson. But this time, instead of cowering or begging forgiveness or waiting for my punishment to be doled out, my brain snapped and I thought, "If he's so evolved, why is he feeling anger? Isn't he supposed to be above emotion? Judgment? Not very Zen of him!"

The veil lifted. His conceit was suddenly clear. I remember thinking, "He's powerful but not pure." That simple sentence propelled me out of the studio. I never returned.

A couple weeks later, one of Eknath's disciples phoned me with a message: "Eknath forgives you."

I slammed the phone down before the voice could reach inside and pull me out of the lonely resolve I had inhabited in my monastic apartment. No one phoned or contacted me from the group again.

Over the years, I've explored my attachment to Eknath and the cult with shrinks, friends, and lovers. Oddly enough, and probably because I made it out, I have no regrets. There's a lot to be learned when you surrender. And the biggest lesson, the one I've never forgotten for a moment since, is this:

I'm the one with the power. All I need to love is an open heart—and the will to hold on.

A Good Struggle Relationship

Jane Smiley

The year I turned twelve, I was five feet one inch, just like all the other girls in my seventh-grade class. The year I turned fourteen, I was six feet tall and still growing—taller than all the girls and all the boys in my ninth-grade class, all but two of the other students in my high school, and almost all of the teachers. I have to say that I didn't feel especially awkward, no doubt because I was oblivious with growth, but also because my preferred love object was always a horse, never a human. I got to college with no romantic experience and no actual information about human reproduction. It was my brand-new freshman roommate who told me the facts of life (as I remember, my mother's only strategy had been to make sure that I knew that "my body was a temple" and that teenage boys "sometimes get carried away"). First base, second base, third base, intercourse, 69—I was astonished. My roommate was astonished, too. But we were not astonished at the same things.

As my freshman year progressed, I made up my mind that I would get a boyfriend somehow. He would of course be a student at Yale University (I went to Vassar—most Vassar girls dated Yalies), and the admissions committee at Yale would have done, I thought, sufficient preliminary screening so that I could limit my own interviewing to the one characteristic that I prized—he had to be at least six feet five, and preferably taller than that. The most convenient thing about these sorts of guys would be that I could see them, and they could see me, from across a dark and crowded mixer.

But the statistical sample of guys over six-five was vanishingly small. Even so, with the first candidate I seemed to have hit a gold mine, literally, since his father was the president of United Fruit and he lived in Hawaii. Not to mention that he was very good-looking, personable, and funny. But it was the end of the year, he was a senior, and I was a freshman. I pined for a week, maybe.

Sophomore year I was more determined. I messed around with short guys (shorter than I was, maybe five-eleven) but they didn't give me the thing I wanted most, which was a feeling that I was feminine, and even, let's say, petite. I wanted to vanish into someone's arms, be enveloped from above, and, ideally, carried across the room and flung onto the bed. At the end of the fall semester, I found him in the newspaper. He was the center on the basketball team, six feet nine, and quite good-looking in a square-jawed way. I went to his room after lunch on one of the last Fridays before Christmas break, and I had decided to marry him (of course keeping this to myself) by the following Monday. I don't remember exactly when he told me he was a Marxist, but it would have been early on, no doubt that first weekend. He was straightforward about and even proud of his Marxist views, and one of the first things he did was to convince me that I was lucky to have escaped the moral taint of that United Fruit guy (not to mention that the Marxist was the starting center on the varsity basketball team, whereas United Fruit had sat on the bench for four solid years—obviously that meant something about manly vigor).

The Marxist's name was John. That seemed an omen, too. John and Jane. And, another bonus, John and Jane were equally retarded socially. John had never had a girlfriend, and possibly never a real date. We were twenty and twenty-two, but our social age was about fourteen.

I made it my job to collect and keep track of our compatibilities. He was a history major; I was a history minor. He was a Sagittarius; I was a Libra. His grandmother was one of the Bookers, from Columbia, Missouri; my grandfather was one of the Graveses, from not far from Columbia, Missouri. Our mothers' birthdays were two days apart. We were both bookish. We were both easygoing (habitually deferential, I see now). But above all, we were both tall. He was so tall that when his high school class went to the Smithsonian on a class trip and looked at the display that demonstrated the range of human heights, the 99th percentile only came up to his ear. I was a great audience for his adventures in height: at a year old, still not walking, he looked three, and women would come up to his mother carrying him in the grocery store and commiserate with her on having such a backward child. At the age of eight, he wore a men's size eight shoe. In second grade, he was five two, sixth grade, six two, etc. Height had shaped him in a way that it had not shaped me. He had cultivated not being awkward; he had made himself athletic.

I don't know what made him a Marxist, but he was the first one I had ever met. I viewed it as an interesting quirk in a medievalist, and I thought it was funny that he would write papers that showed how the reign of Pepin the Short, in the eighth century, demonstrated Marx's aphorism that power comes from the barrel of a gun. I was a little scandalized that he felt in his heart that the president of Yale deserved to be shot, but I knew instinctively that he was too normal to ever act on that feeling. Perhaps more taxing was his love of argumentation, and of taking every sort of contrarian point of view. Once I asked him why he thought he knew everything; he declared that he had thought every thought and chosen the best ones. And I believed him.

At first, we mainly disagreed about the relationship between race and class in America and the importance of environmental concerns. Both of us, of course, had little experience with race and almost no experience with class. To white children like us from the vast middle-American middle class, the United States looked transparent and normal. But I felt strongly that race was the most divisive element in American culture, whereas he thought that in the classless Marxist future, race would disappear as a factor of American society. Sometimes we argued about big cats. I felt that the end of the snow leopards as a species would be a tragedy. He didn't care about snow leopards, or Siberian tigers, or any other endangered species. Our years of arguments never resolved either of these issues to our mutual satisfaction. Needless to say, our friends didn't seem to be engaging in this sort of pillow talk, but we were too busy to notice that.

During the school year, our friends were much like we were—peppery sons and daughters of the middle class who liked to smoke dope, make jokes, play whist, and, most of the time, go to class. In June, though, John decided to join a Marxist commune for the summer and work at the Bilco Basement Door factory. After some hemming and hawing, I decided to move in with him. This new crowd, comrades rather than friends, was commanded by a skinny Marxist economics assistant professor and his less theoretical and more tactical wife. They had one five-year-old son, whose favorite game was "panthers and pigs." In the course of the summer, I pursued my political education on many fronts, not all of them voluntary.

The sociological makeup of the group was not like any I had ever known before. One guy's parents had fled Stalin. They were not happy that he was devoting his time to our group. Another guy was a son of the East Coast ruling class. At one meeting we discussed, as a group, whether he should legally change his name from "Parks" to "Parx." My first job was for a dollar seventy-five per hour (ten cents above minimum wage) at an electronics factory in West Haven. All day long I tested which end of an electrical diode was positive, and then laid the diodes on paper trays with the positive poles to the right. I was not born for this task—it took me a few days to realize that I did not have to test both ends of the diode, that in every case, the end that was not positive was negative. I sat next to a large, friendly fifty-year-old woman with a pile of red hair on her head, and while she was chatting with me, I pondered her political education. Finally, after about two weeks, I had my golden opportunity. The owner of the factory came into the sorting room and greeted the ladies. He was a slender, dark-haired, Italian-looking man, outgoing enough, maybe forty. My companion said, "Oh, there's Mr. So-and-so. He's such a nice man."

I said, "He seems to be. But wouldn't it be nice if we owned the factory, not him?"

She glanced at me, then said, "But that would be communism."

She seemed to know what she was talking about, so I didn't bring it up again.

At the commune, there was trouble. In one of the three houses, there was an unresolvable disagreement about whether one of the members should be keeping kosher. When, one day, the kosher guy was standing in his room, emptying his pockets after work, the two Afghan hounds belonging to other members ran into the room and urinated beside his bed; it was generally felt that the dogs had expressed an undeniable truth about the position of kosher observance in the household. No opiate of the masses for us!

In our house, one of the guys was revealed to be sleeping with two of the girls. The first girl was his longtime girlfriend, plain but well organized and knowledgeable. The second girl was a newcomer, younger, smaller, and with long reddish-blond hair. The entire household discussed, in the course of two evenings, whether one guy's sleeping with two women in one house was good for the commune or bad for it. I was the only one who wondered, aloud, what the girls thought of it. This question remained unanswered. When I asked a similar question a few weeks later, at a discussion of whether one of our members who had received his draft notice should go into the army and do his political work there (my question was, "What does Arthur *want* to do?"), I was disciplined. It was made clear to me that while I was welcome to cook, my input in meetings was not desirable. I stopped going to meetings. I did sit with everyone while we watched men walk on the moon. As I remember, we deplored the whole exercise because American children were living in poverty.

I was not consulted about the split in SDS between the Weathermen faction, who had long hair and promoted armed insurrection, and our faction, a Maoist faction that believed in short hair and more peaceable factory organizing. The last opinion I expressed was that I found it insulting and unjustified that Sandy, the faculty wife, was always telling us how to think. What I could not get past was the idea that a person would go against some deeply held principle if the group required it. The more they tried to educate me to accept that this was the essence of their system, the more I could not buy it. John was caught in the middle, since he agreed in his head with them and in his heart with me. Fortunately the summer ended. After I left, the big bosses from the Progressive Labor Party in Boston came down and administered a "criticism and self-criticism" session right out of *Fanshen*, a book everyone was reading about the Chinese Communist revolution of the 1950s. Although I found such a session impossible to understand, I was pleased to learn that Sandy was reprimanded for being too bossy.

After that summer, we didn't see our comrades very often. John pursued his Marxism in a scholarly and individualistic way and we enjoyed the fruits of class privilege, Yale-style. Once he brought home a book he had stolen from the stacks in the many-storied library. It was a paperbound copy of *The Communist Manifesto*. Inside the front cover was written, "From the library of William Carlos Williams." He kept it for a few weeks before I shamed him into returning it.

We got married because four students at Kent State University were shot by the National Guard and colleges and universities all over the United States went on strike. I had spent that year, my junior year, as managing editor of the *Vassar Miscellany News*. When Vassar went on strike (and Yale, of course, was in turmoil, too, because Black Panthers were being tried in New Haven), I headed up the strike newspaper and met a whole new group of girls. We published every day, usually stories we got from the underground news services about what was going on at other campuses. Our paper was printed by thermofax and ditto, which required a lot of effort, but I had taken incompletes in all of my classes, so I had a lot of time between rallies.

One day we were sitting around the table in the strike newspaper office, discussing the summer, and I complained that my boyfriend and I couldn't figure out what to do. He was graduating, but I still had a year to go. There was no reason for him to go on living in New Haven, but there didn't seem to be anything for him in Poughkeepsie.

It was perplexing. I remember that the girl sitting across from me, who had the admirable audacity to own a Great Dane, said, "Get married; they're sure to give you a car." This was the sort of worldly wisdom my family had sent me to Vassar to acquire but that I had avoided for the most part by hanging out with idealists who could plan for the revolution but never scheme for lucre.

That night, I called him. We were discussing the perennial topic of what next, and I said, "If we get married, they'll give us a car."

He said, "Let me think about it for a night."

The next night, he called and said, "Okay. Let's do it." That was the first time I was scared.

The following weekend, we went to Boston to see what we might be able to put together there. My mother was not happy about my incompletes, the strike newspaper, or American universities in general. I owed her a call, and when I placed it, she started immediately; I was wasting money, doing the wrong thing, going in the wrong direction entirely. She asked me where I was. I said I was in Boston, looking for an apartment. She started in on that. When she paused to take a breath, I said, "We decided to get married."

The line fell silent for a long time. Then she caroled, "MMM-MAAARRRied! How WONderful!" The next thing I knew, we were talking about a car.

We lived in Boston for the summer. We had a cat, whom we took for walks in the park. I worked for a man who lived in a room in a hotel and came up with get-rich-quick schemes. John worked in the warehouse at Sears. Our apartment had a bed, a chair, a lamp, a table, and a sewing machine, where I sewed my own wedding dress, copying it out of *Vogue*. Once in a while, we visited an equally unambitious friend on Martha's Vineyard. We read. We were compatible in every way, and politics only came up once. It was a Saturday afternoon in August, and we had just made love in our apartment. John fell asleep and I went out to buy a magazine. The one that attracted my eye was a new one called *Ms.* I bought it and read the first essay by Gloria Steinem. I read walking down the street. I read crossing at the light, and then crossing at the next light. I finished the essay just below the window of our apartment. I knew now, for the first time, what politics was really for. I looked up, knowing he was in there, still sleeping. I said, "That asshole." But I never did convince him of what I still believe, that race and class inequality are divisive issues, but gender inequality is the most divisive of all.

I had been careful to hide the Marxist element of our relationship from my mother; nor did she really know, though perhaps she suspected, that we were living together that summer in Boston. John was naturally well brought up and polite and his parents seemed to her to be our sort of people, but as our wedding approached, my mother kept looking at us and reassuring herself that our "children would return to the norm." What she meant was that statistically it was unlikely that either the girls or the boys would be as tall as we were. My growth pattern had spooked her, though she hadn't actually pressed me to do what some other girls did in those days, have their legs cut down surgically. The solution to my height that I had adopted, of finding an outsize mate, was, she thought, possibly just compounding the problem. Between ourselves, John and I imagined producing five boys, a whole basketball team. That was a good enough plan for me.

After the wedding, John and I lived in another commune, on a large secluded property beside the Esopus Creek in Saugerties, New York. John and two of the other boys were newly minted Yale grads— John worked as a day laborer for a guy who dug swimming pools, Steve ghost-wrote stories for true romance magazines, and Tom was a clerk in a health food store in Woodstock. Our fourth roommate, the older boyfriend of a Vassar girl, was going cold turkey from the drugs he had taken while living in Jerusalem. He supported himself by playing poker in Tannersville, but he couldn't drive. I would have to drive him to the venue and pick him up a few days later. They were all slackers, but John was the only one whose choices were backed up by theory. I completed my senior year and wrote my first novel. It was about people I knew and ended with a fictional car accident in which the rather annoying female protagonist was conveniently gotten rid of. I considered it Dostoyevskian. In the context of what our friends were doing with their educations, our decision to leave after my graduation and spend the next year hitchhiking around Europe was exceptionally ambitious.

Although John did not admire or share my desire to be a novelist—he thought novels promoted individualism, which they do—he did carry my portable typewriter in his hand for some three thousand miles and some eleven and a half months as we made our way around England, through France, down the boot of Italy, into and out of Greece and Crete, up through the Balkans to Austria and Switzerland, back to Paris, over to Denmark, then across the North Sea to London, and home. He talked Marx but he traveled as a medievalist, from Westminster to Oxford to York Minster to Winchester Cathedral to Notre Dame, St. Peter's, the Duomo, the sixth-century mosaics at Ravenna. In Greece, we visited Corinth and Delphi and Knossos, Mycenae, Athens, and Epidaurus, and it was a history buff's grand tour. He read *The White Goddess* and I read *The Bull from the Sea*, and we applied from abroad to the University of Iowa and the University of Virginia, John in medieval history and me in creative writing. He got in both places and I didn't get in to either one. We chose Iowa because it was closer to Wyoming.

In the year we were gone, we had missed the revolution in Iowa City, which had been the scene of such unrest that the university bookstore, directly across from the administration building, reduced the size of its repeatedly shattered windows to about two feet by three feet. We found ourselves a cheap rural rental, some thirty miles from campus, and began fitting into the history department. It was I who took the working-class job—sewing teddy bears in a home workshop owned by an eccentric female entrepreneur who went on, after her divorce, to join the state patrol. I made two dollars per hour, four hours per day, five days per week. John signed up for two medieval history courses and a course in which the plan was to read all of *Das Kapital.*

The Marxists in Iowa City were, unbeknownst to me, more militant than the Marxists in New Haven had been. John declared his allegiance to them by ordering a woven silken portrait of Marx from

China and sewing it to an American flag. He hung this in our rental farmhouse, though he took it down whenever the landlord came by. Our rent was twenty-five dollars per month. He began telling me that our marriage was unsatisfying to him because it was, as far as I could understand, too peaceful. The ideal was "a good struggle relationship," in which confrontation was the key. He would present, or act out, or express the "thesis." I would respond with the "antithesis," and some sort of conflict would result in a "synthesis." It sounded like a recipe for bickering to me. I thought we had enough arguing about political theory as it was. I think now, and I dimly realized at the time, that he was hoping to fire up our sex life by this means. We both sensed that our sex life, now some four years old, was much in need of some energy, but we were each other's first partners, and neither of us was uninhibited enough to learn anything on his or her own. Besides, Progressive Labor Marxists were about as far from libertines as it was possible to get. They saw that the Left was always destroying itself by choosing sex over class analysis, and so they disapproved of sex. As a writer, I had some theoretical interest in sex, but only theoretical. We had never talked about sex in my family and I wasn't about to start just because men writers did so.

But it was clear that our marriage was in a malaise. John sat around a lot and mildly tormented the cats. He did not enjoy living in the country, though in the November presidential election, he did cast the only vote in our county for Gus Hall, the Communist Party candidate. My symptom was more mysterious. I became irrationally fearful. In October, when election candidates came knocking on the door, I would cover my ears with my hands so I wouldn't hear the knocking. If our puppy ran off, I would be afraid to go find him. I would lie awake in the night, imagining people silently pouring gasoline around the foundations of the house, then setting us on fire. I woke up at every noise. I knew with absolute conviction that as tall as he was, as athletic as he was, he would not save me if we were raided in our house and put to the sword. He might distantly wish to, but he wouldn't have the wherewithal to do it—was it love that was missing, or conviction, or ability? I had no idea, but I felt that I had no protector and was facing all sorts of dangers entirely on my own. In the meantime, I believe, our Marxist friends in Iowa City had picked another, more political mate for him. I don't think they were actively campaigning to get rid of me, but it was clear that my individualism and artistic ambitions put me on the wrong side of the barricades. John's loyalties might have been to me in the first commune, but not so much anymore. One guy in particular—oddly, one I had known in high school—was spending at least some time driving a wedge between us.

In the end, though, it was my fearfulness that broke the spell. A bartender checking IDs gave me a compliment. It was a sexier and more sophisticated compliment than any John had ever given me. It was not a brotherly compliment or a comfortable or a cool compliment. It was a compliment that said *I want to fuck you* and elicited an answering desire in me. I was twenty-three. I got the compliment on a Thursday. I stayed in town that night and the next night, and when John came in to pick me up on Saturday, I said, "I think I want to have an affair. What do you think about that?" Most of the people we knew in Iowa City were sleeping with more than one person, so I expected to be, if not celebrated for my new idea of liberation, at least honored for it. But John said, "No. I don't want you to do that," and I said, "Then I guess I'm leaving you," and that was that. We were broken up by Monday. He moved into town and finished the school year, then moved to Boston. He left behind almost everything we owned together, not only the dog and cats but also the car, the wedding gifts, the *Gourmet* cookbooks, the Marx flag, the furniture, and the television. He took the stereo. Everything else gathered dust in the house while I drove around on the back of my new lover's motorcycle, smashing my fears to smithereens.

A few years later, John and I had two children apiece with other spouses. In stature, they returned (what a relief) to the norm—my daughters turned out to be five-eight and five-nine, and his son got to six-four, while his daughter stopped at six feet. I have often joked that my older daughter must be his child, really, since she is political to the core (in 2002, when she went to Washington to intern for Tom Harkin, a senator from Iowa, she was appalled to discover that the city was jam-packed with Republicans "who aren't ashamed of themselves!"). John's twenty-six-year-old son is working in the very bar in Iowa City where I was plucked from John a generation ago by a bartender. When we were discussing his son's future, John said that, well, it took him until he was thirty-three to find himself. So his Marxist period qualifies as the lost years.

The wrong ones are often so obviously wrong, but in other circumstances, I used to think, in another generation, perhaps, John and I would not have been wrong. We were well-matched physically, educationally, temperamentally. We were a sort of American ideal—promising youngsters plucked out of the middle by meritocratic tests and groomed for leadership. We might never have known what we were missing in our sex lives. He might never have respected my work, but lots of women novelists have been married to men who had no respect for their work. In that other life, we might have ended up as a pleasant academic couple whiling away the years at a nice university somewhere, with a basketball team of boys leaving their giant shoes by the door.

But then, one day a few years ago, when John's wife and daughter were driving around Yorkshire, England, they saw a road sign with their name on it. John's name is an unusual one, so they followed the sign and came to a large estate. They asked around concerning the local history, and were told that that family had fled to Ireland after the Guy Fawkes Rebellion of 1605, in which a group of unreformed Catholics plotted to blow up the Houses of Parliament with a massive charge of gunpowder. John had always wondered why he was a Catholic with an English name. Now he knew. What I saw when he told me this story was our own apparently contingent circumstances nested, the way they always are, in a history that we were unaware of. I saw a tall man in a ruff, his plot foiled and his life upended, and I saw his wife, shadowy behind him in a long gown, who hadn't realized he actually meant what he said about blowing the ruling class to kingdom come.

I Married a Wanker!

Sara Ekks

"I've never told anyone this before," he said, and my mind immediately started racing through the options. My husband stood before me, globes of sweat coalescing on his forehead, twisting long fingers before him. His wedding band was thin and intricate, a handcrafted band with two colors of gold intertwined as a vine. Apparently I was about to receive a confession.

"Is he about to tell me he's gay?" I asked myself, considering that if it was merely homosexuality, I wouldn't be personally insulted, and we could cry and decide whether or not we wanted to stay married and build a domestic partnership.

Marriage, after all, did not originate as a manifestation of romantic love but fulfilled a variety of practical, social, and political ends. Visions of lacy princesses in white are a highly propagandized marketing fiction, Disney meets Kinsey, of the last century.

Unfortunately, the enemy had colonized my mind: I was supposed to be a ballerina and marry a fireman and produce smart and handsome children who could execute grand jêtés and rescue kittens from burning buildings. Things hadn't worked out that way. I was an overweight and depressed clerical worker at a professional association, no tulle or toe shoes in sight. The castle was an unrehabilitated fixer-upper with holes in the floor and cavernous dents in the plaster.

"What if he's a pedophile?" I speculated. That would clearly be unacceptable, and if he told me too much I'd have to decide whether or not to report him. Also, having kids would be out of the question. My head spun. What was he about to say? I tallied ten perversions and vices in a nanosecond: he didn't drink too heavily, too often; didn't smoke dope; owned one fairly nancy pink tank top that I despised but otherwise dressed poorly enough to indicate that he was indisputably heterosexual; we had no money for him to gamble . . . what indulgence was left?

"How do they say it at those meetings?" he continued. " 'Hi, I'm Edward, and I'm hopelessly addicted to bondage porn.' " He stammered and looked at the floor, then raised his right hand to his wire rims and adjusted them as if about to commence a lecture. "This is pornography of the absolute worst kind. It would shock and appall you. It has no redeeming artistic, social, or political aspects whatsoever. I've been this way for as long as I can remember." He paused and swallowed.

"When I was five I used to play 'prisoners' with my cousin, Maryann, where we'd take turns being naked and caged." Edward apparently felt compelled to keep standing before me. I supposed that I had no alternative except to listen, although I was more comfortable gazing at the philodendron behind him. "And I remember getting as excited as a five-year-old could possibly be . . ." He went on to detail highlights from his latency as a bondage porn enthusiast, including a particular episode of *Charlie's Angels* where one of the angels was bound, gagged, and tied to a chair. I wondered how he handled jump rope in gym, or if pursuing a Boy Scout badge in knot-tying held any particular allure. I also cursed my own dumb luck, that I'd managed to find a guy who didn't like to fuck.

"When did this start?" I asked. The prompt was really unnecessary— he seemed to want to talk about it. Also, if he'd been kinked at five, and then preferred pulling the pud to doing the deed upon maturity, perhaps our declining conjugal relations were not due to my innate hideousness. This was the proverbial unacknowledged five-ton elephant in the room. It also explained his undergraduate concentration in erotic literature at a notoriously politically correct design-your-own-program liberal arts college. The capital D of my own denial had been twelve feet tall and neon throughout. Now I recognized my blindness—of course, and the massive argument that we'd had when we first drove out to meet his parents, burning miles of toll road with a fight about porn.

"It really started when I was twelve. I have masturbated to pornography virtually every day since then. It follows a completely addictive cycle. I have some material, and will get more, and get completely disgusted with myself and say that I'm going to quit and throw it all out, but then I'll get one piece, and in no time at all I'm up to full speed." Edward nodded and scratched one of his elbows. I imagined him with a rosy dunce's cap and a placard around his neck that read *Masturbator*. Sure, everybody would qualify, but tweaking one's own meat always struck me as recreational maintenance, not the main course. Something you do out of itchy deprivation, not a legitimate replacement, particularly not if you have a partner with a healthy libido tapping your shoulder. Though it could be argued that having a relationship with a primarily physical component constitutes masturbating on another person. Potentially rude, particularly if the other party harbors romantic notions.

"What's 'full speed'?" I wondered, but didn't want to inquire, not really wanting to know. I was Alice falling down the rabbit hole. I had a moment of proprietary resentment toward those "wasted" erections, the fact that if he could jerk off to whatever his thing was however many times a day, he ought to have possessed the testicular fortitude to give me the vigorous nightly boning that struck me as one of the main motivations for marriage: knowing where your next fuck is coming from.

"What books have *you* been reading?" a girlfriend marveled when I shared this theory with her, that I should be well loved on a daily basis. There's a compelling case to be made for quality over quantity, but why not shoot for both? I have since conceded that perhaps we were just incompatibly addicted.

As more details spilled from Edward's mouth, I wondered how I could have been so blind, that every painful incident that I had chosen to ignore indeed pointed to the fact that I had married a man who was not interested in sex. Well, no—Edward was quite interested in sex, just not the sort that involved coitus between two cheerful consenting parties who were not tied up.

I have heard repeatedly that you're either kinked or you're unkinked. I personally favor plenty of uninhibited athletic fucking and considerate and virtuoso oral attention (hey, I won't complain about well-intentioned attempts). My longest-lasting fuckbuddy was a muscular masseur, and I have had the occasional quickie in a public location. But I would never want to be tied up. Too scary. I'd like to think that I've been both generous and enthusiastic in intimate practice, but I need the option of opting out at any moment. That, and there are enough inevitable humiliations in daily life; it doesn't twirl my turban to seek them out recreationally. In fact, I felt somewhat queasy as he visibly brightened when describing the particulars of his solitary endeavors.

"I'm not into photos. I prefer text," Edward said, nodding, a slight smile unfolding despite the circumstances.

"Yep, that's the undergrad in erotic literature," I thought. "That's unusual, for a male," I said.

His head moved up and down and he went on, warming to the subject. "And I prefer domination stories written from the female perspective, where she's enjoying it."

It was my turn to nod. A year and a half earlier I'd become quite upset when I came home from work for our first married celebration of my birthday and discovered a story entitled "Sharing Wendy" on the computer desktop. A scan of the first page was more than enough. "Is this what he wants?" I'd clutched the sides of my head in anguish and gazed into the blue glow of the monitor. "To not have sex with me but to force me to display my genitals to a platoon of random rednecks? And one among them named 'Eustace,' with a handlebar moustache and a neckwarmer haircut, gets to shave me? Using banana pudding in lieu of shaving cream?"

We fought about it, Edward accusing me of being too easily upset, that it was just something that he'd found online and had downloaded for curiosity's sake. That's entertainment. He made a delicious pork tenderloin with an apricot chutney the next evening, a belated birthday dinner. That night, he had a migraine.

This night, the pain rested in my fatigued heart, and my eyes and hands were miraculously dry, the only thought in my head being, "But of course." I oscillated between sorrow and rage, sad at this ending and irate that he had never told me. It was like there was another woman from day one, even if it was his right hand and some pulp paper. I had even put doing the nasty as an injunction in our wedding vows, or, as the officiant more decorously instructed, "Make love often."

Why *had* I decided to marry him? Possibly because he was the first guy who'd asked, and I hate dating. Marriage was supposed to be different, to make me a good citizen, wholesome and fulfilled. Fucking for the Fatherland, almost. My mind began to catalog the incidents that I had chosen to ignore.

It was early summer, and we hadn't even been married a year. One weekend afternoon, I forget exactly how the interlude commenced, I was surprised and delighted to find myself tossed up against the bedroom wall, not fully unclothed, and going at it. Edward had been cooking something (our common cultural interests and relative domesticity were traits that I appreciated), and the timer went off, a "bing" echoing up the stairs from the kitchen below. He promptly stopped, withdrew, pulled his pants up, and went downstairs to the kitchen. He did not come back. I stood, aghast, and eventually went about my business.

Ladies and gentlemen, I submit to you that there are some times in life when you just burn the biscuits.

I gazed at my spouse as he continued to detail his pastime.

"But you can't say that this is because I'm angry at women, unless it's possible to be angry at women from age five." Edward folded his arms across his chest in indignation and attempted to jut his jaw.

"Honey, it's possible to be angry at women from age two," I replied.

In fact, by age two it might be too late. I shuddered at the thought that my own quirky batch of character defects might be cast in behavioral concrete. Are all sadistic impulses derived from "I hate you, Mommy"? When Edward stumbled in from his initial bout with a recommended and long-overdue therapist, the first phrase out of his mouth was: "I'm not sure how I feel about my mother." The Angela Carter that I've read since said that it is terror of love that drives the Sadeian libertine. But we both had our intimacy "issues."

"I've never been in any relationship longer than a year," he said. I considered, but did not share, that I hadn't, either, really. It tended to be, "It's four—there's the door" or "You're still here, so you might be a boyfriend. Can you talk?" with an expiration date of a year or so. Arrangements more than relationships. The ones who hold my interest don't match my stamina. The ones who can meet my energy are occasionally nonconversant. The notable exception (not a husband) broke my heart. And if I'm going to compromise my aesthetic standards, I might as well find an earner. What is the healthy choice? There's emotional and spiritual growth, but like most, I'm superficial and would prefer emotional and spiritual growth with a materially secure attractive person.

"I'm kind of weird about sex," he stammered. "When it first starts, I'll stop my thing, because I'm happy to be having sex, but after a few months, I start up again . . ." I gazed at Edward, thinking, "My husband, the compulsive masturbator" and "Yep, he looks like a wanker," becoming critical of the previously attractive shaved head (to camouflage a receding hairline), sliding spectacles, emaciated frame, and weak chin. "Wanker," I thought, increasingly appreciating the British term, turning it over in my brain. "Wanker, wanker, wanker. Wanker."

"I can't function sexually unless I'm thinking about it," he explained. "When we make love, I have to think of one of my stories." At this point, I began to feel more sad than angry. I may have had unrealistic expectations of my husband, expecting to be "fixed" or actualized by another person, but I had thought that most males like sex. My previous experience had indicated that this was the case, to the extent that they operate with galling presumptuousness and will do anything with a hole and a heartbeat.

So, not only had we not been having enough sex for my taste, he hadn't even been making love with me, but instead let my body function as a scrim for whatever he had to project in order to get the job done. Whoever, whatever, or however I was was, in fact, completely irrelevant. The lingerie episode surfaced in my memory.

I've always been more conservative than my body count would suggest, enjoying the basics but not finding frills necessary, and I generally dislike any sexual accessory beyond basic black lace. The other stuff strikes me as tacky and a bit off-putting. Perhaps this is more insecurity—"If you want me, you want me as I am, and won't need that other crap." However, after a year and a half with Edward, I was ready to try new things. Not quite up to any hot-pink nippleless studded Frederick's of Hollywood number, I purchased a tasteful matching camisole and tap-pants set in a mauve floral pattern, matte crepe, not satiny fabric. I went to the department store on my lunch break, and that evening pulled the lingerie from its flat green paper bag as Edward watched television in an adjacent room. The ivory tissue paper rustled as I unfolded it to expose the loungewear. It looked pretty, like I wanted to be. I attempted to arrange myself with nonchalant allure on top of the bedspread and cracked a book to read as I waited for him to get through with his programming. The TV clicked off, and I heard his steps in the hallway. Edward stepped into the bedroom. He didn't say anything, at first, but paused, startled, and then uttered, "Hey."

"Hey," I replied. He wandered to his side of the bed and sat down, removing shoes, his watch. He stripped to his underwear, white T-shirt and boxers, and then climbed into bed. At moments like this I liked the routine, the monotony of marriage, as if I'd been suddenly and unexpectedly cast in a black-and-white fifties sitcom version of my life. The "That Wacky Porn Addict" episode had never occurred to me, though.

"Edward," I said.

"What?" he said.

"This," I replied, putting down the book and touching the ribbon trim of the camisole's strap, then the loose pleats on my thigh. "Do you like this?"

"Well, sure, but . . ."

"But what?"

"You aren't doing it right." At this point a siren of confusion exploded in my brain. "Doing it right"? Was I supposed to have tied the underwear around my head?

"What do you mean?" I sat up, crossed my legs, and raised my palms to him in supplication. "What do you mean, 'Doing it right'?"

"I don't know," he sputtered. "Couldn't you ask a girlfriend? Why don't you ask Naomi? Shouldn't you come in and do a little dance or something?"

"Why should I have to?" I was almost in tears. Didn't he want me for me? Did he want me at all? Why did he marry me if he didn't want to make love to me? What was I doing wrong? These questions were answered by Edward's continuing litany of his practice unreeling before me. What I was doing "wrong" included being an actual human with expectations and desires, and, admittedly, a history and an agenda, none of which were served by partnership with a man who eventually found the fortitude to explain why he acted as if I were physically repulsive.

"How did you manage in Honduras?" I asked. Edward had just returned from a scientific expedition with cramped quarters and little privacy. Wandering off into the bush for self-indulgence may have resulted in ill-located insect bites, or perhaps have offended a burro.

"Oh, just fine," he responded. I decided at that moment that the less I knew of the logistical particulars, the better. Frequency, location, and duration were things that I did not need to know. After more than twenty years of continuous practice, he was a pro. Specific events kept coming to mind.

When the lingerie hadn't worked, I'd upped the ante. For our first anniversary, I got my navel pierced. I have never found piercing appealing, but I was in San Francisco on business, and it struck me as appropriate to the spirit of the city and a nice present for him, seeing that he'd said that he found it attractive. A real sign of commitment. And already, then, I wanted more sex. The piercing itself was an adventure, performed by a muscular blond Austrian woman named Hexella. I chose the blue bead instead of the silver. The pain buzz was reinforced by the red-hot chicken vindaloo I had to celebrate the occasion. "Interesting," I'd thought, comparing the two phenomena as I guzzled ice water at the counter of the Siddhartha Café.

"Interesting," Edward said when I peeled back the square band-aid to reveal his treat, my testimony in flesh. "You got this for me? But you said that you don't like piercing."

"Happy anniversary," I said.

It did not have the desired effect. I made excuses, seeing that it was initially infected, and a fetalike discharge could render even a favorite fetish unattractive. If it had been clean right off, he would have showed how much he liked the gesture. He really meant to: he just didn't do it, didn't check it and kiss it playfully to make it better because of the draining and bandage. By the time it was healed, it had just lost its novelty to him. That must be it.

For our second anniversary, I came to visit him in New York, where he was studying for his master's, a degree that I viewed as a selfish indulgence, seeing that it undermined our material security and provided him with absolutely no career prospects in a highly competitive, low-paying field with the necessity of physical separation. He did not meet me at LaGuardia—I accepted that it was a logistical nightmare and didn't complain. The old hotel where he had booked a room was most romantic—a park nearby, original tiling in the halls and bathrooms. We embraced in the lobby. "My sweetheart!" he said, wrapping his arms around me, drawing me to him, kissing me on the mouth, then eyebrow, and carrying my suitcase to the elevator. The elevator actually had a cage door and an arrow that indicated the box's ascent, its brass point arcing from left to right.

The sex was perfunctory. Afterward, he gasped, "That was a good one."

"What do you mean?" I asked. He was already off me and rolling over. I wanted to hit him. "I am not a big, cuddly piece of Kleenex! What do you mean, 'That was a good one'? Did you sneeze into me?" I stared at his back, and then curled up to face the far edge of the bed. What had I wanted? Kissing, an hour of foreplay, or, if a fast one, then a repeat performance, lips all over my body, the assurance that I was beautiful to him, that he missed me, tenderness and passion. Not a pump, a grunt, and "That was a good one." Well, if you want your needs met, you have to tell people what you need. I just wasn't vocal enough. Or maybe it was the weight that I'd put on. It was probably my fault.

He did not respond. I fell into sleep, a stone drifting plumb-straight through chill waters toward an inevitable bottom, instead of weeping.

The next day, we were tourists: Soho, Coney Island, the Empire State Building, and the Pink Pussycat Boutique, something that Edward knew about as a historically pioneering sex-toy shop. We stepped in, and he stood stock-still in the middle of the linoleum shop floor. Display cases full of dildos, vibrators, cock rings, rubbers, lotions, potions, massage oils, and lubes surrounded us.

"Well?" I asked.

"Well, what?" he said.

"Did you want to look for something in particular?" I wandered over to admire a hefty violet jelly double-dong.

"I thought you'd . . ." My husband shrugged as he trailed off, lifting his palms toward me.

"You thought I'd what?"

"I thought you'd know . . ." Edward massaged his forehead with his right hand, as if attempting to assist the last halves of his previous sentences in some sort of telepathic transport.

"Know what?" I said. I settled on a small clear digit-sized butt plug as a souvenir, but we never used it. By the time we'd finished traipsing through the city, we were too fatigued to make love. Once in a weekend does not an anniversary reunion make. But I can only recognize that with time and distance, now that I'm out of that situation, blushingly nostalgic for the rabbitlike enthusiasms of an eighteen-year-old, or a particular Christmas visit from a friend that included five full sessions in less than forty-eight hours. "We're fiery lovers," he'd said. That's a phrase I want to hear again in this lifetime.

Nine months after our second anniversary, Edward confessed his habit. By our third one, I'd gotten myself a lawyer as a present.

Denial is one of the strongest forces in the universe, but that does not mean that I have to live with desire denied, my womanliness rejected. And this knowledge is something that I gained through my ex-husband's courage and willingness to stand before me and tell the truth, to say, "I've never told anyone this before . . ."

I thank you, Edward.

My First Husband's Girlfriend and Me

Caroline Leavitt

For a long time, I didn't know why my first husband, Tom, left me. We had been together for twelve years. We had lots of friends. We traveled and went to movies and restaurants and parties. I thought we were happy.

But suddenly Tom began disappearing, and then he announced that he wanted a divorce. There wasn't anyone else, he said, he was just completely unhappy and wanted me gone. I was devastated. For weeks, I begged and pleaded for a reason, an excuse, for anything that might help me stay this marital execution, but he stayed silent.

I begged him to go to counseling with me and he refused. I asked his sister what was going on, I corralled his friends, but no one seemed to know anything, or, if they did, like Tom, they weren't talking.

Finally, because there was nothing else to do, I left, taking up what I hoped was temporary residence in New York and counting on my absence to make my husband's heart grow fonder. Tom called me every week to see how I was. And although he still talked about divorce, he never served me with papers, and because I ached to get back together, I never got a lawyer, either.

In the meantime, I tried to be happy. I sold a novel. I found new friends, including a man who began to love me, and after a while, to my astonishment, I began to care about him, too. But no matter how good things were, no matter how many months had gone by, I couldn't seem to commit to him; I couldn't cut the cord with Tom.

Not until one night when the phone rang, and the "other woman" called me for help.

I'll call her Stella. She was soft-spoken, and the first thing she said on the phone was, "I've been seeing your husband for four years." She said her relationship with Tom was foundering and she was terrified that he was thinking about getting back together with me. Was this true? Was I still in contact with Tom? Had he ever mentioned her to me?

I was astonished by her audacity. What kind of woman calls the woman she's betraying to ask for advice? Was she crazy? Or just sadistic? I wanted to bang the phone down on her. I wanted to curse at her and then call Tom and curse him. But more than that, more than anything, I wanted to know more. And only she could tell me.

"He doesn't tell me anything," she blurted. "He'd kill me if he knew I called you. But I'm desperate. And you're the only person who can help me."

"I was about to say the same thing," I said.

For three weeks, nearly every night, Stella and I talked for hours. We started at the beginning, telling each other how our relationships with Tom began, the things we did, the way we talked and fought and even made love. We told each other everything, like confessions, filling in the gaps in each other's histories, providing context, explanation, and time lines. We were busy helping each other figure out our lives with Tom.

"Was Tom with you all the time when you first met?" Stella asked me. "And then did it abruptly taper off?"

I felt a sudden shock of relief. It wasn't just me. It happened with another woman, too. Tom, she told me, had met her while buying a present for me. He had talked to her about nothing but me, and then had called home right in front of her to ask me what color I liked, and when I said I didn't need clothes, he had hung up, furious.

"He thought you were rejecting him by rejecting his gift. He asked me to lunch right after," Stella told me. "That's how it began. And then every single day after that, he came to see me. He called me sixty times a day. And now, all of a sudden, he doesn't."

I thought of all the times Tom had been late coming home. I remembered a business trip he had taken to California. "California!" Stella cried. "He was with me! Any trip, any late night, we were together." I felt a flash flood of anger, of shame.

"How could you do this to another woman?" I cried. "He was married."

Stella sighed. "He said the marriage was over. He said you didn't appreciate or understand him."

"Why didn't he ever tell me any of this?" I said, astonished.

"Because he thought, as his wife, you should just know." She sighed. "Oh God, what that sounds like! I guess that's part of my problem with him, too. Maybe he doesn't talk, but I do, and I'll tell you anything you want to know."

I began to call Stella more and more. We were so addicted to each other, we would put the phone down to pee and rush back again. We ate our dinners talking to each other. We cleaned our kitchens with our phones clamped to our ears. And like any couple, we sometimes fought. I yelled at Stella when she told me she had slept with Tom in our bed. "Our bed!" I shouted. "How could you do something so appalling?"

"It was his place to look out for you, not mine," Stella said defensively. "And anyway, how could you not cook dinner for him? Why was your house such a mess? Why didn't you like all his friends?"

"We are so different," I told Stella angrily.

"And so much the same," she quietly responded.

Talking to Stella changed the way I looked at my marriage. It changed me. I didn't lie awake nights anymore worrying what had gone wrong, what had been the matter with me and how I could fix it. Because of Stella's honesty, I knew. I thought of Nick, the man I was now seeing, and how we told each other everything, how different this relationship was from the one I had had with Tom and how, for the first time, to my absolute surprise, I felt good about being out of the marriage.

It felt good to find someone and something so different. I began to feel happier about my life. To see that what had seemed the worst thing in the world might turn out to be the best. One night, when I got off the phone with Stella, I got out the Yellow Pages and found a divorce lawyer.

Everything began to feel different. Even the way I began to look at Stella. She almost seemed a younger version of me. And I began to feel sorry for her because Tom was now treating her the same way he had treated me, disappearing, refusing to discuss anything. There wasn't anything wrong with her, just as there hadn't been anything wrong with me.

I told Stella I was filing for divorce, that I wouldn't make things harder for her by naming her in any suit or even by telling Tom that I had been talking with her. She had helped me. I wanted to help her. And in any case, it didn't matter. All I wanted was a divorce. And suddenly, I was the one telling Stella, "Maybe you should leave Tom. Move on. Maybe you can be happier, too."

"How can I?" Stella said bitterly.

"Because I can," I told her.

I began spending more and more time with Nick. My need to talk about Tom diminished, and with it, so did my need to talk to Stella. "You're happy," Stella said when we finally connected. "I guess I did something right." She still didn't know what she was going to do. Tom, she said, hadn't even told her he had been served with divorce papers. She still loved him. She still hoped he might marry her.

"I want you to be happy," I said. And I meant it. As I began to go out more and more, our calls dwindled. Once a week, then once every two weeks, and then, finally, not at all.

I didn't marry Nick, but I am married again, to a wonderful man, and we have a child. I haven't spoken to Tom or Stella since the divorce was finalized. But just a few weeks ago, Tom's sister called me. I had always liked her and I was happy to hear from her. She told me Tom was remarried now, to a woman whose name was not Stella.

"What happened to Stella?" I asked.

"He left her," Tom's sister said, and I felt sad. I had wanted Stella to be the one to leave, to be strong. "It was awful for her. She went into therapy, but she's okay now. She's doing well, working, seeing people."

"Good," I said, and I meant it. Because when I think about Stella, I feel no animosity toward her at all. Instead, what I feel is gratitude. She wasn't the "other woman" who ended up ruining my life. In the end, Stella was the one who saved it.

I'm Still Waiting . . .

Susan Jane Gilman

I once dated a cute guy in high school who served me spaghetti by candlelight and taught me to play Frisbee. He was a great kisser. He was good at French and geometry. But I had to break up with him because he liked the rock band Journey. Plus, he wore a puka shell necklace.

In college, I dated a gorgeous Rhodes scholar who spent his summers distributing sacks of grain to starving children in Africa. He took me to wine tastings and the opera. But I had to break up with him because his name was Yehuda. Imagine having sex with someone and screaming, "Oh, do me, Yehuda." Just not possible.

After college, I had to break up with a civil rights lawyer because he had a mullet.

I broke up with a pastry chef because he didn't know who C-3PO was. When we were talking about the movie *Star Wars*, he kept referring to him as "that gold guy." I'm sorry, but what thirty-year-old of my generation doesn't know the main characters in *Star Wars*?

I dumped the architect because he had silver fillings instead of white ones.

I dumped the sportswriter because he said "lyberry" and "sammich" instead of "library" and "sandwich."

The stockbroker? A Capricorn.

The junior congressman? Back hair.

As for the stand-up comedian, he simply liked me too much. I'd wake up in the morning and he'd be staring at me the way people stare at wide-screen TVs in appliance stores. Creeped me out.

Today, I am married. My husband is a stunningly kind, strong, handsome man who's actually as intelligent as I am. The Amazing Bob, as I call him, makes me laugh—in fact, we have been cracking up over the same stupid jokes since approximately 1996. When he wraps his arms around me, I feel like I've come home. Even before we got married, the Amazing Bob and I gave money to the same charities, got outraged by the same injustices, shared the same passions for travel, books, politics, art. And oh, do I love him! But eventually, I'll have to leave him, too.

Because for starters, when I first met him, he drove a brown 1985 Ford Tempo with two hubcaps missing. (The fact that he drives a silver Peugeot now is strictly my doing.) If left to his own devices, he'd play his old Smiths and Husker Du albums until everyone in a three-block radius was ready to commit suicide. Occasionally, he uses the word *good* as an adverb. Worse still, he likes to go fishing (snore). Also, his favorite big red Chicago Bulls sweatshirt isn't an item of clothing so much as a billboard.

But most important, when I first met Bob outside a coffee shop, I didn't feel any fireworks, thunderbolts, or butterflies. Afterward, I didn't twirl home to call my best friend and announce breathlessly, "Tonight I met the man that I'm going to marry." Instead, she called me, and I said something vague like, "Well, he didn't seem like an asshole."

Sure, as time went on, Bob and I fell in love. Sure, it dawned on me that we were a great team. Sure, we shared a vision for the future, and had a lot of fun together. And so, eventually, I said "yes."

And so he'll do—for now.

Because as any woman in America can tell you, this Bob may be amazing, but he ain't Mr. Right.

When it comes to Mr. Right, we gals know the hallmarks. We have been inundated with more subliminal messages about True Love and "finding the one" than we have been about anything else in the world (except, maybe, diets). If we'd received half as many cultural messages about, say, how to choose a mutual fund or split an atom, we women would occupy every slot on the Forbes 400 list and have first-strike nuclear capabilities by now. But instead, our central nervous systems have been saturated and encrypted with things like *The Rules, The Bachelor,* and *Bridget Jones's Diary.* Amazingly, it may be the twenty-first century, but finding Mr. Right continues to be exalted as the Holy Grail for females. It's why some of us are writing this book, in fact, and others of us are reading it.

From the day we're old enough to stop teething on our own feet, we're plunked down in front of Disney videos. We then grow up to read roughly thirteen billion women's magazines, Harlequin romances, and *Red Dress* books apiece. We've watched *General Hospital, The Love Boat, Sex and the City.* Most of all, we have seen movies. Thousands of movies. Movies like *Pretty Woman. Pretty in Pink. An Officer and a Gentleman.* Everything starring Hugh Grant.

And so we *know* that when we *do* meet Mr. Right, we'll know it *instantly.* Like almost everything else valued in America, Mr. Right obliterates the need for anything resembling patience or rational thought. He will be Mr. Right precisely because he'll enflame us immediately. With him, we will not have to engage in pesky reason. We will not have to examine our feelings. We will not have to compromise. We will simply see him across a crowded room, feel "that spark we never felt before," and *just know.* (Unless, like Meg Ryan in *Sleepless in Seattle,* we hear him over the radio—in which case we'll know just from the *sound* of his voice that we should call off our wedding to a guy who's committed the mortal sin of having allergies.) Bathed in the gaze of Mr. Right, every doubt and neurosis we've ever had will suddenly evaporate. He will have us at "hello."

What's more, he will have us at "hello" because he will possess two instantly obvious qualities that are mandatory for any Mr. Right:

1. Perfection.
2. Clairvoyance.

Mr. Right will not have back hair because he'll come equipped with the foresight to wax it. He will not need to have his clothes given as a charitable donation to the Salvation Army because he'll already know how to dress. He'll understand that while we may like to watch *Extreme Makeover,* we have no desire to be with a guy who actually needs one.

What's more, he'll instinctively know how we think. He'll understand that when we say, "Do you want ice cream?" what we really mean is that *we* want ice cream. He'll know that when we ask him, "What are you thinking?" we don't want to hear anything except "That I love you."

He will understand by osmosis that sometimes we gals like to go on ad nauseam about our problems without having to consider concrete solutions to them. He will "get" that we often need to talk about our feelings without any obvious point to the discussion.

Most of all, Mr. Right will know that we want him to declare his love for us in vastly public and outsize ways. And so he will wake up at dawn to arrange tea lights and bits of holly in the shape of a giant heart in the newly fallen snow on our lawns.

He will interrupt national sales conferences and school talent shows to serenade us with a cappella renditions of "You Are So Beautiful" before packed auditoriums.

He will, if need be, burst in on our wedding ceremonies at the last minute to halt our marriages to other, less worthy guys.

He will hire a skywriter.

He will understand that having "I Heart U" or "Will You Marry Me?" displayed on a Jumbotron at a sports stadium really won't cut it because, let's face it, that involves sports.

He will be the cowboy in the white Stetson—tough, unflinchingly masculine, and edgy—but never in any way that makes him emotionally remote or truly dangerous. Ultimately, Mr. Right is a stereotypical gay man—but straight. He'll surprise us on Sunday mornings with a bottle of champagne and a basket of homemade muffins—while dressed in Armani and performing cunnilingus on us. He will be a fairy tale come true—part fairy, part tail.

And really: Is this too much to ask?

In the past, I suspect, women yearned for princes and perfect mates because our lives were completely dependent upon wedlock—and we had absolutely zero control over whom we married. Regarded as burdens or property by society, most of us were traded like cattle or stock certificates to all sorts of cruel, hideous, or simply unlovable men in order to secure alliances, stave off starvation, or further the status and ambitions of our tribe. For the majority of women in the world today, these arranged marriages still prevail. So it's no wonder that the ideals of Mr. Right and Prince Charming are so persistent and intoxicating. When our entire fate depends upon a husband selected by other people, riding off into the sunset with the man of our dreams is not only our greatest hope but a profoundly subversive, defiant act.

Yet in the privileged environment of America today, where a woman can get a Ph.D. in molecular biology, backpack to Tanzania, then marry an Elvis impersonator on a whim in Las Vegas, you'd think that someone like me would be hip to the dangers of conflating old-fashioned myths with reality. You'd think that someone like me would realize that there is, luckily, far more to my life than finding a perfect guy. You'd think that someone like me would recognize that the *real* Mr. Wrong is someone like Osama bin Laden . . . or a male boss who invites only male colleagues for a golf weekend . . . or a Supreme Court justice who rules over my womb and my bedroom based on his own religious convictions. You'd think that, free of traditional female strangleholds, I'd be savvy enough to transcend the limited, traditional, wishful thinking that accompanied them. You'd think that, free of an infantilizing culture, I'd stop acting like such a baby.

But! I! Don't! Wanna!

I want Mr. Right! He's what I've been groomed for! Ever since I was little!

I want Mr. Right so that I won't have to look at my husband and see anything close to an actual mortal. I want Mr. Right so that I won't have to see my own imperfections and lunacy reflected in his eyeglasses. I want Mr. Right because I don't want to behave like a sentient, modern grown-up.

And so, I'm holding out. So what if I married a terrific man who actually tolerates me? I'm still yearning for that human asthma attack to sweep me off my feet and into his limousine. I'm still running through the moors in a chiffon ball gown while Mr. Right skywrites love sonnets for me across the horizon. I'm still pining away listening to late-night radio for that one soulful voice that will compel me to throw away everything I've built with the Amazing Bob for a childhood fantasy of perfection.

Unless, of course, my husband is going to reveal himself to me as an exiled Slavic prince. Maybe when Bob's family emigrated to Chicago a hundred years ago, they really secretly stashed away a vast fortune. Maybe they dropped their royal titles just to assimilate, and now live in modest ranch houses and eat chocolates in paneled rec rooms and drive secondhand minivans just to deflect attention. Maybe Bob's just biding his time—waiting to make sure that I've truly married him for his personality and not for his money. Perhaps, on our fifth wedding anniversary, he'll take my hand, look moonily into my eyes, and confess, "There's something I've been waiting to tell you." Then he'll lead me to his Gulfstream jet and whisk me off to Europe for an aerial tour of his estates, castles, and vineyards. And then, I won't have to leave him at all!

Because this, as we all know, is how girls like me *really* live happily ever after.

The Key

Michelle Huneven

I met Mark in an early morning Spanish class I was taking with my friend Joy. Joy fell in love with him first. In fact, I was the only woman in the room who didn't have it bad for Mark Angiers. Even our matronly instructor, Señora Garcia, sighed each time she looked his way. Mark had soft wavy brown hair, big brown eyes, almost ridiculously chiseled cheekbones—movie-star good looks, but coupled with a vulnerable sweetness. He spent every minute in class either taking notes or doodling in his notebook. The faces of our classmates materialized on the ruled pages with startling accuracy.

Señor Marco, barked the señora, are you listening? And he'd gaze up at her with the soulful and adoring look that trusting dogs give their masters. Ahh, she would say, ahhh, muy bien.

And when she called on him to speak in Spanish, Mark would blush deeply, and his eyes would start shining, and he'd laugh a little at his own unconquerable shyness. Then he'd answer her in a barely audible, throaty voice. All around me, women held their breath to hear him.

Not me, though. I had no patience for Mark Angiers. I thought he was a sap, and way too pretty for his own good. I'd had good-looking boyfriends before and knew full well how looks could eclipse the development of character.

Joy simply adored Mark. She and I went out to breakfast every day after class, and every day she wanted to invite him along. And every day she lost her nerve.

I'll ask him, I said. I don't care.

Hey Mark, I said. We're going to breakfast—¿Quiere usted acompañarnos?

He turned a painful and unflattering bright pink and his eyes shone. Yes, he whispered, sí, I'd love to, con mucho gusto, just tell me where.

At breakfast, Joy could neither look at nor speak to him. Ignoring his painful blushes, I proceeded to interview him. He'd been a CEO of a small manufacturing company, he said. He had saved enough to quit that job and go to art school. Now, in his late thirties, he was trying to paint. He was planning a trip to Madrid, to the Prado, the Reina Sofia. Hence the Spanish lessons.

While Joy looked on, Mark and I talked about galleries and museums and artists. Joy liked him even more close up, she said. I invited him to breakfast the next day, and the next, until it became a regular thing. Joy got so she could tease him a little in Spanish. Señor Marco, estas escuchandome? When she got too tongue-tied, I asked him more questions.

One day, we were seated all three in a corner booth and Mark inadvertently leaned against me. A tide of emotion surged through me. Oh, I thought. Now I had an inkling what other women felt about him. He had animal magnetism. Or something.

Mark, Mark, Mark, Joy sighed in one ear.

Hey Michelle, he whispered in the other. Can I talk to you after breakfast?

We went to our cars, and after Joy drove off, he came to me. It's been a very long time since I was drawn to anyone, he said. I hope I'm not being out of line here.

No, no, not at all.

I was wondering what you, uh, thought, he said.

About you and Joy? I said.

By the bright pink incomprehension on his face, I knew I had it all wrong.

I brushed your shoulder, he said, and I knew—it was so emotional! I was astonished and flattered and felt very guilty.

You don't have to say anything, he said. Think about it.

Indeed, I couldn't stop thinking about it. I thought I was done with men who were all unrealized potential. I thought I was done with men who didn't work for a living. Then again, out of all the rapt women in the class, even above and beyond lovely Joy, he'd picked me!

I made a beeline to my therapist. I don't want to horn in on Joy, I said.

Joy should know it's always dangerous to send an intermediary on such errands, my therapist said.

If it weren't for her, I never would've spoken to him. I didn't even like him.

Maybe Joy should've done more of her own talking, my therapist said.

In retrospect, I wish Joy had.

♥   ♥   ♥

On our first date, we went for a walk, and he took me to lunch—to McDonald's. All his budget would allow.

Look here, I said. I'm a restaurant critic. I can't eat this.

Thus Mark became my default dining companion. We also went to galleries and museums. We spoke terrible Spanish to each other, drove up into the mountains, hiked. We planned a trip to Spain. We slowly let go with increasingly intimate details of our lives. I told him how I'd been in love with a married man for five years. Mark said he was in AA. He'd gotten sober seven years ago, but had fallen apart after a breakup. When he first asked me out, he'd been sober for a month without relapse. Now he felt no desire to drink. Having a girlfriend had helped him stay sober before. Perhaps with me . . .

Mark was an immensely sensitive person, respectful, affectionate, generous with his time, patient, kind. He loved my pets, a little dog and a cat. He taught the dog tricks. He fixed my neighbor's faucet. My friends remarked on how sweet he was.

He came to church with me. I was about to start graduate school to become a minister. My own minister and his wife had us over for dinner. The minister's wife, a therapist, couldn't believe how helpful Mark was in the kitchen. Her own husband would try to help, but he'd do such a poor job, she said, it guaranteed she wouldn't ask his assistance a second time. Another older woman in the congregation told me that Mark was my soul mate, she could tell, she saw the understanding and humor in the looks we exchanged.

I told him about my parents' nonstop bickering and quarreling. He described a difficult childhood with an extremely volatile and abusive father. I met his mother, who, the first time she and I were alone in a room together, told me about her ongoing guilt that it had taken her so long to divorce Mark's dad.

Given his struggle with alcoholism and the trauma of an awful father, Mark, I thought, needed a lot of remedial love—which, of course, I would supply.

♥ ♥ ♥

We were more than six months into our relationship when Mark told me he'd been married before—and had a child. He'd gotten a girl pregnant the first time either of them had had sex. He was seventeen, she was sixteen. She threatened to kill herself if he didn't marry her. They married, had a son, and were miserable. Both attempted suicide. In fact, before he got sober, he had attempted suicide numerous times. That yellowish bump on his heel? That was actually a bone pushing through the skin from the time he'd leapt off a four-story parking structure. Oh, and the reason he mostly wore long sleeves? His wrists were welted and crosshatched with white scar tissue.

I didn't know where to start. And where is your son? I asked finally. Do you ever see him?

He's eighteen now. He lived with me for a few years when I was working for the company. Now he's with his mom. In Ventura. I haven't seen him since I started drinking again.

I wanted Mark to call his son. We could drive up to Ventura, see him, invite him down.

I need a little more time, I want to get a little more sober, said Mark. I don't want to let him down again.

A year passed since we'd met, and Mark wondered if we should move in together. Some sternness inside me didn't want to take that step until we could be equal partners—that is, until he could afford half the rent. I was self-supporting, but also on a shoestring. I didn't want to throw my rickety financial well-being in with his.

Still, we'd developed a cozy status quo. He worked in his studio every day. I worked on my journalism and began attending seminary. He spent most nights at my house. He had a key. He kept his clothes in my dresser and closet. We cooked together. We ate out together. We socialized with my friends, often with Joy who, after a month or two, had stopped being angry at us. We talked about contacting his son. Soon, said Mark. Spain was still on the agenda.

One summer day when we'd planned to go shopping together, I couldn't get hold of Mark. He didn't answer his phone and didn't return my calls. I drove to his apartment as planned. He lived in an older six-unit building. His neighbors were elderly Armenian widows, all of whom adored him. His car was out on the street, but he wasn't in his garage-slash-studio and didn't answer when I knocked on his door.

I called from the pay phone at the doughnut shop next door. He was probably out on a walk, I decided, and had a cup of coffee, waited. After half an hour, I left to do some shopping, then came back. The studio had been locked, but there was still no sign of Mark. Troubled, I finished shopping without him.

He phoned that night. He'd been home the whole time, he insisted, he'd had his earphones on. He'd forgotten about our shopping expedition.

Maybe you should give me a key, I said. That way, if you're out I can wait in your apartment. If you're listening to music, we can still manage to connect.

Okay, he said. Good idea.

No key materialized, but I didn't want to nag.

♥　♥　♥

Mark was making art, but was too shy to show it to anybody. His shyness truly encumbered him. I encouraged him to go back into therapy.

His new therapist was an intern accumulating hours to be licensed—all Mark could afford. Their first sessions ran overtime. He'd had a long history of therapy and psychiatric intervention, and could talk about his past with startling and compelling honesty. His ongoing, determined struggle to be a sane, productive person after terrible childhood abuse was one of the most attractive things about him. I understood his new therapist's obvious fascination—to have such a conversant, self-aware client must have seemed a gift.

She suggested he try one of the new antidepressants; she'd seen artists acquire confidence and drive taking them. On Prozac, Mark did seem cheerier and less burdened—though our sex life shriveled up. His shrink started seeing him twice a week, and their sessions lasted two, three, in one case almost four hours. Her supervisor finally intervened and insisted she keep within the prescribed hour.

Mark and I spent most weekend nights together, but when he called one Friday evening to say he was deep into a piece and wanted to keep working, I saw nothing unusual in this. He didn't call around my bedtime, though, nor did he call in the morning. When I phoned him at noon the next day—¿Marco, Marco, donde estas?—he did not pick up.

By early evening, I was worried and drove over. Again, his car was at his house, his studio was open, his apartment locked.

I was there, he insisted late that night when he finally phoned. I just didn't hear you. I was asleep. I'd stayed up all night painting. I'm still beat.

I said, If I didn't know better, I'd think you were drinking.

If I'm drinking, he said coldly, you'd be the first to know. You think I wouldn't level with you about that? I'm not one of your sneaky married guys, Michelle.

Well, I'd feel better if I had a key to your apartment. I wouldn't get so worried if I knew you were fine.

I said I'll give you a key, and I will, if you stop nagging me about it.

I didn't say anything.

Now what's the matter? he said. How can we talk about this if you shut down on me?

♥ ♥ ♥

We got over that bump—he showed up Sunday night for dinner with a beautiful still-wet painting—and soon we were back to our old routine. Dining out on the newspaper. Sleeping together, albeit sex was rare. We went camping together in the Sierras. He drew landscapes, I read theology. We went on a ski trip with his mom and stepdad. I found myself thinking distantly about marriage. He wasn't the man I'd imagined for myself, but I wasn't getting any younger. There were problems—money, for one, and sex—but that could be temporary. We had a nice easy life together. And nobody's perfect.

I went back to school in the fall and after class one day, another ministerial student struck up a conversation with me. Are you married? she asked.

Not yet, I said. But my boyfriend is the nicest person in the world.

That's exactly what I say about my husband! she said. What does your boyfriend do?

He's an artist. And your husband?

Oh, he's a doctor.

A doctor. *A doctor.*

Here I was with a forty-year-old high school graduate with maybe a dozen units of extension art classes under his belt. And here was a woman not unlike myself, who had not only a husband but a nice husband with a grown-up profession. A doctor.

A doctor, it turned out, who had just taken her to Italy.

Perhaps, I thought, I should've set my sights higher than a struggling middle-aged artist whose idea of a date was a burger at McDonald's.

♥ ♥ ♥

We'd been together around fifteen months when he phoned on a hot autumn afternoon. Hello stranger, I said. What's up?

I'm drinking, he said.

The blood turned to ice in my veins. You're what?

I'm drinking, he said.

Since when?

I don't know. Last night. I don't know. It doesn't matter. I just want to die. I give up. I'm just going to die.

Stay right where you are, I said. I'm coming over.

Please don't.

Well then I'm calling the police. I'll tell them to break the door down, that you're killing yourself.

Silence. Then he said, I'll come over there.

But you're drunk.

Not so much right now, he said. I'll come over there.

If you're not here in half an hour, I'm calling the police, I said. Then I called the suicide hotline and told the man who answered that my boyfriend was threatening to kill himself.

Okay, well, have him call us, the man said.

I couldn't believe how cavalier he sounded. Isn't there something I should do? I said.

Ever hear of a program called Al Anon? he said, and began to spell it.

When Mark showed up, I told him to call the suicide hotline. He looked at me blankly. What for? he said.

The rest of that afternoon, we sat on the bed and talked. He talked, that is. I wept. He told me about his suicide attempts. He told me about jumping off the four-story parking structure. He'd been in a mental hospital at the time. He'd charmed the nurses into bringing him alcohol and drugs. He'd charmed his psychiatrist into prescribing hypnotics and barbiturates. Eventually, the hospital's director forbade any female staff to go near him. Only male psych techs and psychiatrists could interact with him. Mark learned how to sneak off the grounds to get high. He was in the process of sneaking off when two security guards saw him and gave chase. He ran into the parking structure, up ramp after ramp until there was no place else to go. As the guards closed in on him, he jumped. That's how his ankle and foot got so screwed up.

Another time, he went on, he put his fist through a plate glass window. Somehow, he got to the hospital. He doesn't remember how. He came to in the ICU, but was so drugged up he couldn't move or speak. A doctor and nurse were playing with the severed tendons flying around at the end of his arm. They would touch the severed ends and the tendons would snap back and coil up.

Once, when he was a baby, he said, his mother had gone to the store and left him alone with his father. He doesn't remember this, he was too young, but it came out in a family therapy session. When Mark soiled his diapers, his father beat him almost to death. He'd spent months in the hospital. His mother and father split up, of course, but then his mother went back to his father, and they had another child, Mark's sister.

I wept and wept.

Mark said that once he had sneaked a look at his medical file. One of his psychiatrists had written about him, personality incompatible with life.

If only he could stay sober, Mark said, he could keep a grip on himself. If he could stay sober, he had a chance. His sobriety wasn't perfect, but it was something. He hoped I wouldn't leave.

His relapse frightened me, as did the newly revealed breadth and depth of his emotional history. But somehow we managed to recapture a daily rhythm and move on with our lives. He made art. I studied. We spent most nights together. He was going to meetings and not drinking. Things were good, except that I was having trouble breathing. I couldn't catch my breath. I'd try yawning. I tried breathing into paper bags. Once, twice, three times a week, I'd have episodes where I simply could not breathe normally. I thought something might be wrong with my heart and went to the doctor.

When the nurse touched my arm to take my blood pressure, I flinched.

Later, when the doctor looked in my eyes, I flinched again. The doctor said, You are suffering from severe anxiety. He wanted to put me on antidepressants. Me! Mentally healthy, spiritually advanced me. No thanks, I said. I'll cut down on the caffeine. I'll exercise more, study less.

Mark was the one who needed pills. He was the anxious depressive, I told my therapist.

Well, couples often assign each other roles, she said, and polarize. If one gets to be sick, the other gets to be healthy. Maybe you two are ripe for a little couples counseling. She wrote down the name of someone we might see.

I wasn't game for couples counseling, until Mark drank again.

Same deal—he stopped answering the phone, wouldn't come to the door—only this time it went on for three days. It's over between us, I said, unless we go into therapy.

Like Mark's therapist, our counselor was another small, pretty, forty-something actress who'd given up on Hollywood and turned to psychotherapy. She, too, was earning hours toward her license and therefore budget-priced. She asked me to talk first.

Mark virtually lives at my house, I said. His art is up on my walls. His clothes are in my drawers. He has a key, free access, he comes and goes as he pleases, whereas I'm not welcome in his house. He keeps it as a drinking den. For me to feel safe in this relationship, I need to have equal access to his life and house. Then I'll believe he doesn't intend to drink again. It may be symbolic. I want a key.

The counselor turned to Mark.

I love Michelle with all my heart, he said in his soft, throaty voice. And she tries really hard in our relationship. But she has intimacy issues and I need to get away sometimes, just to get my bearings. It has nothing to do with drinking. She doesn't really know how to be close to someone. But she's so willing, and tries so hard, I really want to stick it out. When her issues surface, though, I need a place to retreat and sort things out.

What about these intimacy issues, Michelle? said the counselor.

Gosh, I said. I'm sure I have some issues, but this is the first I've heard of them.

Which is why you're here now, said the counselor.

Yes, I said, but frankly, if you look at how I've welcomed him into my house, and how he has made himself at home there, while I've been in his apartment exactly twice, ever, it's pretty obvious which one of us is better at intimacy. That's why a key to his house . . .

We're not going to talk about a key, Michelle, the counselor said sternly. We're talking about your intimacy problems.

I was so stunned, I don't remember much else about the session, except that at one point the therapist said, You keep talking about Mark drinking. So what? I drink, you drink. What do you mean by "Mark drank"?

I was, again, at such a loss for words that Mark himself explained. I'm a sober alcoholic, he said. When I drink, it's a betrayal of everything, like I'm having an affair.

Oh! she said.

Afterward, we had left the office and gone only a few feet when Mark knocked me with his elbow. Boy, you really had no idea what you were doing in there, he said, whereas I'm on home territory! Another elbow knock, and chuckling. In this particular situation, he said, you, missy, are way way way out of your league.

♥   ♥   ♥

My own therapist told me I had to go back to the couples counselor and tell her why I didn't want to continue. Being the good therapy patient, I complied. First of all, you don't know anything about alcoholism! I told our petite couples counselor. And you don't know how thoroughly you were manipulated, either.

She apologized. In the last week, she'd done her homework on alcoholism. Now she was more prepared. Could we try it again?

Mark was willing. I went along. The three of us conversed in a more equable fashion, so I agreed to keep coming.

Mark drank again when I was in the middle of finals. Our counselor suggested we see it as a slip, and we tried to be light about it. Indeed, he climbed back on the wagon, and we moved on. He worked in the studio; I finished my finals and welcomed winter break. Mark had some dark days over the holidays, but stayed sober. At Christmas, his sister told me he'd been struggling with alcoholism for more than twenty years. The whole family had gone into counseling with Mark many times, in many different treatment programs. If I eventually left him, she added, nobody would ever blame me.

Perhaps I'd been waiting to hear exactly that. The next time Mark went incommunicado for two days, I told him, Enough. I wanted out. I was not keeping him sober. I couldn't. I didn't want to try anymore. The drinking was more frequent. The emotional roller coaster was not the life I wanted.

He didn't try to talk me out of it. He asked if we could speak from time to time.

We spoke every day, in fact. Just checked in on each other. Told each other our news. Sometimes we talked about meeting for coffee, normalizing—not getting back together again, but not avoiding each other, either. Maybe a month after we broke up, my car ended up in the shop a few blocks from his apartment. I called him and impulsively asked him to meet me at a nearby coffeehouse.

I arrived first, ordered a coffee, and waited. I'd read most of the newspaper when I noticed a ripple go through the room.

Mark stood inside the doors panting, as if he'd burst in at a dead run. He wore a holey white T-shirt and paint-smeared jeans. His hair stuck out in clumps, his eyes were wild. The whites showed under his irises to an alarming, even bizarre degree. He looked possessed, insane. Two men in business suits stood up, ready to deal with him. I threw a five-dollar bill on the table, grabbed my purse, and herded Mark outside. I smelled the booze on him. Are you drinking? I asked.

No, he whispered in his throaty voice. I have a cold.

Keep walking, I said. People in the coffeehouse were still watching us. Mark headed toward the street. Following, I put my nose almost against his back and sniffed deeply. He reeked of alcohol. We stopped at the crosswalk. Can you look me in the eye and say that you haven't been drinking? I said.

His irises looked like two dull dimes. I haven't been drinking, he said. And please, don't start.

As he spoke, I had the distinct impression of a door shutting in my chest. An abrupt but complete cessation of interest. He was in the grip of something huge and horrible and disgusting. My love couldn't change it and my pity couldn't touch it. From that moment on, I wanted only to get away from him. I never wanted to see him again.

♥ ♥ ♥

A psychiatrist I know has since suggested that this sudden shutting off of concern and affection indicates that there may have been no authentic bond to begin with, that the relationship I had with Mark may have been compulsive, codependent, addictive, and not about real love.

Perhaps. I certainly don't feel compelled to argue love's case.

I have had no nostalgia for Mark and the months we spent together. But for one large beautiful canvas stored in my garage, I have kept no mementos, no gifts.

When I stopped taking or returning Mark's calls, he turned to Joy. She was the one who brought cookies and paperback novels to the treatment center he entered. She went to the group meetings and the family counseling sessions that his own mother and sister now declined to attend. Marky, Joy took to calling him. Marky, Marky, Marky, she'd sigh, and sound more like a weary mother than a besotted wannabe lover.

Joy told me about Mark's new counselor, a large, intimidating Native American woman named Wilma. Wilma was tough on him, Joy said, really tough. No more nonsense. No more charm-o-rama for Marky. When he graduated from the program, Mark moved in with Wilma. Joy, who may have imagined another outcome, was shocked.

♥ ♥ ♥

A year or two after that, when he was in yet another program, Mark called me. He owed me amends, he said. Those times I'd suspected him of drinking? Well, he had been. It was uncanny how you knew, he said. Every time, you nailed it.

Not so uncanny, I thought. The mystery to me was how willing I was to believe his narrative, how willing I was to lie to myself, even when I couldn't breathe.

But I'd been up against a real pro. Better women than I, women whose profession it was to recognize and treat such behavior, had fallen for him, too, hook, line, and sinker.

♥　♥　♥

Seven years ago now, I was in an art supply store buying ink for a fountain pen, when I noticed a man staring at me. Going by his cheap Hawaiian shirt, ratty jeans, worn-down cowboy boots, and clay-toned complexion, I pegged him for a two-bit gambler, some barfly down on his luck.

Is that you? the man said, and I recognized the throaty, soft voice. Mark?

We spoke for a few minutes. He was still making art, he said. And hadn't had a drink in six years. He thought of me often, he said, but was afraid to make contact.

Through the store's front window, the sun glinted off cars in the parking lot; a gray haze hid the foothills. Since Mark and I had been together, I'd learned a few things. I was not, for example, the paragon of mental health and spiritual sophistication I once took myself to be. Therapy, I'd learned, was not the forum to show off my mental health, but quite the opposite; it was the one safe place where I could reveal the sickness in my soul. Yet another romance with a good-looking charmer and borderline psychopath brought me to see that I had my own share of irrational fears and plunging moods and emotional stall-outs. The relationships with Mark and his successor in fact had served as a kind of key to what I wasn't facing about my-self, the broken, neurotic, and unconsolable parts. With better ther-apy and heaps more humility, I'd learned to recognize these sad and faulty parts of my personality. As I did so, the compulsion to annex a deeply damaged person to express my emotional pain thinned and vanished.

I turned back to the ruin of the man I'd known and summoned what warmth I could—a small, mostly sad smile. I have to go, I said.

I phoned Joy when I got home. He's alive, I told her, but there was no trace of the beautiful man we used to know.

Oh Marky, she sighed. Marky, Marky, Marky.

Professor Wrong

Marge Piercy

I believe that in love you are entitled to a great many mistakes so long as you aren't making the same one over and over. I have friends who seem to always fall for the same man in various guises. One dear friend insists that she must have the right chemistry, a template in her brain that must match up for her to fall in love. That template ensures that the man will never be faithful or loving in the long run.

I have managed, however, with persistence and gullibility, to commit a great many different mistakes, a whole galaxy of flaming errors. It is with difficulty, therefore, that I select just one bad star to describe. We will call him Oscar because that was not his name. Oscar was an intriguing mixture of bad boy and respectable professional. He taught literature in a good enough university. He was very "political," as those of us who work for social change use the word, meaning in this particular case that he had the vocabulary of a revolutionary but wasn't one. He could sound quite the rebel, but he taught his classes and graded his papers on time, paid his taxes, was good to his parents, and in truth was an upstanding bourgeois son from an upper-middle-class family. His students liked him and he got on with his colleagues unless he chose not to. I was living on the Upper West Side of Manhattan, and I met him when he interviewed me for some periodical. He flirted with me and I flirted back, but at the time I wasn't open to a relationship, so nothing more happened until two years later, when I had moved to Cape Cod after an acrimonious divorce.

I do many gigs—readings of my poetry and occasionally prose, workshops for aspiring writers, and speeches or the odd lecture. I don't know if Oscar actually arranged for me to give a poetry reading at his university or if someone else on the faculty suggested my name, but certainly when I arrived, he took credit for the invitation. He chauffeured me about, was attentive and charming. He was quite deferential in soliciting my opinions. "If a man can be a feminist, then I'm proud to be one," he murmured. One of his colleagues was annoyed that I had been invited instead of a respectable male poet adorned with establishment prizes. "Who are you to address our students?" he demanded over supper.

Oscar defended me with passion and wit. I was grateful and intrigued. We made love in his Brooklyn brownstone apartment. I didn't know what would come of this event—whether it was a one-timer or something more engaged.

He came to visit me in Wellfleet, staying in my house, bringing me presents of books he thought I must read. They were always by men, usually academic radicals like Marcuse and Chomsky. As a writer, I always have at least ten books I am reading at any given time and a list the size of one of my pine trees to be read soon. Books to be blurbed come in the mail almost daily. I would rather have been brought Godiva chocolates or a pretty scarf, but oh well. He would not have thought such presents sufficiently correct. Once we had been to bed a few times, his deference wore off.

He was a man of great self-confidence, a trait that I, like many women, tended to find attractive, although after Oscar I was less wowed by assertiveness. He could not see why I always walked to town a certain way, taking half an hour. Why not go straight across the green area in between? I explained that the area was partly wetlands. He saw no obstacle in that and led the way. At first the going was difficult but passable, as we picked our way through brush and jumped a creek. By the time we had penetrated well into the area and thrust halfway through an enormous patch of bull briar, it was too late to turn back. Two hours later, soaked and caked with mud to the thighs, lumpy with mosquito bites and, it turned out upon later examination, crawling with ticks, scratched to bleeding with briars, we emerged in town. People passing us averted their eyes. We fought the marsh and the marsh won. We bought our lunch—takeout because no place would have seated us—and went home via the road. After this, I picked our routes.

A particular bay was posted as off-limits to shellfishing. Oscar announced that this was nonsense and they just were trying to keep regular people from enjoying the clams. We didn't need a license, he argued, to reap the bounty of the sea. It should be free to everyone. He had grown up in New Jersey near the ocean and he knew. Who was I to argue? I grew up in center-city Detroit, saw the ocean for the first time when I visited New York my senior year in college, ate my first shellfish and lobsters then, and had been a full-time Cape resident for only a year and a half. We waded in and dug clams. It was new to me and interesting. We were sick for two days.

That was the usual digestive trauma caused by eating polluted clams. Oscar insisted it must be the way I had cooked them, but after that, I ignored his statements about the natural world. Still, I was fascinated by him. He was physically strong—had played football in high school—and was quite a different type from the scientists and poets I had been involved with. He was energetic and opinionated, as am I, so our evenings tended to be lively. As a lover he lacked finesse but offered enthusiasm—at times a bit too much pounding, but at least he was ready and able at a moment's notice. I like to cook and he liked to eat. I don't do well with men who are finicky trenchermen or on weird diets.

Our relationship went forward sporadically but intensely. I lived in Wellfleet; he lived in Brooklyn. He came to me oftener than I went to visit him, but we always managed a long weekend or most of a week every month. Sometimes when I had planned to fly down, he would announce the day before that he had to go out of town suddenly to see someone or interview somewhere. I am not by nature possessive and I am busy and actually like to write, so I would cancel my reservations—something one could do freely in those days of easy and comparatively inexpensive plane travel—and we would reschedule. We were both busy, and a part-time relationship seemed to work. I was open about my ex-husband's infidelities and how they had hurt me. He was sympathetic and described his pain when his wife left him. I thought of us both as injured by love but in recovery. We were well suited, I thought, for such a partial commitment that might well grow into full-time over time.

One problem I had was his desire to have sex outdoors. I am not an exhibitionist; I believe beds are built to be comfortable for purposes that do not only include sleep. However, I was more malleable in my early thirties than I have ever been since. We joined our bodies somewhat clumsily together in blueberry patches, in the dunes, on a deserted (we hoped) stretch of beach, under the pines and, memorably for him—I was on top that time—in a patch of poison ivy.

All this time I had supposed we were open about our lives. He was divorced, as was I; in fact, I knew and liked his ex-wife. They did not seem to be at odds. But everything blew up when I was offered a short residency at a New York university. It paid rather well for the time involved. I had expected that he would be delighted. I was not anticipating moving in with him, for the university was providing housing. I would be teaching a workshop, giving a reading, a lecture, and several seminars, so I wouldn't have much free time, but obviously we would see quite a bit of each other while I was staying so near him.

When I called to tell him, I could sense that he was not pleased, but I wasn't in the habit of asking his permission and I had already accepted the residency.

I did not have time to see him until my third night in the city. He came to the apartment that had been provided for me in what by then had begun to be called the East Village instead of the Lower East Side. I had lived there years before it was gentrified and still had a couple of friends in the neighborhood. I assumed we would go out to eat, but he brought some Chinese takeout and a six-pack of Tsingtao.

I didn't need great intuition to see that he was angry, although I had no clue as to why. "You shouldn't have come to New York and parked yourself here for weeks," he said, grimacing. He put the takeout on the table but stood, looming over me.

"I don't need your approval to come to New York. I lived here for seven years before I ever met you."

"But you expect me to eat with you, sleep over, run around to flicks. You expect to call me any time and drop in."

"I assumed you'd want to spend time with me. But I'm here making a living." I reiterated what I'd said on the phone, that I was not dependent on him. "I like New York. And I thought you'd be pleased to have some unscheduled time together."

"Unscheduled? Unwanted, you idiot."

"What's with you?"

"Jennifer won't like it. She's going to be pissed off. You've put your foot in it this time. How can I keep her from finding out when you're staying here?"

"Who is Jennifer?" I tried to remember his mother's name. Laura, I thought. Why would this Jennifer be annoyed? He didn't have children by his previous marriage, and his ex-wife's name was Carole.

"Only my girlfriend . . . my fiancée."

"Your what?"

"We're getting married in June."

"But I've been in your apartment lots of times. She doesn't live there."

"Of course she lives there. She's a flight attendant and she's gone half the time. I always put her things away when you came. But now you've blown it! You've really blown it!"

"You've been carrying on an affair with me for nine months and you have a fiancée you're living with? And you never thought to tell me?"

"I didn't tell her, either. Obviously! She's gone a lot. Do you think I'm stupid?"

"No. I am. You're a liar. You're as bad as my ex."

He turned red as a radish and raised his fist at me, shouting that it was all my fault for insisting on coming to New York. "You've messed everything up! How am I going to keep her from finding out?"

"Simple. Get out and stay out. I hate men who lie!"

"Shut your face or I'll shut it for you," he said unoriginally but with emphasis.

I was afraid for a moment, then picked up a chair. "Get out. Get out now. I never want to see you again. If I see you, I'll cross the room to avoid you." I tossed his take-out food into the wastebasket.

Snarling, he took his six-pack and left, slamming the door so hard every loose object in the room shimmied and rattled. I fished the Chinese food out of the trash and sat down to eat it. After all, I was still hungry. I took some pleasure in the image of him packing all of his fiancée's things before I arrived and scrubbing away the traces of my presence before she returned.

I felt humiliated. I had been having an affair with a man who belonged to another woman, not with her knowledge but behind her back—some feminist! I refused ever to see him again. To my surprise, my reaction annoyed him. I don't think he had anticipated when he arrived that our argument would be our last conversation. Perhaps he expected me to apologize, pack up, and go back to Cape Cod, where he could periodically appear.

Of course he got his revenge. He reviewed my books negatively for years in various small publications, always with some sort of dig about my man-hating. But I didn't hate *him*. I felt tricked but lucky to have gotten out when I did. I had been an idiot; he was right. After that, I did a little detective work on any man I considered bedding. I didn't intend to get fooled again. Of course I was, but never quite so badly.

Almost Homeless

Christiane Bird

*H*e was sixteen years older than I was—younger than I am now. I was in my mid-twenties and relatively new to New York. He had been around.

He couldn't hold down a job. He had no money. He was essentially homeless. But he was also witty and charming, sexy and smart, sophisticated and sensitive, and enormously sad.

We met at a writers' event, where I was immediately smitten with his thoughtful eyes, his expansive brow, his long and sensual body, his courtly and worldly-wise ways. I followed him home through the tail end of a surprise snowstorm. He was pushing his bicycle. I was slipping along in flirty leather shoes.

He was house-sitting for a friend in the Village, he'd said, and we turned down a genteel, brownstone-lined block muffled with snow. It was after 2 A.M. and the plows hadn't been through yet. Our footsteps and his bicycle tires made the only marks in the suddenly all-white world.

We climbed up a stoop and he unlocked the door. We stepped inside. I felt a stab of fear. Although the lights were still off, I could tell that the house was completely empty. I could smell it in the air echoing around us. Who was this man? What was I doing here?

There are no lights, my companion said apologetically as he lit a candle, shadows dancing around us in a molten golden light. My friends haven't moved in yet or turned on the electricity. But come, let me show you around, it's a spectacular house.

It was a spectacular house—all three empty floors, connected by a curved staircase. The only furniture was on the second floor: a mattress, a rickety table, two straight-backed chairs, and a broken-down armchair. A picture window looked out onto a backyard centered on a tall, gnarled tree, black limbs limned with white etching the night.

Do you want some coffee? he asked.

I shook my head. I was thinking about going home. But it was cold and snowy and late, and I was already here. My fears had abated.

We must have had sex that night, but that's not what I remember. What I remember is waking hours later to an empty bed. My companion had disappeared. Halfheartedly I called out his name, but I knew it was useless. I was completely alone in a dark, deserted house. Except for the mice. I could hear them scampering around me and I shuddered, imagining hundreds of them spilling across the dusty parquet floors. Would they come up onto the bed? Desperately I wished I could turn on a light.

I can't believe this, I cursed. Where did he go? Why did he go? How dare he?

Again I thought about leaving, and again I stayed put. I didn't want to search for a cab in the dark of a snowy night. I also didn't want to make my way down the unlit stairs, through real or imagined mice. It would be safer to wait until dawn, now not far away. Besides, I was curious. Would he be back by then? Had he had some sort of emergency? Or had he perhaps gone out to get breakfast? (Though even then, less than twelve hours into our relationship, I knew that that was unlikely. He wasn't that sort of man.)

Just before dawn he returned with a flimsy excuse. He hadn't been able to sleep, he'd needed to get some air, he said—later, I found out he often needed to get some air. My anger at being left alone was silly. My fears about the mice were ridiculous. There were only a handful of them and besides, they were his pets, white mice. He'd kept them in a cage for a while, but they'd found their way out and now he let them roam, which probably wasn't wise. Two of them had already disappeared.

I think I went home that morning planning never to see him again. He was just too odd—and old; red flags were sticking up all over the place. Nonetheless, I had to admit to myself, he did intrigue me.

A week or so went by before I heard from him again. Then, and throughout our relationship, he had a good sense of timing, seeming to sense exactly when I would be receptive to seeing him again. If he had called right away, I might very well have ended it then and there. But he knew enough not to push too hard too soon, or try to come too close. He always respected the natural distances that lay between us.

We met for coffee one afternoon later that week, and then he came up my stairs. That marked the real beginning of our relationship.

In our earliest months together, I didn't yet know (or didn't let myself know) about his complete inability to cope with the world. All I saw was his charm, his intellect, his sexiness, and, perhaps most tantalizing of all, the window he seemed to offer me into the artistic and intellectual circles of New York. Most of my friends were just like me, young and new to the city, and I was eager to reach beyond the parameters of that small world. He knew people, he knew things. He also didn't take anything at face value. He was always thinking, observing, analyzing—just like me.·

Because he told me from the start that he was in need of work, I tried to help him. I occasionally heard of freelance jobs, and knew of some that might be appropriate for him. He had gone to Harvard (though he'd never graduated); he knew about science and computers. I helped him land a few minor assignments with an encyclopedia and an obscure newsletter. He started each article off with an enthusiastic bang, writing a few stunning paragraphs, but then got lost in a maze of details and digressions, never completing anything. Feeling responsible, I finished the articles for him while he complained about how stupid the assignment or the editor or the publication was.

At first, I sympathized with him. He was smart, and the jobs were beneath him. Besides, I knew about the writer's inability to finish things. Other more serious writers I knew suffered from the same affliction. As long as what you write remains unfinished, it has the potential for greatness. But as soon as you say it's done, you're done, your lack of genius exposed for all to see. Better not to beg the question.

With no work to fill his days, my companion spent much of his time roaming the streets of New York, perusing flea markets and secondhand bookstores. Before long, I became the recipient of his many "finds"—mostly huge, heavy, and slightly soiled editions of the classics; they were my courtship flowers and candlelight dinners. Along with dozens of other volumes, he brought me three nicely bound volumes of *Moby-Dick* because I'd mentioned one day that I'd never read it, and a collection of discarded but first-rate dictionaries. He knew a great deal about dictionaries and disdained the edition that I'd owned since college.

For a time, he also brought me typewriters. Computers were then replacing IBM Selectrics in offices all over town, and he'd find the old machines out on the streets. Often, though, something was wrong with them—perhaps the well-working ones were turned in for rebates somewhere? At any rate, he'd lug the broken machines, which he always promised to fix but never did, up the stairs of my five-story walkup, to my pleasure the first time, my resignation the next, and then to my gathering fury. I didn't want the clunky things jamming my small apartment. Bags of secondhand books were already half-blocking the door. Sorry, sorry, he'd apologize every time I exploded, looking so hangdog that I inevitably felt guilty and apologized as well—though the machines still had to go.

He was always making me feel guilty, usually over the simple fact that I could cope with the world and he couldn't. Was that his fault? I wondered over and over again as months slipped by. It never really seemed so to me. Maybe some people just don't have the stomach for life's daily battles, I thought. Maybe that's just the way they are made. Can they help that any more than people born with misshapen limbs or limited intelligence can help who they are? My companion had a good heart. Why didn't that count for more?

Because he made no money and I made little, we seldom went out. Sex was the glue that held us together. On a typical "date," we made love for hours and then lounged around my apartment, talking, reading, and drinking the strong coffee that he brewed. Making coffee was one of the few practical things that he did well—years ahead of Starbucks—and my apartment became the breeding ground for secondhand espresso machines as well as IBM Selectrics.

Talking was another of my companion's great talents. He seemed to know something about everything, and I delighted in the way I could ask him about almost anything and he'd not only know the answer but also be able to elaborate on the subject in a highly entertaining way. He wasn't always the best listener, but he was psychologically astute and gave me a few insights into my character that I mulled over for years.

When we did go out, it was seldom much fun. He couldn't stand the noise in most restaurants and didn't like the movies or outdoor events. Theater and concerts were out—way too expensive. Occasionally, I'd volunteer to buy us both tickets to some event, but he always refused the offer. Things are bad enough as they are, he'd mutter, giving me one of the few indications I ever got that he knew things were askew between us. Usually we avoided talking about our relationship; he never brought up the subject and I rarely did. I knew that we had no future together, which is not to say that I didn't daydream, at least during the first few months. He'd get a good job, we'd get a place together, cultivate a brilliant social circle . . .

He had been different once, I knew. He'd told me about his motorcycle trips to Europe, prestigious early job offers, friendships with the near famous—and his stories had the ring of truth. As a young man, he'd been filled with promise. How could all of that be irrevocably gone?

Throughout our relationship—which lasted, on and off, for more than three years—I continued to have my own separate social life, going out with friends and on occasional dates with other men. Though I seldom admitted it to myself, part of me was furious at my companion for not being a "real" boyfriend and for apparently taking me—an attractive younger woman who could do better (!)—for granted. Sometimes, too, I was ashamed of him and of myself for being attracted to him, and ashamed of being ashamed.

Yet whenever I did go out with other men—mostly younger professional types with seemingly bright futures (i.e., just like me)—it never went very far. Compared to my idiosyncratic companion, they seemed so mundane, their conversation so unoriginal, their paths so predictable. Dates with them made me flash ahead to five or ten years hence when we might be safely married with kids and even (gasp) a house in the suburbs. The thought made me blanch—and run. I didn't want anything predictable. I didn't want anything safe. Better to stay with my almost-homeless middle-aged guy with a talent for solving the *New York Times* crossword puzzles in under ten—or was it five?—minutes.

He also had his separate social life, which seemed much more glamorous than mine. As a good-looking and entertaining single male, he was constantly being invited to dinner parties, for which he sometimes dressed in tuxedos he'd found in thrift shops. The parties were given by moneyed friends and acquaintances whom he'd met mostly through family connections. Every once in a while, especially in the beginning, I'd ask him to take me along, but he never would. This isn't fun for me, he'd say petulantly, this is work. I need to network for jobs and places to live.

Work my ass, I would think, but in truth, I didn't really want to go along and eventually stopped asking. I imagined being the youngest person present and the object of much bemusement, as the other guests tried to figure out what had brought the two of us together. I also recognized that I would be a liability should he need to flirt his way into a future house-sitting gig. These I desperately wanted him to find, especially as time went on. I couldn't let him move in with me. I was already in far too deep as it was.

I had let him stay with me for several monthlong periods during the middle stretch of our relationship, and each time the experience had brutalized me. I cared deeply about him by then, but the daily contact made me both furious—everything he did was wrong, wrong, wrong!—and despairing. His depression was all too clear to me by then, and I couldn't see how he was ever going to get out of it. He didn't seem to have any will to change, and try though I would, I could think of nothing to help him. I was too young then to know that you can't really help others; they have to do it themselves. What will happen to him as he grows older? I worried. What will happen to him if I leave him? How can I ever leave him?

When I stopped letting him stay with me and he had no house-sitting gigs, he would contact his last resort: his mother, who owned an apartment on the Upper East Side. I met her once, a diminutive and elegant woman who, despite everything, doted on her son and gave him a small allowance. Well, at least he has that, I thought. And when she's dead and gone, he'll have her apartment.

I can't remember now at what point I gave up hopes of my companion ever introducing me in New York's artistic and intellectual circles. Was it before or after I gave up on all other things, including the possibility of a future together? But although ours was an extreme case, it seems to me that that's often the way it goes in relationships. We all enter into new unions with the highest of hopes, imagining all our daydreams coming true, and then slowly scale back, as the object of desire disappoints. Tick, tick, tick, we cross off one item after the next, although, if we're smitten enough, we're elated when even one or two of our imagined prerequisites remain alive and forgive the rest.

Whenever I watch television shows like *Sex and the City* or listen to certain types of women talking, I feel as if they and I belong to different species. Marrying for money or position never occurred to me when I was in my twenties and thirties. I was looking for Romance, writ large. Now that I'm older, I can better appreciate the advantages of "marrying well," but I continue to think, as I've always thought, that such a union too often carries with it too high a price.

Long before the novelty of my relationship with my almost-homeless guy had worn off, I began obsessing about all the possible unhealthy psychological reasons I might have decided to be with him:

a desire to save him, a fear of commitment to someone more suitable, a possible lack of self-esteem, a sexual addiction to the other that often afflicts women. I knew that, despite my sometimes frequent dating, his presence in my life was keeping me from seriously seeing other men. I also knew that I was "enabling" him. Perhaps, I thought in my lowest moments, we were bad for each other.

I tried to break things off again and again, almost from the very beginning. But it never seemed to work. He'd get upset, he'd leave, I wouldn't hear from him for days, sometimes weeks, even months. But then he'd call, his voice husky, sexy, and sad. Couldn't we just meet for coffee, nothing more? he'd ask.

Coffee, nothing more, I'd finally reply after an unbearable silence, and traipse down the stairs, promising myself that this time I wouldn't let him come back up. But, somehow, I always did.

I finally ended it by writing him a long good-bye letter and then not answering or returning his phone calls. By then I was completely fed up with the way things were, but I can still remember how acutely painful it was to hear his voice on my answering machine and not respond to its suffering. I had finally recognized that we were stuck in a limbo that had no exit, that some problems have no solutions, that I could not move on with my life without moving out of his, and that romance, alas, can carry a couple only so far. He would never change; I needed to live in a more realistic world.

Over the next few years, I saw my ex-beau from a distance once or twice, but met him face-to-face only once, about seven years ago. He was older, of course, but otherwise seemed much the same, which both saddened and relieved me. So he was still all right. I was happy to see him. He gave me the number of the apartment where he was house-sitting and I meant to call. But I never did. The moment passed. I never saw him again.

I could blame my infatuation with my almost-homeless guy on my youth, and it is true that my age played into it. I wouldn't have as much patience for someone like him now. His sadness wouldn't seem so appealing. Back then, I think I equated sadness with wisdom. I know better now.

But my youth is only part of the answer. Most of the men I've ever been with for any length of time have been "inappropriate," in conventional terms at least, in some major way. I've never gotten over my fear of entrapment, and although I've been with the same partner now for fifteen years and we have a daughter, we have never married.

What is it that we look for when we look for a mate? Sexual attraction, mutual understanding, trust, and the ability to have fun together are central, of course. But among countless other things so difficult to articulate, we also want someone who will enlarge our world, expand life's possibilities, make us more than the sum of our parts. And sometimes the best person to do that is someone inappropriate. Sometimes Mr. Wrong is Mr. Right.

Minding My P's and Q's

Harriet Brown

He was a sweet man. Still is, I suspect. I'm not going to tell you too much about him, because I'm sure by now he's someone else's Mr. Right, and I'd hate to blow his cover.

I met Q. at the annual all-night New Year's Eve contra dance in Brattleboro, Vermont. I liked his lean, competent body, his sideburns and gold-rimmed aviator glasses, the way his smile parted his walrus moustache suggestively.

I'd come up from New York City with another man, P., one of the many Mr. Wrongs who accompanied me through my twenties. This particular one was like Velcro, sticking to me grimly when I didn't want him, peeling off the minute I did, able to rip away several layers of skin at one go. What we shared: an appreciation for his penis, neurotic Jewish families (at one Thanksgiving dinner I watched in horror as his mother nearly decapitated his father with an electric carving knife, on purpose), an interest in the arts (I wrote poetry, he played classical guitar), and the ability to match each other step for step in a waltz, scottische, or reel. That night, as on many nights, he picked a fight and went off to dance with other women, and I, too, went looking for other partners.

Q. smiled a lot. Used to the intensely erotic stares of P., I felt myself relax in response to Q.'s white teeth and the crinkly lines around his eyes. He was a little tall for me, but he leaned his shoulders forward when we swung around and around, so that by the end of the dance I didn't have a crick in my neck. When the music stopped, he bowed low, then tweaked the end of his moustache and flew across the dance floor to his next partner. I admired the shift of his tush in his tight blue jeans.

By the next morning I'd forgotten all about Q., reabsorbed in the nightly drama of my relationship with P.—lust turning to grief and then rage, the hottest sex I'd ever had followed by smashing crockery, the occasional slap, the inevitable passionate reconciliation. But a month or two later, when P. and I were in one of our more distant phases—in other words, when he was back to screwing the woman he'd been screwing since before we met and whom he would continue to screw long after we split up—I caught a ride up the Thruway with a couple of other dancers and found myself on another dance floor, face-to-face once more with Q. This time, after our turn on the floor, we exchanged names and life stories. He was a welder; his hands were rough and calloused, unlike the hands of any other man I'd touched. His parents were dead. He had never been to New York City.

He called a week later, the first of a number of conversations that neither lit any fires nor set off any alarms. They were a relief, frankly, from the Sturm und Drang of my relationship with P., who refused to hold my hand in public, say he loved me (though we both knew he did), or break up with me. So a few weeks later I was on the train, heading north to spend a weekend with Q. I told P. I was unavailable for the weekend. *Fuck you, buddy,* I meant.

Q. met me at the train station with a handful of dyed carnations. I was charmed and unnerved; P. had never brought me flowers, and he would never have bought carnations. A Venus flytrap, maybe. Carnations were cutesy, I thought, then felt ashamed of my snobbishness. Maybe this traumatized bouquet was all the florist had left. Maybe it was all Q. could afford.

Or maybe he just liked dyed carnations. I got another shock when we pulled up in front of his house, which was actually a trailer. I'd never been inside a trailer before. This one was small but neatly kept, and smelled of dirty sneakers and fabric softener. The best thing about it was the woodstove; I imagined lying on a quilt in front of it, feeling the delicious heat warm my skin.

That weekend we went to a dance; we cooked; we made love. I don't remember the details, which as much as anything foreshadows the end of this story. I remember that I went back two weeks later, and soon I was taking the train every other week to see Q. And I remember P.'s reaction: with tiresome predictability he grew more interested, not less. We had sex three times a day, lying tangled in my sheets, the sweat prickling our skin. Still flushed and panting, we'd reach for each other again. We couldn't get enough of each other's surfaces—like an itch that can't be scratched, no matter how hard you dig at the raw skin.

After about six months Q. and I spent a weekend at my aunt and uncle's lake house in upstate New York. He gave them a pair of candlesticks he'd made, which still sit on their mantel, twenty-two years later. My uncle revved up the motorboat for water-skiing, and while Q. was in the boathouse putting on his life jacket I said to my aunt, "I don't think he's the one for me."

I *wanted* him to be the one. I'd been miserable for two years. I was sick of the game I was playing with P. But I couldn't imagine stopping. I wanted to be happy. But I didn't know how.

Q. was a gentleman. He was considerate and kind and a sexy dancer. He read, when he read at all, the kind of book you pick up in an airport and leave on the plastic seat. He listened attentively when I read him poems, but he didn't understand poetry or why I wrote it.

One Friday night, as we cruised the grocery store, shopping for the weekend, he stopped the cart in the cereal aisle, his brown eyes solemn. "Are you serious about me?" he asked. We were surrounded by bright boxes of sugary nothings. "Because if not, we should stop right now. I don't want to get hurt."

I knew what I should have said: *Listen, this has been a lot of fun, but I've got to be going.* But I couldn't bring myself to be that kind with either of us.

Two weeks later, when I swung off the train, he gathered me in a hug. "I have a surprise for you," he said. We covered the twenty miles to his trailer in half the usual time, pulling up in a cloud of dust. "Close your eyes," he said, and led me up the steps and inside.

I opened my eyes. In one corner, previously piled with boxes, he'd built me a small desk, big enough for the portable typewriter I was lugging back and forth. There was a wooden cup for pens and pencils, a gooseneck lamp, a vase with a single rose in it. A rose, not a carnation.

He had made a space for me in his life. How I wished I wanted to move in.

That night we lay in bed in the dark. The trailer had no curtains; it was far enough away from other houses that no one could see in easily. The new moon shone through the window, a sliver of brightness.

"I have something to tell you," he said. His tone made the hairs on my arms stand up. "But you have to promise not to laugh."

"Okay," I said, glad of the covering darkness.

He drew a breath. "I . . . dress up sometimes," he said quietly.

Silence; I didn't know, yet, what we were dealing with, what to say.

"What I mean is," he went on, "I dress up in women's clothes."

My brain and body went into survival mode, as if we'd just been in a small, nonfatal car crash. *Okay, just stay calm, keep breathing, it's going to be all right.*

I had to respond, but how? "Um, where do you get them?" It was all I could think of.

His voice warmed with relief—I hadn't run screaming out of the trailer. "When my mother died last year I got a whole box of her clothes," he said, and laughed, a marveling, knee-slapping kind of laugh. "Can you believe it? They fit really well. We must be the same size."

I sat up in bed, pulled the sheet up to my neck, and turned on the light. "That's *sick,*" I said, and immediately wished I hadn't. Q.'s face crumpled, then hardened. We turned our backs on each other and lay there for the rest of the night, not speaking.

Playing at Lady Chatterley was one thing; dating Norman Bates was another. The next morning I put myself and my portable type-writer back on the train. I never saw Q. again.

I went back to P. For a while, anyway. When I finally left him—for the man who, twenty-two years later, is still my husband—he took it badly, as I knew he would, calling at all hours, hanging around my apartment, falling into step with me on the way to work. "We had something special," he would say in his deep growl.

"Emphasis on *had*," I'd say, and keep walking. In the end I had to get a lawyer friend to write him a letter and make him leave me alone.

I heard two things about Q. in the years that followed: that he'd gotten married, and that he'd lost two of his toes in a welding accident. I hoped he could still dance. I hoped his wife didn't write poetry or mind being married to a cross-dresser. I hoped I hadn't trampled the sweetness out of him.

Most of all I hoped I would never run into him. What would I say—"Sorry I was such a bitch twenty years ago"? I moved halfway across the country and had two daughters. Later I heard that P. had moved to New England and was living with an old girlfriend—a different old girlfriend, not the one he'd been seeing when we were together—but still wasn't "committing." I wonder if he still plays guitar, if he has ever longed for a home and children.

I wonder if Q. still puts on his dead mother's clothes, and how it makes him feel. Would I react the same way now, presented with that same confession? Or would I make my voice soft and sympathetic, and say, "Tell me all about it"?

Isn't that, after all, what we do with the people we care about—swallow hard, open ourselves to their peculiar longings, their ecstasies and griefs?

Senior Prom

Roxana Robinson

When I was thirteen, I entered the local public high school. I was both excited and alarmed by this: excited that I would be moving into a life that was faster than mine, alarmed because I was not sure I could keep up the pace.

Until then my life had been quiet. I had always gone to a small, private, Quaker school. My family was Quaker, and in fact my father was the head of the school. We lived out in the country, surrounded by farms, and my older siblings were away at college. We had no television set, and I spent most of my time alone, reading. Of course I knew all this was wrong, I knew this was not the way a normal teenager would live. I had read teen magazines, and I knew from the advice columns that normal teenagers spent their time driving too fast, drinking too much, and having unprotected sex. I was looking forward to doing all these things at my new school. I was looking forward to being picked up by a fast current and carried out of my silent Quaker pool into something turbulent and thrilling. My chance would be brief: the following year I was going to my mother's all-girl boarding school. I had one year in which to enter the wild teenage world, to become normal.

The local school held both junior and senior high, grades seven through twelve. This meant that all the lower classes took the same buses and used the same classrooms and breathed the same air as the seniors, who owned the school. The seniors moved confidently, they called out to one another in the halls, raising their voices and taking possession of their space. The rest of us were in their thrall. Between periods, when everyone changed rooms, a senior hall monitor stood at the end of each long hallway. The monitor was there to remind us of the rule of law, and we passed the upright figure respectfully, our books hugged to our chests, our eyes straight ahead. The seniors were our aristocracy. We did not look at them directly, but from the side, with deference.

In the fall, I tried out for the school play. The auditions were open to everyone, though the principal roles all went to the seniors. I was given the role of a child. It was a small part, but it thrust me into a new circle, and I became friends with two senior boys.

The play's hero was played by Donny, who was president of the senior class. He was tall and lanky, with a long, friendly, irregular face. He drove a red secondhand convertible, and he was applying to Stanford and MIT. I did not care about the colleges or the convertible: what I loved was Donny's easy, offhand manner. One day in the drugstore, Donny came up behind me, bumped against my shoulder, and said agreeably, "Sheesh, they let *anybody* in here."

I was enchanted by this. In my family we did not banter. We argued, we told jokes, or we were silent. I hardly knew what banter was.

I was enchanted by Donny, but I was far too awed to consider him in a romantic way. He was a senior, and also, of course, he had a girlfriend. I didn't know her, but I knew who she was. She was a senior, too. Her name was Carol.

Once, outside, waiting for the late bus, I saw Carol waiting, too. She had perfect skin, a pure profile, and an air of calm. Her light-brown hair was in longish loose curls. She wore a pale blue sweater set with the sleeves pushed up, a full skirt, and little white sneakers with rolled-down white socks. When her bus arrived she walked toward it. At the curb, she set her tiny sneakered feet neatly side by side on the edge of it, and then she rose slightly up on her toes and let her momentum carry her forward, over the lip of the curb, as though she were about to fall, her books held modestly against her chest. It was a very small movement, private, discreet, and almost unbearably romantic: the unexpected yielding, the sweet surrender to the air.

Watching her, I was mesmerized and humbled. "That is what Donny wants," I thought. "A girl who would do that, hold her books to her chest and pause, poised on the edge of the curb, and let herself fall, gently, into the next step. That's what he wants in a girl." It made me feel helpless and respectful: it was not something I would have done, nor would it have occurred to me. I was thirteen.

My other senior friend was Ralph, who was short, breathtakingly handsome, and not the president of anything. He was barely taller than I, with dark sunny skin, black eyes and hair. Ralph was funny, in a quirky, restless, nonverbal way. It was mostly expression and timing—just seeing his face made me start to smile. Sometimes we had lunch during the same period, and we sat together. Sometimes we ran into each other in the halls, after school. All we did was laugh. We never met outside school, or talked on the phone. Ralph had a girlfriend, too, with fluffy blond hair and a wide mouth. She was a junior. I was a ninth-grader, and without expectations.

In my own class I had no boyfriends, and not many girlfriends, either. At the beginning of the year all the girls had been friendly, but around midwinter the popular girls sent me a long handwritten letter, signed by them all. They had made a list of my flaws, with prescriptive suggestions. These girls had all gone to school together since first grade, and I was a newcomer, and they thought—who knows what they thought? They thought I had many flaws, and they were right. My response was energetic and uncooperative, and after that, my only friends were two girls who were not popular enough to have been asked to contribute to the list, though much nicer than the ones who had.

In any case, we were all in the "advanced" section—9A—and we were all, I am afraid, dorks. I looked longingly at the bad boys in 9E, who wore heavy black boots and motorcycle jackets, and missed classes. They did not return my longing looks—why would they? I was straight as a lath, with short mousy brown hair, and not allowed to wear makeup. As the year went on it was clear that no wild current was about to sweep me over the falls. Ralph and Donny, elevated though they were, were not bad boys, and anyway they did not ask me out. The wild current coursed along through the school, but I was still in my backwater.

In the spring, the main event was the senior prom. The halls were covered in posters, and assembly was full of announcements. We all watched the seniors to see who would go with whom. By then we knew their names, we had watched their romances bloom and fade, we gossiped about their lives. We knew who had been thrown out, who was flunking, who drank too much. Who had gotten into college. Who, among the girls, was "fast."

There were two famously fast girls: one had straw-white blond hair, pulled back in a wispy ponytail, and one had very dark hair, cut short with bangs. They were both very buxom, and wore bold colors and tight sweaters. They weren't beautiful: the blond one had bad skin, and the dark one was duck-footed and rolled from side to side when she walked. In the halls they were always together, their books clasped to their big chests. They walked fast, with their heads high. It was said they would sleep with anyone. They were deep in that current, tossing in its foam.

What did the ninth-graders know about who the seniors slept with? We knew nothing, nothing at all, but we told one another these things with fascination and reverence. At my elementary school no one had slept with anyone. Gossip about sex between people you actually knew was stunning to me: these were people who had actually done it. The seniors were another race; the lives they led were not like ours.

A few weeks before the prom, Ralph called me at home one afternoon.

His voice was subdued and formal. "This is Ralph," he said carefully, as though we had never met.

At once constrained by his constraint, I answered in the same tone. "Hello," I said soberly.

"I'm calling," Ralph said, "to see if you would go to the senior prom with me."

"Hold on," I said. "I have to ask my mother."

I was upstairs, in my parents' bedroom, and I sped downstairs and out to the back lawn, where my mother was hanging up laundry.

"It's a friend of mine," I told her importantly. "He wants me to go to the senior prom."

"Who?" she asked, mouth full of clothespins.

I had never told her about Ralph—why should I? I told my mother nothing at all if I could help it.

"His name is Ralph," I said. "He's a senior. He's really nice. He's really responsible."

My mother looked at me.

"*Really*," I said fiercely. "Can I go?"

My mother felt she had no control over me, and I knew that. She did have control over me, but she did not know that. Now I stared at her commandingly, aware that there were all sorts of questions she might justifiably ask—who would be driving, what was Ralph's last name, why had I never mentioned him before—but under my ferocious stare she asked none of them. I was commanding her not to. This was my chance to enter that rapid stream.

"He's waiting," I said, adamant. "I have to tell him."

"Oh, well," my mother said in a yielding voice, "the senior prom. All right." She smiled at me.

I knew that my mother believed that, if she were accommodating enough, at some point I would stop being fierce, but this was not true.

I turned and sped back inside, into the kitchen, through the dining room, and up the stairs, two at a time, to the phone in my parents' bedroom.

"Ralph?" I said. "I can go." I tried to quiet my breathing.

"Great," he said cautiously. "That's great."

There was a silence. We didn't know what to say next.

"See you tomorrow."

There was much discussion at home about the dress. I had no idea what to wear. The senior girls would know, but I couldn't ask them since I didn't know them. The popular girls in my class might know, but I couldn't ask them since we no longer spoke.

Between my two remaining friends and my mother, we decided that the dress should be what my mother knowledgeably called "ballerina-length." I hated it when my mother seemed knowledgeable about anything that was in my territory. My territory contained everything in the world except being a mother and having children. My mother's knowledgeability about the dress meant that I couldn't permit myself to ask her any more about this, for fear she would start telling me about the dances she had gone to, the coming-out parties and the proms (neither of my parents had grown up Quakers; they had grown up normal and then imposed Quakerness on all of us later) and what people wore to these events, and I knew all that would make me feel crazed in some puzzling way. I would feel torn by admiration and love for my mother, torn between my pride that she had had such a rich and golden life and a desperate need to keep her and all of her offerings at a remote distance, not to acknowledge that she might have, or might ever have had, anything that I might need at any time.

It seemed that if I admitted my mother's knowledge of anything, or her right to advise me, I would be opening some kind of floodgate, and all would be lost. All the careful work of my separating myself, establishing my own fresh green-leafed stand on my own hillside, would be ruined, and I would be engulfed once more by her towering green crown.

My friends agreed with my mother about the length of the dress, and so it seemed safe for me to do so. We cut down a dress that had been worn by my older sister. The dress was pale blue, with a full tulle skirt, a silky underskirt, and a tight strapless bodice. It was floor-length, so we shortened it to the famous ballerina length, which turned out to be mid-calf.

I don't know why Ralph hadn't asked his girlfriend to the prom; maybe they'd fought or broken up. It did not occur to me that I might actually *become* Ralph's girlfriend. He was about to graduate, and I was about to leave for boarding school, and anyway I felt utterly distant from the seniors. There were layers and layers of mysterious experience that lay between us—between me and Donny's girlfriend, who had done that graceful balancing thing on the edge of the curb. Between me and the two buxom girls in tight sweaters, their chins high and their big breasts jouncing around as they hurried through the halls, on their way to have sex with anyone who asked. I had no idea of how to be a senior, and no wish to be one: I was only thirteen. But I wanted to go to the prom. It was like a promotion—you didn't turn it down.

On the day of the prom I spent the entire day preparing. I knew, from my magazines, that this was what a normal teenager did. It was a ritual. I shaved my legs to marmoreal smoothness. I washed and conditioned my hair. I put rollers in it, and then I sat out on the back lawn and let it turn soft and glossy in the sun. I had a crisp transparent packet of new pantyhose. I had new, low heels (so I wouldn't be taller than Ralph), a strapless bra. I believed that all this meticulous preparation would make it possible for me to enter the world where the seniors lived.

When Ralph arrived that evening I was glimmering with anticipation. Ralph looked handsome and unfamiliar, his white dinner jacket glowing against his caramel skin. Moving carefully in the stiff tulle skirt, the unnerving bra, I introduced him to my parents. My heels made an odd tocking sound on the wooden floor. My father, the headmaster, shook hands with Ralph and looked stern. He asked what time he thought we'd be back.

Ralph stopped smiling. "By midnight," he said.

I was pleased that I'd produced someone so responsible, but disappointed that we'd only stay out until midnight. Weren't you supposed to have more fun than that? Even my mother's coming-out parties had gone on past midnight.

My father nodded to us, and my mother smiled and told us to have a good time, and then Ralph and I said good night, and we stepped into the lilac darkness. We walked across the bumpy lawn to the driveway, where Ralph had parked a small, light-green sedan: clearly the family car. He came around and opened the passenger door for me and I thanked him and slid carefully onto the front seat. I had never actually sat down in the dress before, and I was afraid of destroying the stiff sheets of tulle. Ralph got in and turned on the engine. Our driveway was long and narrow, with high hedges on either side. Ralph had to turn over his shoulder as he backed carefully out, his attention elsewhere.

By the time we had gotten onto the road, the silence had been unbroken for several minutes, and it seemed to grow more and more powerful as it lengthened. I waited for Ralph to speak. I watched the stands of white pines sweep past us, tall windbreaks along the edges of the big fields. Ralph, eyes on the dark road ahead, said nothing. It was twelve miles from our house to the school and we drove it in silence. Ralph was a senior, and he would know when to initiate conversation. When he was ready, we would talk.

At the school, we parked, and I watched Ralph as he got out, to see if I should get out myself or wait for him to open my door. I saw that he was coming around, so I sat and waited for him. It felt strange, sitting alone in my stiff skirt, waiting for him to do something that I could so easily do myself, but I knew that different rules applied here. I was in another world, watching for clues.

"Thank you," I said as I got out. Ralph put his hand beneath my elbow and we walked to the entrance of the gym. We stood in line. Ralph had our tickets. We didn't speak.

Inside, we stood together, apart from the others. I didn't know the other seniors, and perhaps Ralph didn't want to introduce a ninth-grader to his friends—despite the (as it turned out) proper length of my dress, my impeccably smooth legs, my shiny hair, my satisfyingly invisible bra. We stood together for a time, with fixed, pleasant expressions on our faces, and then Ralph turned to me and spoke.

"Would you like to dance?"

"Yes," I said, interestingly, and lifted my arms.

For hours and hours we danced without speaking. We danced fast and we danced slow. We stopped for refreshments. We stood silently side by side and drank punch; silently we ate cookies from big round plates.

"Would you like some more?" Ralph asked, and I shook my head and smiled.

We danced again. The longer we went without speaking, the less possible it became for us to speak. The silence had become so dense that breaking it would require words of particular potency and precision. The words would have to be remarkable, words of great fascination, shimmering with genius and charm. As time went by I became less and less sure that I could produce words like this, and finally I became certain that I could not.

Halfway through the evening we went to have our photograph taken. We were told how to stand: close together, my back to Ralph's front, my head leaning lightly back against him, his arm around my shoulders. Behind us hung a glittering moon and stars, and in the picture we are both smiling. Ralph's teeth are very white, and so is his dinner jacket. My hair is curled exactly as I'd wished, my dress just the right length. We look happy. When the photographer told us we were done, we stopped smiling.

At the end of the evening Ralph delivered me home, well before midnight. "Thank you," I said, smiling, when he opened the car door. We walked back across the bumpy lawn to the house. I knew enough to ask him if he'd like to come in, but he knew enough to say no, and then he left.

I went quietly up, walking on tiptoe and trying not to let the stairs creak, but my mother was awake and heard me. She called my name. I knew she wanted me to come into their room and talk, and tell them all about it. "Did you have a good time?"

"Yes," I called back. I went hurriedly into my room and closed the door, as though I didn't want her to know how drunk I was, or how wild the evening had been, or how much unprotected teenaged sex I had just had.

I never told her what happened. I could not risk receiving her sympathy, or learning that she had experienced something similar, or that she knew something that could help me. I knew that I should have been in another world by now, doing something wild and perilous that my Quaker mother knew nothing about, and where she could not help me. I did not want her to know that I had failed to enter that other world.

Several weeks afterward, Ralph came up to me in the cafeteria, with an envelope in his hand.

"I have the pictures from the prom," he said. He wore the same sober expression that he had worn when he arrived that evening, and that seemed never to have left him. We had not spoken since the dance.

"Thank you," I said, taking the envelope. I wondered if I should offer to pay for my share. Or would that be gauche? Was this all part of the larger expense of the prom, assumed by the boy? I should know about this, but I did not. "Are all these for me, or would you—?"

At once Ralph put his hand up, palm out, as though to forestall absolutely my offering him any of the prints, or payment, or my offering him anything else, really, at all, ever.

"Please," he said.

It was the last time we ever spoke.

Ralph graduated in June, and I went away to boarding school in the fall. Who knows what happened that night? Who knows why Ralph asked me to the prom in the first place? Who knows why my mother let me go? Who knows why I thought I ought to go? Who knows why both Ralph and I were struck across the mouth by the goddess Mute at the start of that silent evening? It was a mystery to me, as was almost everything in my ninth-grade year: the romantic haze surrounding the lives of the seniors, the giddy approach of sexuality, the great mystery of boys and how they work.

I knew that I was responsible for the evening's failure: I knew from my reading that it was the girl's responsibility to provide charm. That's what girls did, from Lizzie Bennett to Daisy Buchanan, and I had failed. I had failed to create the right mood, one that would have carried us, light and buoyant, through the evening. Something in me had frozen stiff. The strangled silence was my fault, and I was ashamed. I had failed as a woman, and sometimes I wondered if the girls in my class had been right about my flaws. Banter was not in me.

For a long time afterward, whenever I thought of that evening, I thought of my failure. But years later I had a revelation: it occurred to me that Ralph, too, could have spoken. He could have said something. I was not, necessarily, responsible for everything. It was not just me, it was both of us. We were both shy, we had both been struck dumb. We were both kids, even though Ralph was a senior.

Now, when I look back at that night, what I feel is affection for the two of us, so carefully prepared for the momentous evening, the great occasion, both top-heavy with expectation. Stiff and silent, circling the dance floor, courteous, wordless, waiting for something to make us come alive: we were like hapless creatures in a fairy tale, under a malign spell, hopefully, helplessly longing for it to be broken.

I should have known when I saw Carol let herself fall so beautifully into space over the curb that the seniors knew things I could not know. I should have known when my mother frowned, her mouth full of clothespins. I should have known that even my mother, who knew *nothing, nothing, nothing* about my world, had known something then that I did not.

But I was confused about what I knew and what I did not, and so I spent that long evening circling and circling in silence with handsome, black-haired Ralph, waiting for someone to speak; waiting for the spell to be broken; waiting, simply, though I didn't know it, to be older.

Good-bye to the Gaiety

Marilyn Jaye Lewis

*L*et's say I'm twenty and the year is 1980. The place is a clinic for poor people on some bombed-out corner in Brooklyn. It's nighttime, pitch-dark outside. The clinic is nearly deserted, and at this late hour, it's supposed to be closed. However, tonight they've stayed open late for us. I'm there with my very first husband-to-be and we're getting our blood tests done in order to apply for our marriage license. We've known each other only a handful of months, really. He's come to this clinic in Brooklyn by way of Singapore, London, Paris. I've come less illustriously—by way of Ohio. Neither of us has lived in New York for a year yet.

"There is good news, my friend!" The Pakistani doctor announces this with great relief as he joins us in the poorly lit examining room. I've never seen this doctor before, never stepped foot inside this dilapidated clinic until now. "We were wrong, my friend; it's *not* syphilis."

He's directing this heady comment at Liu, my intended. Apparently they've met before. Liu is glancing at me uncomfortably, caught with his pants down, as it were, and I'm doing what I did best back then: politely acting like I hadn't just heard something terrifically alarming and unexpected. Never mind the fact that it was indeed "good news."

Let's fast-forward to spring 2005. The Gaiety Theatre, a male strip club and hustler bar in Times Square, is finally closing its doors after thirty "wonderful years" of notoriety.

I'm not feeling at all wistful about the news. I'm glad to see it go.

Somewhere in those two seemingly isolated events, events separated by twenty-five years, no less, is the crystallized essence of a marriage—mine. Or what came to be called, in my head anyway, the incredibly true disaster of Mr. & Mrs. Liu Man Rui.

♥ ♥ ♥

It's safe to say I was born a Kinsey 3; I came to it by birth. A right-down-the-middle bisexual, I could go either way with an equal amount of fervor and had been that way since before puberty, falling hopelessly in love with my female babysitters as easily as I fell in love with the boys at school or the male lifeguard at the community swimming pool. I had no idea that this was in any way unusual. I just went with it and let the often-strange responses I received to my various confessions of love just roll off my back. It was everybody else who was weird. It wasn't me. When I was in my teens, frustrated with the classmates who regarded my open bisexuality with contempt, but still getting plenty of action from both sexes, I decided that these classmates were just jealous of me and lying to themselves; that *everyone* was bisexual, that some were simply afraid to admit it.

By the time I met Liu, my world was populated mostly with gay men who sometimes fell in love with girls, and bisexual women who, like me, were all over the map. (It's prudent to recall that this was New York City in 1980. The dawn of AIDS was on our horizon but we didn't yet see it coming, that dawn that would eviscerate everything we loved.)

My deep-rooted belief that people were liars about their sexuality held true for Liu as well. When he said he wanted to marry me, I knew he still wanted to sleep with men. Why not? I still wanted to sleep with girls. In 1980, we were all sleeping with everyone; married people, single people, straight people, gay people. Sex did not necessarily go hand in hand with love, marriage, or commitments to a lifestyle, nor did it discount those things. But it never once occurred to me that he had never been intimate with a woman in his life and wasn't about to start anytime soon. It was one of those wedding-night rude awak-enings, of the rudest variety imaginable. "I don't love you, you know," he confessed over the roast chicken and the white wine. "I feel a deep sense of gratitude toward you for becoming my wife, but I'm never going to love you in any way." And then he spent our wedding night on the floor.

In my fashion, I acted as if it were okay, those piercing words I'd just heard that had torn my heart to pieces. I'd just *married* the fucker. Why had I *bothered*?

They say people come to New York City to escape reality, or at the very least to rewrite it for themselves. It was certainly why I'd come. Terrible things had happened to me back in Nowhere, Ohio. After that, I couldn't get to New York City fast enough. The folks at home warned me of the terrors of the Big City. But by then nothing could be as frightening to me as simply staying at home.

What had brought Liu to New York, I learned after our wedding night, was his homosexuality. Had I known before our wedding that he was "totally gay," that not everyone was secretly bisexual and just lying about it, I doubt I would have married him. Which is not the same as saying I *regret* marrying him. I don't. And I stayed married to him for nine years, just refusing to live under the same roof with him for seven of them.

It wasn't so much that he was gay that exasperated me. It was that he was closeted about it. Nobody else I knew was closeted about it. Yet it was the sole reason he'd married me, I soon found out—to have a beard, a lovely Caucasian wife to hide behind so that he could conduct business as a straight man, could present himself to his parents, his family, as a straight man.

In Singapore, where Liu had grown up, gone into the army, been educated, where his family still lived as part of the aristocracy com-plete with live-in servants in a grand home right next door to the prime minister's, it was a crime punishable by imprisonment to be ho-mosexual. Coming to America didn't take away Liu's innate fear of being found out to be homosexual. It simply enabled him to have many, many male lovers outside the confines of his acceptable-on-the-face-of-it marriage.

I felt sorry for him, for his need to keep his true self locked so tightly in a closet while everyone else I knew had been liberated. But what was worse is that I loved him, and so part of me was in that closet with him. After a respectable period of not necessarily grieving but of being in stupefying shock over having agreed to this crazy marriage, it soon became way too close for comfort in that god-awful closet.

♥ ♥ ♥

With any luck, we can each look back on our lives and have a favorite person come to mind. For me, that favorite person was Paul. We met in the high school theater department when we were seventeen. I was introverted and moody but smart, with a keen sense of humor. He was buoyant, outgoing, campy, and side-splittingly funny. We became fast friends. When we realized we were both "out"—actively having sex with partners of our respective genders—we became inseparable. Two freaks of nature stuck together in a high school of hostility. Paul became my very best friend on the planet. The kind you are guaranteed to have but once in a lifetime. That kind of friendship *can't* come again because your youth, and all the excitement and crazy insecurities of it, can't come again. After nearly ten years of being ravaged by AIDS, Paul died in the fall of 1999, on a crystal clear and cool October evening. The nurse told us that at around eight o'clock, he'd smiled at something in the corner of the hospital room and waved, then he'd said, "That's my grandma, she's waiting for me." He passed on peacefully, guided to heaven by Grandma. It probably doesn't get better than that, comfort-wise.

Let's rewind to 1982. Let's say I'm living in the theater district with my closeted husband, Liu, and that my best friend Paul, a blatantly gay guy who works in the theater professionally now, has come to visit us. Let's say it bothers me not one iota that they have sex together right there in Liu's bed while I sleep in the next bed over, or that they carouse together through Times Square until all hours. That they really hit it off in that way gay guys do—inseparable, at least until the minute they are separated.

Let's say both of them are already infected with the deadly virus that will savagely rob them of life, very slowly, due to all the new and unpronounceable drugs the doctors will be experimenting with. Now let's say a prayer of thanks that we didn't know it yet—how it was going to go for them, the merciless way it was going to end.

Amen, we say. *Thank you, God. I'm glad we didn't know. And God, as long as you're here,* I pipe up, *that misery I used to feel because my own husband steadfastly refused to sleep with me? Well, now I see it was a gift, God. With every fiber of my being I also thank you for that.*

♥ ♥ ♥

Thanks for the memories, Liu. And here they are now, those memories, those reasons I loved you, why I hated you, why I don't regret the day you walked into my life.

The first time we met, I was bowled over by your very presence. I'd been in New York only a matter of weeks but I was already pregnant. Already running from myself again. I was looking for a place to live, to hide out from the man who'd knocked me up. He'd been superb in bed, but he was twenty years too old for me. He claimed to be in love with me, nonetheless. What he wanted more than anything, he'd said, was to get married to me, have a baby with me; a future together. But he was involved in organized crime—specifically, a hit man. He killed people for a living. On the day he decided to ask me to marry him, he confessed his profession to me over a light lunch in a local delicatessen.

"Don't worry, I'll teach you how to use a gun," he'd assured me, not noticing I'd stopped eating and was in horrified shock. "You know, so you can protect yourself when I'm away."

Instead of cluing him in that we were already pregnant, I made a run for it and never looked back.

In the crumbling, unrenovated town house where I would soon be renting a room, I met you, Liu. A Chinese man who was as tall as I was—not something I'd encountered before. You dressed impeccably in designer clothes, clear down to your Yves Saint-Laurent socks. You spoke with a very formal British accent and had been educated in London and Paris. You extended your hand to me and said, "My goodness, aren't you beautiful. It's so very nice to meet you. It will be such a pleasure to have you living here."

What were you—continental, cosmopolitan? I mean, what were you besides secretly more feminine than I was, opening like a delicate Asian flower when you were with a man, *any* man, behind closed doors? I'd never met anything like you in Nowhere, Ohio. And you were so damned considerate of me. After I'd moved into the building, where we all lived in communal fashion, and you surmised I was pregnant, you never once mentioned the pregnancy. Yet you brought me saltines and soda water from the bodega across the street. And you brought me a tiny bottle of eucalyptus oil from a shop in Chinatown.

"The women in my country use this," you explained cryptically, handing me the tiny bottle. "They rub a drop into their navels when they're feeling, you know, like they're going to vomit."

You never once asked, was I going to keep the baby? Get an abortion? Or even why I was pregnant in the first place, so obviously without the benefit of marriage.

Instead you sat next to me while I lay on the sofa in nauseated misery, and you chatted with me, asking about my dreams, my goals, about what I was planning to do with my life. You didn't judge me and you were so incredibly kind.

On the afternoon you asked me to marry you, I was no longer "with child" and we were no longer living in the same building. I was now living in a walk-up in Hell's Kitchen. When you came to my apartment that day, you were dressed impeccably, as always. As you sat on the small sofa, the only sign of your nervousness was the way you twirled your slender black umbrella while you spoke.

You handed me a handwritten list of all the reasons why I should marry you. And then you said, "If you become my wife, I will always take care of you. You will never want for anything. All my life I've dreamed of coming to America and having a beautiful Caucasian wife like you. You simply have to say yes."

You believed in me, you'd said. You wanted to help me achieve my dreams, too. You couldn't imagine me not marrying you.

Ten days later, feeling friendless and at loose ends in New York City, I wrote you a brief note and mailed it to you, saying that yes, I'd marry you.

On our wedding day at City Hall, the sun was shining like mad. After we'd said, "I do," you told me that I was nothing less than a gift to you from heaven. That you always knew you were going to meet a woman like me one day, that we'd be together.

I was swept away by your intoxicating romanticism. At a lonely time in my life, I suddenly felt loved. I felt like you were my destiny, too, and I said as much. It didn't occur to me that I'd never once dreamed of being with a man like *you*. In fact, I never spent much time thinking about getting married at all. Then, of course, later that night, as wedding nights go, ours was that complete disaster.

♥ ♥ ♥

Our First Christmas Together. So many Hallmark Christmas ornaments display this commercially viable sentiment. In our happy home, our first Christmas together cut me like a knife.

That year you were having a platonic "flirtation" with the actress Nastassja Kinski. You'd met her at work, remember? In that chichi health food restaurant on Fifty-seventh Street. You were smitten with her and you spoke to me about it constantly. She wrote you harmless little love notes on paper napkins, which you'd squirrel away in your dresser drawer, for me to find later when I was alone.

"She's so beautiful," you'd rave breathlessly. "She reminds me so much of you, Marilyn, dearest, before you put on all the weight." And: "Her skin is like porcelain, honestly—even up close. I'm *certain* your skin would be just like hers if you didn't drink quite so much, dearest."

Oh et cetera, et cetera, et cetera. It never stopped. It tortured me. It was bad enough that you insisted on calling me "Marilyn, dearest" while the campy *Mommie Dearest* was all the rage. I couldn't compete with a fucking movie star, and I was vain and egocentric enough to *lament* that I couldn't, so I drank more.

In a light snowfall, we went to the Times Square Woolworth's, long gone nowadays, and bought an artificial Christmas tree. Lights, glass ornaments, tinsel—the works. I was silly enough to feel excited about having your complete attention, about decorating our first tree together.

You helped me assemble the tree in the living room. The eggnog was ready; Christmas records were on the record player while I waited eagerly for you to come out of the bathroom and help me start decorating our tree. You seemed to be taking an inordinately long time in the bathroom—even for a fastidious man like you.

When you finally emerged, you were dressed exquisitely in a black suit and tie. "What's going on? Why are you dressed like that?" I needed to know.

"I have a date, dearest," you explained, throwing on your black, tailor-made cashmere coat. "I'm meeting a chap in Chinatown. Don't wait up for me; I'm not coming home tonight. Enjoy your tree."

I tried so hard not to hate you as you walked out the door that night. I took it out on myself instead; you'd rescued me from loneliness, hadn't you? You *believed* in me when not many people did. With a splitting headache, I decorated that goddamned tree.

Two days later, I awoke from a mid-afternoon nap, staring at "our" Christmas tree, and realized with a start that this was not the tree I'd decorated. While I'd been out the day before, you had completely redone it and now it looked fucking fabulous. Once again, I'd failed where you'd succeeded. God, I *hated* you.

♥ ♥ ♥

Two years into the marriage. You sleep with men. I sleep with girls and occasionally with other men now. For some inexplicable reason, though, I still live for those private moments when we're alone together and you find even a shred of a reason to praise me—like you did on our wedding day. To give me a reason to pretend, as if this marriage weren't a complete self-destructive mistake. You're good about giving me gifts—clothes, jewelry, chocolates. You leave little surprises of cash on my night table. However, you frequently wish aloud that I would "grow up" and stop running around with musicians. I'm a professional singer by this time, so it doesn't seem likely to happen anytime soon.

And look! Paul is visiting us again.

One afternoon, Paul and I take a walk. He angles us over to West Forty-sixth Street and we come to a stop in front of the Gaiety Theatre. Paul points up at it—it's on the second floor of a tall building.

"That's a hustler bar up there," he notes.

"So?"

"So, you know how come I know that?"

"No, how come?"

"Your husband took me there last night."

"Did he?" It's not fazing me. "What do I care about the gay clubs you two go to together?"

"Marilyn, he *works* there."

I look at him blankly.

"Your husband's a hustler—he turns tricks at night."

Your husband's a hustler. He turns tricks at night. My goodness. You don't know how incredible that sounds, how foolish it makes you feel, until someone who cares about you is saying something like that to you in earnest.

What haunted me most was that I couldn't understand *why*. You were a businessman with a master's degree. You had a wealthy family back home that frequently wired money into your account at the Bank of Singapore in Rockefeller Center. Why this need to turn tricks, to get fucked by men for money? Were you really that hardhearted?

You didn't know yet that I'd found out, so it was hard to figure out how to ask you to explain yourself. From then on, though, when you left gifts of cash on my night table, the money disgusted me. Not that I would have judged you if we'd met and were friends and you'd confided in me that you were a hustler—so many guys I knew back then were hustlers—but why did you have to *marry* me?

Eventually I confronted you with what I'd found out. You cried when I told you I was leaving you, but I left anyway.

For the next several years, each time I tried to so much as broach the subject of a divorce, you'd cry again. You'd sob, actually. "You're *my wife*," you'd rant. "You're supposed to stand by me. I need you."

For what, exactly? To hold your ring?

Like that night many years earlier, when we'd stood together in a ticket line outside a movie theater in Times Square. "Here!" You'd suddenly panicked, pulling your wedding band off your finger as a man came toward us, waving happily at you. "Hold this," you'd said, slipping the ring to me, "and act like we're just friends."

As always, to protect you, on instinct I did what you asked and acted like your denial of me hadn't hurt.

That was not one of the nights I felt fond of you.

After we'd been living apart for three months, you took me on a "date." We met on Mulberry Street, in Chinatown, and popped in at a Buddhist temple because you wanted to say a quick prayer. Then we went on to dinner together, to a place only the Chinese people frequented. Everyone around us was speaking Mandarin. In those years, I couldn't speak a word of it. After you died, I painstakingly taught myself to speak it, to read and write it. It gave me a degree of comfort, a measure of joy.

In the restaurant, you said, "Do you know what these people around us are saying?"

"Of course not," I said.

"They want to know why a beautiful Caucasian woman like you is in a place like this having dinner with me."

For some reason, we both found this very funny. Perhaps it was because we knew it was a question of cosmic proportions; that it was a question of destiny, a question of primal need and maybe even of unconquerable fear.

After dinner, we went for a winding walk through the busy, crazy streets of Chinatown.

"You look good," you said to me.

"I stopped drinking," I replied.

"It suits you—being separated from me, I mean."

Then you handed me a small gift-wrapped package. "It's for you," you said offhandedly. "I just wanted you to know I think of you now and then."

I unwrapped the gift. It was a cassette tape of Willie Nelson's song, "Always on My Mind."

Later that night, alone in my new apartment, I played the song over and over again. Of course, I cried.

▾ ▾ ▾

Fast-forward to here, to now.

I still have the Willie Nelson tape, although I know I won't have it forever. Cassette tapes disintegrate and crumble over time, and it's already been twenty-two years since Liu gave it to me. Not even cassettes are meant to last forever. I guess nothing is. By now, it's no real surprise to me. Even a veritable institution like the Gaiety Theatre eventually closes its doors and vanishes into the outrageous night.

I take no issue with men loving men. I support it. I'll go so far as to say I celebrate it and always have. But I don't think it's a woman's place to marry into it. I feel sorry for those women I sometimes see on tabloid TV shows, who find out, in front of the televised world, that their husbands are raging queers after dark and the poor women are the last to know. I haven't been spared too many travesties in my life but at least I was spared that particular one.

In the last note I received from my (by then) ex-husband Liu before he died, he wrote, "Marilyn, dearest, I am forever grateful to you. I will never forget you and all you did for me." He was referring to how I'd petitioned the Naturalization Services to help him become an American citizen, even though we were legally separated; and how, after he'd been raped by a deranged Filipino man and wound up in an emergency room in Honolulu, I'd stood by him; or how I'd held his hand while he'd wept uncontrollably, having just been unceremoniously dumped by his much older Brazilian lover for a much younger Chinese boy. Those types of things. The types of things any wife does in a pinch, I figure—right? Liu's note indicated he was grateful for all of it and then some.

Why did his last note to me leave me feeling so defeated?

Still that darn gratitude, I realized, and not a speck of the word *love*. Was I still expecting it after all that time? Always a bit of a romantic, I'm ashamed to admit it; I was.

The Ten Most Wanted

Marion Winik

When, at twenty-seven, I married a good-looking and funny, though penniless, gay bartender who had recently lost his job as an ice-skating coach due to his drug problem, not everyone understood that this was a sensible choice, or at least a significant upgrade. While we usually think of a "bad boy" as some charming roué with a few bad habits, in my younger days I really didn't need the charming part. What I liked was simply bad. Moral turpitude created an allure that was completely independent of good looks or personality.

Unlike other girls with this proclivity, I did not suffer from the Jane Addams syndrome—where the secret goal is to reform the guy, to shine the bright light of your love and middle-class morality into his life, rehabilitating him. This was not my approach. I was more likely to try on, rather than cure, his flaws. A scary thought, as you will soon see.

Perhaps it is my parents' fault for bringing me up in comfort and ease, with my own shag-carpeted bedroom, ballet and piano lessons and new clothes each fall, ice-cream cones at the beach club, family trips to Disney World. What were they trying to do to me? To rebel against kindness and generosity, I had to seek malevolence and dysfunction. And I did, with a single-mindedness only recently tempered by advancing middle age.

One time, when I was between my first and second husbands, a gorgeous, wealthy, physically fit, and socially conscious doctor—yes, friends, a millionaire M.D.—became infatuated with me. He wanted to take me to Hawaii and entertain me at his marble-floored mansion. I found all this rather unconvincing and gave him no encouragement (though during a particularly screwed-up period, after his crush had petered out, I tried unsuccessfully to get him to write me a Vicodin prescription).

Gone is the doctor and longer gone still are the boys of my youth. If by chance, however, you have seen any of the following shady characters—now grown men—you could either notify the authorities or just send me an e-mail. I'll take care of them. I always have.

1. The Boston Strangler

How can it be that when I was too young to have a real boyfriend but not too young for fantasies, I attempted to initiate a pen-pal correspondence with jailbird Albert de Salvo, the Boston Strangler himself? It was 1967, I was nine years old, and I had just read Gerald Frank's true-crime bestseller, *The Boston Strangler*. (This was typical of my reading material at the time, consisting mainly of books my mother had requested from the library for herself.) What you may not realize is that de Salvo was never charged with the thirteen killings he is associated with; he was in the pen for something else. And if you had read the interview in this book, and found out, as I did, about his horrible, sad childhood and marriage, you'd probably want to write him a letter, too. Too late—he was murdered in jail in 1973.

2. The Boy from the Boardwalk

Donna Benoit and I both loved him, though I can't remember anything good about him except his shoulder-length blond hair, which was very straight and shiny and hung in his face. Perhaps this is why I don't recall much else about what he looked like. I think of a missing tooth. Donna and I met him on the boardwalk in Asbury Park, New Jersey, the town next to ours, on a particular bench where you could always meet guitar-playing hoodlums. Guitar was our bond. Good thing, as he was not much of a conversationalist. From him, I learned the opening bars of "Stairway to Heaven." Soon after, he stole my guitar.

3. The Twins

Buddy and his brother Bobby also came from the boardwalk. Bobby was strawberry blond and freckly, Buddy raw-boned and hazel-eyed. They had an apartment on the top floor of a rattrap building called the Santander. This was an early experience of bad sex on a bare, possibly insect-infested mattress. Also, they stole cash from my father and steaks from our freezer. My sister dated Bobby, but Buddy was all mine.

4. The Guy with the Convertible I Bailed Out of Jail

Who remembers anything about him except that the bail was $150?

5. and 6. My Ivy League Loves

As an undergraduate, I completely lost my heart to my housemate M-, who had a nervous breakdown and a cocaine problem but was the focus of my hopes and dreams for many years. Also at Brown I met Jan, in many ways my first grown-up boyfriend. Just as I had had my enthusiasm for the Boston Strangler, Jan had a fixation on Squeaky Fromme, spokeswoman for the Manson Family and would-be assassin of President Gerald Ford, and had even thought of a plan for springing her from jail. Jan was devoted to bringing down the capitalist state by making free long-distance phone calls, and figured out a scheme to steal money by pretending traveler's checks were lost that involved ordering IDs for babies who would have been the same age as we were if they hadn't died at birth. We actually planned to rob a bank, for God's sake.

7. David Rodriguez

David Rodriguez was an authentic Mexican-American street person whom my sister, my best friend, and I met in Austin, Texas, at an art opening. All of us were at the opening for the free food, and in the months to come he would teach us many, many more ways to get things for free. Hopelessly in love, I hitchhiked with him to Colorado to a creative writing conference. He went to an outdoor concert where he was arrested while trolling the grounds for pills people had dropped. When the police searched him, they found someone else's ID in his pocket, someone who was wanted for grand larceny in the town of Junction, hundreds of miles away. I hitchhiked out behind the police car to spring him. Ultimately, he stole our stereo.

8. Eddie Gonzalez

Eddie Gonzalez was my sister's first husband Steve's friend from high school, and I think he may have been the original link in the chain that got us all doing intravenous drugs. Since he is now many years dead of AIDS, I don't want to go on too much about his terrible complexion, his tedious conversation, or his addiction—all of these I was only too eager to share at the time. It was he who realized how inappropriate our relationship was.

9. Liverpool Dave

Foreign travel provides many opportunities for inappropriate liaisons, as word of a female American tourist passing through town with her easy virtue and her MasterCard will bring out the crème de la crème of any country's freeloading sleazebags. In fact, they're not all sleazebags, some are quite nice, and for this reason it is possible to think of yourself as doing charitable work overseas rather than just being taken advantage of by the uncircumcised. Dave and his friends were a group of on-the-dole Liverpudlians my friend and I met in a bar. They gave us cigarettes and took us to what seemed to be their home, a tent in a field outside Cambridge. Mine was sallow, hollow-cheeked, and so thin I feared I might accidentally suffocate or break him. Though he and his friends stole our camera right after we took the group photos, when I got home there was a letter from Dave suggesting he come to the States and live with me. In a trailer, he said.

10. Tim at the Fiddler's Convention

It was a mistake to go with my bluegrass-loving friends to the Fiddler's Convention in Union Grove, North Carolina, in 1977. I didn't like bluegrass as much as they did, and I soon found live banjo and fiddle combined with very strong LSD to be a form of psychological torture. Even today I cannot hear bluegrass without experiencing a nerve-jangling acid flashback. This unpleasantness was dwarfed, however, by my decision to sleep with a guy named Tim. I remember little about him except his first name and that he looked something like Gregg Allman. I met him that evening when he fell into our bonfire. The rest of our romance is a blank until the next morning when, in his tent, he woke me up by pissing on me. Truly, I am sorry to have to tell you this.

Russian Lessons

Catherine Texier

*I*t was the way he looked at me, I think. His pale, gray gaze had an intensity, a naked knowingness that you wouldn't expect from this hunk of a guy who looked like a marine or an ex-convict—decidedly *louche.* He was standing by the buffet table in loose black pants and a T-shirt, as though he had come straight from the gym—unless it was his idea of a disguise.

We were at a Carnival party at a photographer's loft in Williamsburg, Brooklyn. The loft had a wall of windows overlooking Manhattan in tight close-up. The view was spectacular. Everybody was turned out in silly getups—Roman toga, Marie Antoinette, Tarzan—except him and me. As soon as he opened his mouth I knew he was Russian. Those rolled "r"s, those "w"s that slip into "v"s are unmistakable. "From Siberia," he said, coolly appraising my low-cut top and high-heeled boots with his pale eyes. He might have just been out of the Soviet army. Red hair buzzed tight, thin scar running across his right cheek, massive shoulders, thick hands with square, flat nails that brushed against mine when he brought me a glass of wine, apologizing because there was no more vodka: it all fit, except his question when I told him I was French.

"Did you see that French movie about a young barman and an older woman?" His thin lips stretched in an ironic smile.

I knew exactly which movie he was talking about, *The School of*

Flesh. Isabelle Huppert plays a successful fashion designer who falls in love with a young, penniless bartender. I didn't expect this ex-marine, or whatever he was, to watch art films. But I was impressed by his mix of intuition and cunning. He could play the young, lower-class immigrant while I could be the older woman—a French novelist in New York. And he sensed that I could easily make the leap. Since my divorce, which had left such a huge hole in my life, I'd felt dangerously young again, accumulating flings with a vengeance to make up for the loss of my husband.

"You often go to the movies?"

"No. But I like French movies. And I liked that it was about an older woman and a younger guy." His gray eyes took on an intense, metallic light. "I like older women."

"Why?"

"Because they are deeper, more interesting."

He knew I was older than he, although he may not have known by how much—twenty years, by my calculations, since he had told me he was twenty-four. And he wanted to make sure I knew that he knew.

He held me brutally on the dance floor. Each time he slid his arms along mine his muscles felt like steel ropes. During the next dance, which was a slow one, his sex pushed against my stomach, as stiff and unyielding as the muscles in his arms. The sexual energy between us was so intense, I was sure that if we kept dancing he wouldn't hesitate to fuck me in the middle of the floor. I thought of those working-class Mediterranean men who would press themselves against us, the French bourgeois girls, in the darkness of the Côte d'Azur nightclubs. The urgency of his desire was embarrassing. I decided it was time to leave and went to get my coat.

He was watching me from the edge of the dance floor, waiting to see what I was going to do. "Can I take you back?" he asked. I said no. My car was parked at the curb. But I scribbled my phone number on a piece of paper, and he gave me his card, which was engraved in red, with the words *The Spy Who Came in from the Cold,* a phone number, a P.O. box number, and his name, Yuri P. He was not an ex-marine, after all; he sold pirated videotapes and DVDs at cultural events and fairs.

Now, from my table by the window of the East Village diner where I am waiting for him, I watch him cross the street, in jeans, big black leather coat and a Kangol cap. Now I think: *mafia*. He'd called me in the morning. He was in New York for the day. He had a present for me. Could we get together? Under his arm is a package wrapped in a Russian newspaper, which he carefully deposits on the table. It contains two bottles, tall and narrow, with long necks.

"It's very good wine from Moldavia, sweet. For dessert." He watches me attentively. "Do you drink wine?"

"Yes, of course. French people drink wine."

I am touched that he's brought me an offering, that he's run all over Brighton Beach to find a second bottle because he had only one at home and he didn't think it was enough. He picks up the bottle of Rolling Rock I have ordered, studies the label, and sniffs it.

"Try it."

He takes a sip and twists his lips. "Tasteless. I prefer Guinness."

"So you live in Brighton Beach?"

"Just the last few months. When I came here two years ago I worked on a farm in North Carolina for three dollars and fifty cents. Imagine that? Three-fifty an hour! At the time, coming from Russia, I thought it was good money. I hated it there. The boonies. For five months I couldn't even get laid. Not even those fat women, those water buffaloes, would touch me."

His eyes twinkle with provocation. I don't mind his vulgar frankness. I find it refreshing in the stuffy air of a city where everybody constantly watches their tongue for fear of offending. He pulls out a pack of Parliaments from his pocket and lights up. Then he pushes the pack toward me. It's before Mayor Bloomberg has decided to cure New Yorkers of their vices. It's before September 11, even, when the city is still naïvely forging full speed ahead. I take a cigarette out of the pack and he leans to light it.

"How did you end up in the States?"

"I met an American woman on the street in Moscow. It didn't work out. She was playing games with me. Always push-pull. American women, they boss everybody around. Like men."

He looks at me to gauge if I, too, play games with men. His pale eyes are both candid and shrewd, like those of a salesman who plays innocent. See: I have nothing up my sleeve. "I don't play games," he adds. "I'm honest." He says "hoooonest" with a long "o." "You don't believe me?"

I laugh. How honest can he be if he advertises it, especially with this long Russian "o"? But I play along. I am intrigued by him. I've met enough New York men who can't make up their mind about a second date for fear it might be construed as a commitment. His directness is a relief. I glance at his strong shoulders, sculpted under a gray-green T-shirt the color of his eyes.

"I don't know. I don't know you."

He shrugs. But he's caught the way I looked at him.

"What do you think makes someone sexy?"

His skull is too flat, his eyes are too small, his forehead is narrow and stubborn, his scar alarmingly long. And yet, in profile, he has a thin, interesting nose, a strong chin. He can go from plain to handsome with a swift shift of expression. There's something primitive and incandescent about him. That's sexy.

"Sexual confidence," I say.

His face lights up and immediately afterward his eyes become probing. I push my chair back and slip on my coat.

"I have to go. Make dinner for my daughter. She's eight. Thanks for the wine."

He follows me outside and wraps his arms around me but the bottles are awkwardly clutched under my elbow and I quickly pull away. I remember what it felt like when we danced. It would come back in an instant if I let it happen.

"I will call you in a few days," he says. It almost sounds like a threat.

It's dark already. A fine rain has started. Puddles reflect the streetlamps in a kaleidoscope of red and yellow; the pavement shines. I pull away from his arms and run to catch the light.

Our first date is in Brighton Beach, in an apartment he shares with
a computer programmer from Minsk. Yuri's small room, crammed
with piles of VHS tapes and DVDs, overlooks the ocean, which rolls
pewter and copper in the setting sun. The sense of strangeness is intensified by the tin of black caviar and the chilled vodka on the table,
and the raucous voice of the singer Vussotsky, his "hero," whose black-
and-white poster hangs on the wall. Evidently eager to establish his
credentials as a wild, oversexed outlaw, Yuri proceeds to entertain me
with tales of his Russian parties. I admire his choice of details. Moon-
shine vodka. Bottlenecks hit against the wall when they couldn't be
bothered to unscrew them. Two chicks for ten guys. Girls' underwear
hanging from the chandeliers, and so on. I have a vivid image of him
standing in the middle of a cavernous ballroom, grabbing a woman by
the crotch with his thick hands, lifting her like a bird and impaling her
right on the spot, kneading her with both fists, ramming into her till
she gives herself up in an orgasmic scream.

A cheesy porn scene, but set in the Moscow unhinged by pere-
stroika, it takes on a forbidding allure, with Yuri playing the kind of
dark, primitive character—violent and naïve—who fascinated me in
the Russian novels I read as a teenager. He reminds me of a man I
knew when I was twenty-one, an older graphic artist. The excitement
was like a drug. Yuri is a cruder version of him. And he has seen,
right away, that I recognized his type. He is what I want: the more
vulgar and less educated, the better. The gap between us, social, intellectual, cultural, attracts me with the same mix of fascination and fear
I experience when I stand at the edge of a cliff, overwhelmed with
vertigo: What if I let go?

He grabs me by the waist and sits me on his lap with the same bru-
tality as when we danced. Then he probes me with his thumb, pops it
in and out, and enters me without pulling my pants all the way down.
No finesse, but a hunger so ferocious it takes my breath away.

"I am not too rough?"

"A little," I whisper.

We're on the couch, then on the bedding he's dragged onto the
floor, then against the wall, where he supports me with only one hand,

and I rock under him like an origami paper girl, pliable and docile, yielding to the sure hand of a master until my flesh melts and abandons all resistance.

When I come to, the big rectangular window frames the night sky and a sliver of a moon. A Pink Floyd video is playing in a loop, a swirl of psychedelic shapes. Yuri pulls a cardboard box from a shelf and takes out a stack of photos.

"My mother. She died when I was fifteen."

A black-and-white shot of a plain young woman with short hair. Her skin is pale, her eyes transparent. No makeup. She looks like she comes from another era. The fifties, maybe, though the picture probably dates from the seventies.

"I loved her. I could never love a woman the way I loved her."

More photos: his father, his older sister, him, grinning with a Grand Canyon T-shirt.

I pull the blanket over my shoulders. I am touched but a little embarrassed that he's opening his life to me so easily after the unbridled sex we've just had. I lean against his chest out of exhaustion. He cups my breasts in his hands, tweaking my nipples hard.

"Ouch!"

"You've got to learn to take pain," he says, and laughs.

Then, like a kid who passes without transition from brutal to childish games, he squats next to me and pulls tiny animals carved in a clear, gold-orange resin out of a plastic bag. An elephant, a cat, a frog, a monkey, a dog, none bigger than my thumb.

"It's amber. I collect them. Choose one."

They feel like plastic, light and smooth, except for the dark veins and crystals flowering inside the resin. I pick the frog, because I am French.

In the morning we go out and buy two cups of coffee on Ocean Parkway and we carry them back to a bench by the ocean. Couples dressed for winter weather, the women in fur coats and hats and the men in heavy overcoats, stroll, arm in arm, on the boardwalk.

"I'd like to buy a house on the New Jersey shore one day," he says, "and a Mercedes." He sets his cup of coffee on the bench between us and opens his hands a foot apart. "The extra-long one. Do you know which one?"

I shake my head.

"And then one day, maybe I'll get married and have kids. But first I have to get legal status. I know this Russian woman. She has U.S. citizenship. I pay her six thousand dollars. I move in with her and get married so that I can have my papers."

My heart sinks when I remember my own dreams of a green card and marriage and kids, when life was opening up and everything was still possible.

♥ ♥ ♥

Cyrillic characters run across most of the awnings of Brighton Beach Avenue. On the weekend, when I come to see Yuri, I decipher them one by one, remembering them from my Russian classes at the School of Oriental Languages in Paris. His cell phone hooked on his jeans belt, his leather coat flapping about his legs, his Kangol cap tilted over his forehead, Yuri picks salads and meat at the international food store and haggles over fish with the Russian fishmonger whose shop is tucked under the boardwalk. "A Jew," he informs me one day after we've left the store. "See how he sucks up to me? They're all like that. You can't trust a Jew!"

A flicker of forbidden thrill flares in the pit of my stomach. All these years celebrating Hanukkah, Yom Kippur, and Rosh Hashanah, attending seders, bar mitzvahs, Jewish marriages and funerals with my ex-husband's family, to end up in divorce. "You can't trust a Jew." I've heard the slur before, in Morocco and Algeria, from the mouths of the friendliest and most hospitable young Arab men. I shudder, ashamed of my brief, terrible instant of bigotry. Who is ever to be completely trusted? A Jew or anyone else?

"I was married to a Jew." I say in protest. "Anyway, you can't speak about Jews that way. It's anti-Semitic, prejudiced."

He shrugs. "Russians are prejudiced," he says, as though it's a fact of life. Then he pulls on my tightly curled hair suspiciously.

"You are not Jew, are you?"

To even answer the question feels like a betrayal but I do. I tell him the truth: "No, I am a good Catholic girl."

His eyes open wide and he grins, although he has no idea what it means: that I don't want him to meet my daughter or any of my friends because I would be too ashamed of being seen with him. That he is my secret sin, my secret sexual kick. That if he comes to my East Village apartment when Lulu is at her dad's for the weekend, I erase all trace of his passage after he leaves. That my life is tightly compartmentalized. How could I explain it to him?

▾   ▾   ▾

Yuri spends most of his time on the road. He calls me every two or three days, usually when he is driving, lonely hours at night on the interstates listening to the radio. Then I don't hear from him for a whole week, and one night he calls me and tells me it's over: "I'm getting married. For love." I am stunned. We've spent the previous weekend together. Who is she? It isn't the same woman he was supposed to marry "for his papers." That one, I know, hasn't worked out. This one is a former dancer, a "beauty," he says, with whom he's slept once a couple of years earlier. Russian, but a U.S. citizen. "Tasha." She has money from her ex-husband and drives a second-hand Jaguar.

"So you're giving up on the ultra-long Mercedes?" I ask, acerbic.

He ignores my barb. They are looking at houses to move into upstate with her daughter. He's in love. They are going to have a family. His voice is jubilant.

Yuri and I have no future, I have made sure of that. But to end like this, without any warning? It stings.

"You're hurting me." I don't know what else to say.

"I know." He tries to console me: we can still see each other when he comes to the city. But we can't have sex. He wants to be a good, loyal husband.

I snicker. "At least make sure you get your green card out of this." That hurts him.

After we hang up I look at the little amber frog he gave me, which is perched on the base of my desk lamp, and I cringe. Yuri has been more generous with his emotions and his time than the men I have been with since my divorce. He hasn't held back. Maybe it's for the best. To end before we get attached.

When I visit my mother in the south of France in the summer, I tell her about Yuri. "He is a hothead," I say. I know she'll understand. She was a hothead herself, and a Russophile. She had been a pro-Communist sympathizer in the fifties, selling encyclopedias written by the poets Louis Aragon and Elsa Triolet, door to door, to raise money for the French Communist Party—enraging my *gaullistes* grandparents, with whom we lived. "He must be interesting, then," she says. I think I want to show her that even after a long marriage I haven't turned into one of those dreaded *bourgeoises* she abhors. I can still be as wild as she has been, even more. Talking about Yuri with her gives him more substance, a weird kind of legitimacy. I miss him.

In October, while I am waiting to pick up Lulu at school, my cell phone rings and it's him. His voice makes me joyous. Excited.

Can he stop by and see me? The marriage is over.

He is gaunt—which makes him look great—all dressed in black, as though he's on his way to a funeral. He lies down with me in my bed with his socks and underwear. "No sex," he announces with a mournful tone, flicking his limp penis. "I'm finished." The promise lasts only through the morning. By then I have heard all the details of the breakup. (It involved a bout of anger on his part, at the door of a Russian restaurant, and which resulted in his being thrown out—all because "Tasha" had provoked him and made him jealous. She has filed for divorce and threatened to have him deported if he doesn't comply.) Though his convoluted explanations suggest a violent temper—clearly "Tasha" has decided she wants no life with this loose cannon—I choose to believe his version: "Tasha" has overreacted.

♥ ♥ ♥

Yuri has moved to New Jersey, halfway between Atlantic City and Philadelphia, in the ground-floor apartment of a run-down Victorian house. After dropping Lulu off at her dad's, I turn on the stereo and coast down the Garden State Parkway for the two-and-a-half-hour trip in a state of languor, pulled by some strange magnetic force.

The place can only be described, with my own big-city prejudices, as white trash. The yard is surrounded by carcasses of old cars the owner meant to fix in an indeterminate future. And Yuri's apartment is discouraging. A hallway in which he stores his "merchandise," a little kitchen, a dark bedroom with just enough space for a bed and a dresser on which perches the TV, and a living room with a desk and a big Naugahyde swivel chair for his bookkeeping and paperwork. They clash painfully with an astonishing fake Louis XV sofa upholstered in gold and ivory, left over from a set he had bought when he was planning to keep house with his first Russian fiancée.

We cook breakfast and dinner together when he isn't taking me to the sushi restaurant in a nearby shopping center. I have always found the America of strip malls deeply depressing, but with Yuri it takes on an exotic allure. In his apartment with a view of a maple tree and a rusted truck devoid of tires and steering wheel, I bury the wife I used to be, who has been so painfully rejected. Nobody knows I am there. I become again the French girl who arrived in New York twenty years earlier.

♥   ♥   ♥

Nights run into days. Yuri has no sense of time. We fall asleep when we've had more sex than we can handle, we wake up famished, then talk for hours. *He* talks, mostly, about his difficult childhood and his runaway episodes when his mother died and he moved in with his aunt. We debate about women's and men's roles. He is vehemently antifeminist and holds firm opinions about men's need to dominate. I make fun of his old-fashioned views, but they remind me of my childhood, when my grandfather and my uncles asserted their manhood without apologies. In any case my so-called power in an equal-rights marriage has ultimately amounted to an illusion.

There's always a bottle of vodka in the freezer, along with a tin of frozen black caviar, which he saws with a knife and lets defrost on the bread. And the kettle is always steaming on the stove for another pot of tea, which he likes to drink in a black mug: "Black like my life." He has a sardonic sense of humor.

Sometimes I wake up in the middle of the night and he's sitting in the kitchen over a mug of tea, chain-smoking, lost in thought. When he notices I am up, his worried look turns into a grin, and he ravages me until I pass out again.

He is intense, and intensely present. He is more real than the half-life filled with cultural events and dinner parties I have in New York. His laugh is resonant, his slang colorful, his bragging bombastic, his jokes truculent. He can be teased without taking offense. If he has drunk too much vodka one evening he won't get on the road before noon, but when he's finally set up, at one of the events he attends, he generates more energy than all the other vendors, sometimes ending the day with a devilish Russian dance. Along with his stacks of video-tapes and DVDs he sells KGB and NKVD memorabilia. Once, a skinhead stopped by, he lifted the red-sickle-and-hammer flag hanging at the back of his stand and discreetly shows his secret stash of neo-Nazi posters. When I see the posters I walk away in fury, swearing never to come back, but he runs after me and spins me around. "Don't take it so seriously," he says. "Someone gave them to me to sell."

"I am sleeping with the enemy," I think. Like Charlotte Rampling in *The Night Porter*, who has an affair with the Nazi officer who had been her tormentor when she was in a concentration camp. Is it the thrill of the forbidden that I find exciting? But Yuri is mostly a provo-cateur, and I know all about provocateurs from my mother, who loved to walk around my grandparents' house in suggestive *négligés* spewing a string of curse words worthy of a truck driver. Yuri, with his dirty mouth and his wife-beater tank top, is the personification of the angry misfits I write about in my novels.

On Monday morning when I drive back, I am as exhausted as if I have run a marathon, my mind wiped clean. I can take only so much of Yuri, of his intensity, of the acrobatic sex. I long to get back to New York, to my daughter, to my desk.

"You're like a bird," he says. "You forget everything the next morning and you take off." I have taught him the French word *amant*, which he likes better than the English *lover*. He isn't my boyfriend, he is my *amant*.

For a few months, through the winter and spring, the arrangement works well. I drive down to New Jersey or I meet him at a motel near the events he attends, or the stores he sells to in Philadelphia, Baltimore, or Boston.

The motels all look the same, although they belong to different chains: Lucky 7. Super 8. International Motel. Econo Lodge. They are in strip malls, right off the highway, sometimes tucked away in a cluster of other motels and restaurants. I like the motels for their anonymity. To me they are the true symbols of American freedom. Yuri parks his van at the bedroom door and I slip in incognito. I want the rooms to be as plain and nondescript, as characterless as possible. I want a certain feeling of seediness. A certain shade of neglect. I disappear more to myself that way.

I don't tell Yuri about these fantasies. He would find them perverse, attributing them to my decadent bourgeois upbringing. He, on the other hand, holds these rooms to certain standards. He likes some better than others. He finds some cleaner, others dirtier, although to my eyes they seem interchangeable. He frets about the dirt, runs a finger over the dresser like a fussy housewife, picks my bra or my underwear off the floor, checks the towels in the bathroom, makes sure the glasses have been properly wrapped in paper. Meanwhile, I lie on the bed, studying the intricate pattern of the bedspread, analyzing the various shades of green of the wallpaper, marveling at the muddiness of the colors, at their aggressive dullness, waiting for him to finish his inspection and spread my legs open.

In the morning, he turns on VH1 full blast and drags the sheet and blanket on the floor as he did the first time in Brighton Beach. He hates to have sex on beds; beds are boring. Once, after a breakfast of muffins and coffee from the motel reception, he opens the door and gestures toward the trees lining the parking lot, pointing to a branch at the end of which a flower seems to be blooming.

"My baby."

I take a couple of steps out and realize that he has hung a few of the condoms we've used during the night.

"I didn't want to waste my sperm." He laughs at my face. "Sperm is good. Look, it's dripping into the soil."

His sperm worship and his need to advertise our affair so crudely while I go to such lengths to keep it secret alarm me. I make a show of being disgusted, hurrying to pack my bag and ordering him to throw away the pathetic receptacles of our night's activities—contrite, he promises to remove them—but secretly I am amused by his provocative schoolboy humor.

In my rearview mirror, when I pull away, I see him standing by his van, waving good-bye to me, looking lonely and sad. Behind him, the condoms are withering like pale, translucent flowers, or jellyfish hung dry after a tidal wave.

♥ ♥ ♥

During the whole time of our "relationship," I have been dating other men, going out for drinks and dinners and the occasional fling, in the hope of meeting someone who could become a "boyfriend" and put the Yuri "episode" behind me. Invariably, though, things are cut short, either because I am not interested enough or because, as they say, the man is "playing the field." A journalist from San Francisco seems promising and I tell Yuri about him. I want to prepare him in case things get serious. Yuri listens calmly, only expressing doubt that a long-distance relationship could work. When I find out the journalist is involved with someone else on the West Coast, I am crestfallen. By contrast, Yuri shines with steadfastness. Why not, I think, let him come a little closer, stay at my place for a few days, for instance, when he has to do "business" in New York, meet his "suppliers" in Brooklyn?

It's a subtle change, but he doesn't miss the significance of it. I have opened the door a crack and he has pushed his foot in. He sleeps in the guest room, and he still doesn't meet any of my friends—except inadvertently. Once or twice someone stops by while he is at my place, with disastrous results. Either out of insecurity or jealousy, Yuri shows his worst argumentative self—playing the part of the angry Russian—or sulks.

Meanwhile, he has been pursuing a young American girl, a "virgin" who lives in Maryland, in the hope of getting her to marry him. He has met the family, brought them presents, but can't resolve himself to sleep with her. "I can't fuck her," he whines. "She doesn't turn me on. She thinks I am gay!" According to him, she has a good body but an ugly face, and they just engage in tepid fooling around. I am fine with that—especially with the "ugly face" and the no-sex arrangement—and I encourage him to go ahead with the marriage and finally get his "status."

It's summer again. We've been together for more than a year. When I come back from my annual visit to France, Yuri is very agitated. There is a new law, a deadline before which he has to get married in order to benefit from a possible amnesty given to all illegal immigrants—at least that's what I understand. The American girl has been ready to give up her virginity to him, but he is just not attracted to her—and in frustration she has broken up with him.

This isn't good news. A few days later he calls from his van, one of his rambling night phone calls, driving down I-95. "La Vida Loca," Ricky Martin's hit, is playing in the background. He asks me if *I* would marry him.

I can't take the idea seriously. It's preposterous. I am not a U.S. citizen, it would take a long time for him to get his green card with me, if I was twenty-five I might do it, but I am a mother, I need to protect my daughter's interests, and so on. He listens gravely and drops the subject, but every other week he brings it up again. The deadline is approaching. Couldn't I help him? I, too, have gotten my green card by marriage. If I loved him, wouldn't I marry him?

How much I hate the word *love* used in that manner! First he has announced that he could never love a woman other than his mother. Then he married the dancer "for love," and that didn't work out. He is finished with love. What we have isn't love, is it? What we have isn't clear to either of us. He has once warned me not to get "addicted" to him sexually. Another time he has said that it wasn't a "sex affair." One night of mist and drizzle in New Jersey, we walked outside and stood under a tree. "I wish I had been in love with a girl when I was twenty," he said. "Instead I got into sex." Diffused by the fog, the headlights of the rare cars on the road bathed us in an eerie light. The earth smelled of moist soil. We were in the backyard of a dacha, in the outskirts of Moscow, holding each other tight like teenagers. Another time, very late, he was sitting on his big swivel chair with me on the floor, leaning between his legs. The Pink Floyd video was playing on the VCR. "*Ya tebya lioubliou*," he whispered. Did he even say that? I wasn't sure. The words came out a little slurred; he had been drinking. My Russian was shaky. I didn't answer.

But now he is flinging the word *love* around in order to get what he wants, and I resent it. I reason with him. I humor him. Perversely, I encourage him to get back with the virgin and give her what she wants. She would make a good wife, he has said so himself. But his arguments are sharpened to a fine and poisonous point: I am selfish, I only see him for sex, I am using him. Each point lands with wicked accuracy. When I am about to drive back to the city, he leans into my car window and complains: "I am your part-time lover. You're always in and out, going back to your life." I start having nightmares about being held captive in a room, with a German shepherd attached by a leash at the door keeping guard.

The following May, my mother has a cerebral hemorrhage. Although she has already had a mild cerebral accident once, it's a shock. She is a force of nature, still camping and traveling all over the world at eighty-five. I fly to Nice. Before leaving I tell Yuri about her, and, guessing she is a kindred spirit, he gives me a picture of his to show her. I can't bring myself to take the picture with me into the ICU, but I tell her "Yuri" is sending his best wishes. It makes her smile. Four days later she has a second, fatal hemorrhage.

At JFK when I get back, I turn on my cell phone and find eighteen frantic messages from Yuri. My mother's death reminded him of his own mother dying when he was fifteen. The next time I drive to New Jersey I bring with me the cashmere scarf that I found on my mother's bed, still smelling of the fires she made when she camped outdoors. We wrap ourselves in the scarf on his bed. My American friends didn't know my mother in her prime, and it's hard to make them understand who she was, but Yuri, intuitively, gets her.

I will pay a price for that moment of closeness. I go back to France in June for a family wedding, and when I reappear at Yuri's door after being gone for a few weeks, tanned and relaxed, in a sexy dress and mules, his eyes have that metallic light that doesn't bode well.

"You came to provoke me," he says, running his hands down my stomach and pushing them between my legs in a crude way. "You travel all the time and I'm stuck in the States. I couldn't even go to Novosibirsk to put flowers on my mother's grave!" I am dumbstruck. I take such care to keep our worlds separate, it hasn't occurred to me he would be so upset at our different lifestyles. But I resent his use of his mother's death to make me feel guilty. He has asked me to bring a bottle of vodka and he starts drinking right away. By the time we go to bed he has gone through half of it. He is supposed to fly to California the next morning to sell a new stock of DVDs fresh from Russia, and I am going to drive him to the airport. Instead of packing he sits down at the kitchen table with a glass and the bottle of vodka.

I stand by the bedroom door, watching him get drunk.

"You should pack," I say, sounding like a stern mother. "Otherwise we'll never make it on time to the airport."

He gets up and curses, picks up a full jar of Tide detergent that is by the chair, and throws it against the doorjamb of his room—barely missing me. The spectacle of him slumped on a chair, wearing a wife-beater, his bare feet swimming in the blue, sticky gel covering the kitchen floor, is sordid. Even more sordid is his drunken order to get on my knees and clean up. Having stepped out of a Dostoyevksy novel, he is now a movie character (didn't Marlon Brando wear a similar T-shirt in *On the Waterfront*?) in his own kitchen sink melodrama. I want no part in it.

I leave him to deal with the mess and check into the Gramercy Hotel instead of going home. I am afraid he will chase me into town and set up siege in front of my building. In the morning, while he is sleeping off the vodka, I leave him a message to tell him it's over.

It's another sultry summer. Lulu is spending the month at the beach with her dad, stepmom, and half brother. I am in New York, working on a historical novel that I can't get a handle on. My mother is gone. The loneliness is unbearable. I don't believe I am sexually addicted to Yuri, but without his constant drama I feel empty. I call him one morning. He sounds bitter and incoherent, and as soon as I hang up I know I have made a mistake. But when he phones me at the end of the month, he sounds serene. He has stopped drinking and smoking, he announces, he's calm, stable, and would I pick him up at the airport? I agree. In a bizarre mix of guilt and longing, I wait for him at Newark airport and drive him all the way back to his apartment. In my state of delusion I convince myself I am only giving him a ride.

He has become unpleasant, angry, demanding. He makes me pay for dinner at the Japanese restaurant, he orders me to press his shirt or wash his socks when I meet him at a hotel. The slightest annoyance throws him into a rage. By going back with him I have tacitly agreed to behave as a girlfriend or a wife. Perhaps it all comes down to that moment in my mother's hospital room, when I talked to her about him as she lay dying. But the wheels started to turn decades earlier. I, the docile girl who played by the rules, was in awe of my mother's gift for setting ablaze my grandparents' household, while she berated me for toeing the line and always "caving in." Now is my chance to prove her wrong. Yuri has come to test me so that I can finally show my mettle and save a communist from deportation. Didn't Jesus himself stand up for the rejected? Hadn't he been tortured and nailed to the cross for his beliefs? I lend Yuri money (which he will eventually repay) to pay a sponsor for a nonexistent job—even though we both know it won't pass muster with the INS. And then I agree to talk to a lawyer.

♥　♥　♥

The weather is still gorgeous in early September. The Tuesday after Labor Day, like every morning, I drive Lulu to school, and on my way back I turn on Z-100, but instead of the usual morning banter of disc jockeys, a grave voice announces that a plane has crashed into the World Trade Center. I turn around to pick up Lulu. We spend the next two days huddled together in front of the TV and walking the deserted streets of downtown. Of all the phone calls that come to us once the line is restored, Yuri's is one of those that comforts me the most. His voice sounds upbeat, ironic, as though he has booked a front-row seat at the world theater and is enjoying the entertainment. When I tell him how nervous we are, waiting for the other shoe to drop, he laughs at my paranoia and invites me to come up the following weekend. Once again, I drop Lulu off at her dad's and drive to New Jersey. As usual Yuri is waiting for me at the door, Kangol cap screwed on his red hair, a cigarette dangling from his lips. I flick my fingers at it.

"I thought you'd quit?"

"It's crap, I know."

But he still hasn't touched liquor in two months. I put great stock in that. Perhaps he can reform?

We make dinner with the food I have brought from New York, and I sleep for twelve hours straight. My anxiety is gone the next morning. In Yuri's world there is no fear of terrorist attacks, only an ironic detachment about America.

♥ ♥ ♥

The matrimonial lawyer has been recommended by a friend. The consultation is at her home, a sunny apartment by Lincoln Center. It's a relaxed, intimate conversation. She tells me she had once been involved with a man not unlike Yuri. She married him and later divorced him. She explains how a prenup agreement works. "It's doable," she says. "You can protect yourself, and then divorce him when his papers come through. Unless he wants to go after what you own. But why would he? All he wants is his papers, right?"

I walk all the way home after the meeting. The streets smell acrid

from the smoke at Ground Zero. Manhattan is still a ghost town—
even though by now the cars have come back—the walls covered with
photos of the WTC victims. Candles are burning, surrounded with
sprays of dahlias and mums. I see Yuri's face at every street corner, his
freckled shoulders slumped in his wife-beater, desperate.

He comes over a few days later, cheerful, carrying a bunch of Mr.
Bean videos, and pops in *Mr. Bean's Christmas*, the one in which he
tries to cook a monster turkey and sticks his head in the bird's butt by
mistake and then walks around with the turkey on his head, frantically
trying to pull it off. When his girlfriend shows up, Mr. Bean hides in
the kitchen, and through the door she asks: "Do you have the turkey
on, dear?"

Yuri is in stitches.

After the video I make tea and we sit at the kitchen table. He takes
out his keys and cell phone and sets them next to him. Perhaps he's
waiting for a phone call.

"I am thinking of buying a little house upstate," I say, pouring the
hot water into the teapot. "To get away from New York. It was too
scary to be trapped here during the attack."

"You have enough money to buy a house?"

"I might sell my mother's apartment."

"Really?"

I take cheese out of the fridge and lay it on a plate. He helps himself to a slice and shoves it into his mouth.

"So," he says, "have you talked to the lawyer?"

"Yes."

"You did?"

He looks surprised and thrilled. Hopeful, even, as he stirs sugar
into his tea.

My heart sinks. By going back with him after the summer, I let him
throw a noose around my throat and now he's tightening it.

"It's not a good idea. You should forget about it."

He freezes, his spoon suspended in midair.

"Is that what the lawyer said?"

"It's not what she said."

He drops the spoon and picks up his keys.

"You're playing with me. Like a puppet. One day yes, one day no." He waves the keys back and forth between us with an air of menace. "Like this. You're manipulating me."

"No."

"No what?

"It's no. I won't do it. I won't marry you. My decision is I won't do it." I know that once I have said those words, I have to break up with him, that it's the natural outcome of my decision. But he beats me to it and explodes with rage.

"That's your *decision*?" He emphasizes the word with forced sarcasm. He cups his keys into his palm, grabs his cell phone, and gets up, toppling the chair under him, and leaves without a word. It's over. I will never see him again. I feel a huge sense of relief.

The relief is short-lived. He calls to apologize a few days later. He had no right to get so angry with me. Sometimes the frustration is just too much and he loses it. He'll find another way. But he wants to keep seeing me.

I can't tell whether I am caving in as per my weak nature or whether I feel terribly guilty for having let him down. Or if the constant drama he provides is irresistibly attractive to me. A blur of confusion is blinding me. The next Sunday, my head full of the terrifying warnings in the latest *New York Times* article on bioterrorism, I take the Mr. Bean videos he has left at my place and a shopping bag of food and drive up. He is waiting for me at his door, as usual, watching me park my car. But when I tell him I have to be back in Manhattan early the next day, he turns testy.

"So you just came here to eat and have sex and then you'll leave tomorrow morning?"

He prepares a pot of tea on the kitchen counter, his rage simmering.

"In and out. You're always in and out. I want a woman who's with me. Who cooks and shares a house with me. You don't want a man. You don't need a man. You just want sex. Why can't you be hoooooonest?"

▾ ▾ ▾

My backpack is leaning against the Louis XV couch, three steps away from me, my car parked in the yard. And yet I don't leave. A force of inertia, the magnet that has pulled me here, is keeping me glued to the couch. In fact, Yuri is the one who picks up my backpack and holds it like a war trophy, pointing to the triangular Prada label on its flap.

"That costs eight hundred dollars," he says, his voice snapping as though I have spent his own hard-won money. How does he know that? Has he been reading *Vogue*?

"It doesn't. More like four hundred dollars. Anyway, I bought it secondhand and paid a hundred bucks for it."

I hate myself for even offering a justification where none is called for. Already he's laid out the rules of the game. I have put myself at his mercy by refusing to marry him and not breaking up with him right then and there and on top of that walking right into his lair. He dangles the backpack as he has dangled the keys another day, taunting me. Who knows if he's planned this or if holding the backpack gives him the idea? He pulls the cord loose, rummages in the bag.

"Where are your keys? Give me your keys."

Adrenaline pumps in my heart. He opens the two outside pockets one after the other. In the second one he finds the keys and brandishes them. I don't try to grab them from him. I am mesmerized, paralyzed with fear. He is twice as big as I am. With one swipe of his hand he'd throw me to the ground. I know no karate moves, I have taken no self-defense classes. I have only my wits, what's left of them. I was dumb enough to come here today. I try to hide my fear by playing it cool.

"You'll have to give them back to me. I told you I have to leave early tomorrow. I have a class to teach at eleven."

He goes to the bathroom, then to the bedroom. He moves powerfully, his body almost as tall as the doorways. When he comes back my keys are not in his hands anymore.

"If you leave."

I sit back on the couch, forcing myself to calm down. He sits next to me, as though nothing has happened, and plays the Christmas video again. Mr. Bean is running around with the turkey on his head. The fiancée asks, "Do you have the turkey on, dear?"

Yuri laughs on cue.

"What are you going to do with the money you'll get from your mother's inheritance?" he asks suddenly. "Do you still want to buy a house upstate?"

"I don't know."

"I saw that there are cheap houses around Millville."

I tense up and say nothing.

"My landlord wants to get the apartment back for his mother," he goes on. "I don't have a lease. He can kick me out anytime. If you buy a house I can live there. I'd pay you rent. That would help you pay the mortgage."

My heart races. So he has it all figured out.

"I don't know what I am going to do with the money. There's not much anyway. It's not a good time to bring francs into the States. The dollar is too strong. I should wait until they convert to the euro. I might buy a studio in Paris."

Mr. Bean is offering a picture to his fiancée instead of the diamond ring she was dreaming of. She looks devastated.

"What about me?" His voice turns menacing. "I need a house to open a showroom. I am sick of being on the road all the time."

"I don't know. I can't tell you what to do."

What has he heard in my voice? That I'll never help him with his dream? That it's finally over?

He takes one step toward me and hits me on the back of the head, just behind the ear, maybe because it doesn't leave any mark there. Hard. One side. My eyes black out for a second. The other side. I fall on the couch, then sit back up, my heart pounding. Mr. Bean is now alone in his apartment, listening to the kids singing Christmas carols to his next-door neighbor. His girlfriend has run off, outraged at not getting her diamond ring.

Yuri is towering over me again.

"You said you'd buy a house."

"It's a possibility. I don't know. I haven't even sold my mother's place."

"How much can you get?"

I don't owe him any explanation of my finances, but I don't want to oppose him head-on and provoke him.

"I don't know how much I'll end up with. Depends on the inheritance tax."

"An inheritance tax? Another capitalist dirty trick!"

Suddenly he's at me again, his two hands around my neck, dragging me off the couch, choking me, his whole body, 185 pounds of him, weighing down on me. Then, just as abruptly, he lets go of me.

"Don't," I say, uselessly. "Don't touch me."

The kettle whistles. He disappears in the kitchen to make more tea. I go to the bathroom, which is adjacent to the living room, and close the door in case he is tempted to throw boiling water at me. I feel safer that way, which is ridiculous since the door doesn't lock, but I am grasping at straws. I do a quick survey in case he's hidden my keys there, but I see nothing.

"*Chai? Budish?*" he calls through the door.

I come out and sit back on the couch to drink the tea. I talk to myself: Don't antagonize. Keep things fluid and calm. Try to control the situation until his rage and his paranoia subside. Try to find an opening. He's your jailer and you are his hostage. You need to outsmart him. It will take you the whole night, at least until he falls asleep. Be prepared to wait. Considering the difference between your weights and muscular abilities, that is your only way out: putting the giant to sleep and escaping behind his back.

"You're not saying anything?" he says.

"I am tired. Don't you want to sleep? Let's go to bed."

That was the wrong thing to say. He jumps up again and drags me off the couch on my knees all the way to the center of the room and circles my throat again with his hands.

"You're not a Jew, are you? You didn't lie to me when you said you were not a Jew?"

He pushes both his thumbs into my throat until I choke. In a flash, the poor communist I must save from deportation has turned into an SS officer about to send me to the gas chamber.

"Are you Jew?"

The pressure of his thumbs is suffocating.

"*Maman,*" I talk to her silently. "*Maman,* help me survive this. Protect me from up there, wherever you are."

"No." I feel like a traitor again, like the first time he asked me that question. "No, I am not a Jew."

"Swear."

"I swear. I am not a Jew."

He hits me again, same place, behind the ear. And then above my temple, in my hair.

Before my scream has a chance to explode, his hand's on my mouth. With his other hand he grabs a bandanna that was lying on the desk and stuffs it into my mouth.

"If you make noise, if the landlord hears anything, I'll kill you. If you try to call the cops, I'll kill you."

He places his thumb on my throat again, just like he's done before, and presses hard.

I shake my head and try to get the gag out of my mouth.

"You swear?"

I nod forcefully. He drops the pressure on my mouth and throat and the bandanna falls to the floor.

"You swear?"

"Yes."

"I'll kill you."

We are both speaking in forced whispers. He pulls me to my feet, drops me into his big leather chair, and looks at me with disdain. His eyes suddenly cloud over.

"I'm going to bed. Don't even try to call the cops or look for your keys because I'll hear you. I'll hear you and I'll kill you. Come with me."

I follow him and lie down on the bed.

"Get undressed."

I get undressed except for my underwear and my T-shirt. It takes him a long time to fall asleep. Every time I make a move, he senses it and seizes my wrist or mumbles something. It's only when the birds start to chirp and a dirty light washes away the night that sleep overtakes him. He snores lightly on his back. I slip off the bed and look around the apartment for my keys. Nothing. I go through the pockets of his jeans and his sweatshirt, run my hands over the shelf in his closet. Nothing. I pull on a pair of pants, pick up my backpack, tiptoe outside, and take my cell phone out. 6:15. I am afraid to call 911 for fear he might hear me.

Suddenly he is at the door.

"What are you doing?"

"Nothing."

"Were you calling the cops?"

"No. I . . . I just wanted to see what time it was."

"Outside?" His voice is sarcastic.

"I couldn't sleep."

He shakes his head suspiciously.

"How about breakfast?" I ask in a fake breezy tone to create a diversion.

While I chop onions and tomatoes to make fried eggs, he boils the water for tea. The silence in the kitchen is heavy. At least alcohol took the edge off his rage. Now it's raw, smoldering again, although not as intense as during the night. We sit down wearily. I need to keep soothing him until a new opening occurs. After we finish breakfast, I propose a walk. I'd be safer outside than alone with him in his apartment.

My car is there, bright red and shiny. I glance at it longingly. We walk in silence for a while, following the tracks of a disaffected railroad I never knew was there. When we reach a little wood, he stops and points to the left.

"You see those trees?"

"Yes."

"If you died nobody would find you. If you were buried here."

My heart leaps up in panic.

He stands tall, his chin up, his eyes lost in the distance, his legs slightly apart, stiff.

"My mother died younger than you are now. You deserve to die."

Is that what a murderer looks like? Rigid, his features frozen? He could have killed me during the night. With just a little more pressure from his thumbs. He could strangle me now. He would be methodical in digging the grave. He is right, nobody would come and look for me. Nobody knows I am here. Not my daughter. Not any of my friends. He hesitates for a moment, holding me in his cold gaze. Do murderers kill in cold blood?

"I want you to go to Novosibirsk," he suddenly says, breaking the tension. "I want you to put flowers on my mother's grave for me. Since I am trapped here and can't leave the country."

"Yes," I say. "I will." Does it mean he's going to let me go? I try to calm the beating of my heart and take a tentative step in the direction we came from, to test him. He calls me back. He's still standing the same way, his legs apart, his eyes lost, although he looks less fierce now.

"Let's go," I coax him gently.

He follows me all the way back to the apartment. He goes straight to the bedroom. His fury seems to be spent.

"Come lie down with me."

This is the moment I've been waiting for all night.

"I have to go back soon." I speak in a very soft voice, so as not to break the spell. "I'll need my keys back." It's a gamble I'm taking. The question might infuriate him again.

But no. He looks at me for a second, then runs his hand under the mattress and pulls them out, showing them to me in his half-cupped hand.

"Promise you'll lie down with me for a while first."

I hold my breath and say, "Okay."

He hands me the keys and I put them in my backpack and go back in the bedroom to lie down next to him. The hard mask of his face has loosened, revealing a brutish carnality. His narrow forehead, his long gash across the cheek, his thin lips repulse me. But I have to play the game till the end. After a while he unzips my pants, lies down on top of me, and enters me. He moves inside of me with a rare gentleness and comes almost right away. A feeling of immense sadness and pity overwhelms me, as though we were both abandoned orphans.

"I can't believe I did what I did," he mumbles. "What I did to you . . ."

I roll over to the side, letting myself off the bed.

"Don't," he whispers, half asleep.

I touch his forehead with my fingers and leave the room. I pick up my backpack and put on my shoes and let myself out. It's five minutes after ten.

My car starts right away. I slowly pull out of the yard, but just when I am about to turn onto the road, he appears and leans into the passenger window, which I have already pressed open. My heart bangs in my chest.

"You're leaving," he says.

"Yes."

My hand is on the gearshift, my foot on the gas pedal.

"You're leaving for good."

I say nothing.

"I'll never see you again."

His face is creased with sleep. On one side of his right temple the sheet has left a pink line, which looks like a fading scar, paler than his real one. I slowly let the clutch go and ease into first gear. The car moves just a notch but his arms are still leaning at the window.

"*Do zvidannya*," I say. I press the gas pedal down. The car jumps. He lifts his arms off the window and steps aside.

I make the turn on the road without looking back.

♥ ♥ ♥

When I got home, I packed a bag for me and one for Lulu and drove to a friend's house. The next morning, when I turned my cell phone on, there were six missed calls from Yuri. I erased them one by one without listening to them and booked a seat on a plane for Paris. Lulu would stay with her dad. Then I called the lawyer and asked her to write a letter warning Yuri to stay away from me or I would take legal action. I didn't want to call the cops, because they would denounce him to the INS and he would probably be sent back to Russia. I couldn't bear to crush his dream. I asked the lawyer to wait to mail the letter until I'd be on the plane. I didn't want to take any chances.

nothin' from nothin' leaves nothin'

Ntozake Shange

*f*or many years i have lived in a state of suspended disbelief as well as elaborate models of the cinderella complex & just plain old guilt that i had done so much better than my peers, especially my male colleagues. a self-identified feminist, my work reflected—& to this day reflects—a sense of urgency in complex examinations of the nature of heterosexual relations in the first decade of the 21st century.

but i must confess i have not always or virtually ever lived up to my own ideals. what a mess i have made. & then there is my faulty memory of what i was complicit in as well, & relationships i had no intention of honorably participating in. now i find myself chuckling about situations. so many years have passed & i have moved on & started over again with no male helping or at least contributing to the running of the house. i find myself raising my eyebrows & doing strange things with my eyeballs now that i have to reveal my malice & begrudging in situations i knew to be unsettling & humiliating to my so-called partner of the moment.

it was inevitable. my career had peaked way before those of my alleged peers & created an entire slew of gigolos, sycophants, & an angry slew of black and puerto rican lovers whose aim was to get whatever they could wrangle from me before i understood betrayal. yet i survived again. the concerted attacks on my commitment to african americans & black latins took a terrible toll on me. i grew to be suspicious of the intentions of many who crossed my integrity boundaries. yet i was not always able to stand my ground. things just moved too fast for a young woman to catch.

for instance there was a black puerto rican independisto who came to me seeking a safe house where his wounds could be nursed & arrangements made for transporting him out of the city swiftly. luckily i could do all that, but months later after he returned to the city, i loaned him $200. many months later, the check he wrote back to me was for "mizfullashit." there are many instances of that kind of exploitation. a man who i had begun to love went into a rage because i had several hundred dollars on hand when i went to buy fresh crabs at a harlem fishery. this fella wanted to know how come some woman could have all that money to buy fresh crabs for a party i was giving to which he had not been invited because he was a definitely married man & i had no need to bother his wife or children with the fact that i was briefly this man's mistress. nevertheless, this same guy kept up this chorus of "whose pussy is this," which i found laughable, but i replied ever compliant "oh so & so this is yours" & he would settle down. he really lost my respect & understanding when he flew into a fury as i prepared myself to be the mistress of ceremonies at a celebration of cuba's moncada barracks, a day of singular importance to the cuban people as the day fidel first landed on the shores of western cuba. this man actually believed that his tirade as a black anglo saxon could shake my resolve. the last thing i remember hearing from the top of the stairs was "what about me, what about me?" this is not the last time i'd hear this query.

there are so many instances of my acquiescence to bizarre behaviors and i'm sure many will show up in my creative endeavors, but i want to help unmask the terror of the patriarchy as it manifests itself in our lives.

i almost forgot a fella who gave me a day at the spa with manicure, steam baths, hairdo, the works & i thought that was wonderful until i found a wonderfully decorated box at my hotel room that held a black leather bustier & a ping-pong paddle. then there was another one who kept a machete in a loft above my head & he was very forceful during sex to the extent that my gynecologist told me i had to stop seeing him because of the black & blue marks on my arms that indicated to her domestic violence. this scared me so he had to go. i haven't lived with a man or chased after one for many years & i have been reasonably just fine. i survived & any woman who is living with one of these men: tread softly, get out & shut the door. when a fella attempts to take control of our bodies, our politics, or our god, believe me he might just kill us.

Mr. Wrong Meets Mr. Wrong

Whitney Otto

One early autumn evening, as I sat in the nearly empty middle-school cafeteria, permeated with that same singular smell as the school cafeterias of my youth, one of the other parents, a married man, taller than average with unfashionably long hair, folded himself into the chair beside me and announced, "I'm a bad guy. No one should be married to me."

Our relationship (friendship? acquaintanceship?) did not warrant the confidential nature of this remark, even though I happen to be one of those people to whom other people, regardless of how well we know each other, like to lay out their secrets. I used to think they found me trustworthy or sympathetic; then I thought it was because I have a kind of generic quality, physically speaking. I also wondered if it was evident that I'm pretty socially nonjudgmental and like to be enter-tained. Now I believe this tendency to tell me the intimate details of their lives is something more primal, more animal kingdom. Like the way the herd knows to cut loose a lagger that invites the attention of a predator, my animal quality invites confession.

Because I slightly knew this man's wife, I knew quite a bit about him: He was unpredictably unfaithful, and he needed to be loved and admired. He made you love him, then he went his own way until you threatened to leave, then he came back with words of adoration and remarkable, touching gifts, the sort of offerings that aid in forgetful-ness and trust. It was the way he tried so hard for your love that made you think you were safe with him, until you understood, unequivocally, that you weren't. And his wife wasn't like most of the other moms in that she had kept her dancer's figure despite three kids, as well as possessing a kind of sexiness that was completely innate, independent of clothing (or shoe) choices.

He and I were in the cafeteria watching our kids learn how to fence. If you happen to be a borderline recluse, you will never go wrong in the fringe sports area. You will be able to catch up on your reading, crosswords, and daydreaming. You will never be asked to bring juice boxes or organize car pools. You will be pretty much left on your own if your child chooses to learn the finer points of waving around an épée. There I was, lost in the lull of a parent observing her child, wondering if fencing is a step above or below Latin Club, when I heard, "I'm a bad guy. No one should be married to me."

Perhaps I should mention that this man and I have virtually no social contact, with the exception of the occasional party on the street or school event. Once, he asked me if I would mind watching his kids when his wife was out of town and he had to attend a business dinner. When he dropped them off, as we stood in the doorway of my house, somehow the conversation went from pickup times to literary pornography. It was actually alarming to be talking about one thing, then something completely different, without any sense of the transition.

His normal social mode was distraction and boredom, not the calm focus of our exchange. It made me realize that I had never witnessed, let alone been the object of, his undivided attention. Though the whole encounter lasted minutes, abruptly ended by my quick, uncomfortable good-bye, it allowed me a glimpse of what his wife must have been dealing with, what she had always dealt with.

♥　♥　♥

He continued speaking. "You know about the Internet thing, right?"

The thing is, I didn't know what I was supposed to know or not know, confidences being what they are, so I just kept looking straight ahead, nodding in what I hoped was a noncommittal manner. In fact, his wife, S., had mentioned something about some Internet thing that had occurred a few months prior, and I figured I was now going to hear his side of things even though I just wanted him to leave so I could get back to my crossword. Except the story he told wasn't the one I thought. This is what he said:

"Two years ago I bought this vintage movie theater, you probably know it, classic Deco with all kinds of architectural detail even if it was pretty beat up. I wanted to bring it back, you know, a real movie palace, and I thought I could maybe work on it myself with this good friend of mine who's a contractor. I planned to take a six-month leave of absence from my job and thought it would be a nice change of pace for me. Anyway, this is how I ended up on this website devoted to building codes for disabled access. You know, seats, ramps, wheelchair allowances. There was a girl online that I got talking to about disabled issues. She was very helpful.

"A few days later, I had another question, returned to the site to check something, and this girl and I met up again. Again, she answered my question, saying if I needed anything else she was more than happy to help.

"The third time I went to the site she wasn't online, so I left her a note on the message board. It took about a week to get a message back from her. She said she was usually on in the afternoon, but she could just leave a message for me if that was inconvenient.

"The next time I went on, it was the afternoon; she was there; somehow we got to talking, you know, one thing leading to another, and our conversation drifted the way they do, on to other things. I can't say what it was about her, she just seemed smart, and sweet. I wrote a couple of funny things—we just got on, like we had known each other for a much longer time. I asked her if she was an architect or contractor and she said no.

"I learned that she worked at a local university and that she was thinking of applying to graduate school in sociology because she thought she might want to teach, though she had trouble with shyness. She was twenty-eight years old and separated from her husband, a successful surgeon, whom she had met when she was in a car accident in college. The accident had left her in a wheelchair, paralyzed from the waist down, which depressed her for a while until she stopped being depressed. She told me that she wasn't a naturally depressed person, even though I said it seemed natural to be depressed in her situation. That's behind me now, she told me. Life goes on. We exchanged e-mail addresses.

"Eventually our e-mails got friendlier. This was when she said that if I wanted to let her know I was going to be online to call her fax number, let it ring twice, then hang up before the machine answered. We did this often, usually in the mornings after my kids were in school because of the three-hour time difference. She lived in New Jersey.

"We talked about anything and everything. You know, people always think that it's what you talk about when you have someone else to talk to that you aren't married to, but that's not it—it's how you talk, the way you talk. I mean, no one gets all sensitive—there's no resentment because you didn't mow the lawn and crap. Christ, marriage always feels like being endlessly censored. We would talk about my day and my work and I was never boring with her. And nothing I said ever started something, like with S.

"Most of all, I cared about her. I mean, really loved her. She made herself so easy to love. Hearing from her always made my day. It *was* my day.

"She sent a picture, at my request. She was in a wheelchair and she was beautiful, with a beautiful smile. She said her husband took the photo right before they split up.

"She told me that I helped her, too. We talked about her school plans and her current job. She said that since her husband had left she didn't get out as much as she knew she should. Even though I encouraged her to go out and have a life of her own, I didn't want her to fall in love with anyone—by now, I was in love with her.

"I said I wanted to see her. I'd fly out for a few days and we could just hang around together, no big deal. At first I didn't tell her I loved her because I wasn't sure how she'd feel about it—we had never talked about loving each other. She said she thought that my coming to visit wasn't a good idea because I was married.

"I said, Well, what if I wasn't married? Then I told her I was in love with her and that I couldn't imagine a life without her. I would leave my wife for her. Whatever she wanted. I love you, I said, You've changed me—and it was true, I was really somebody else with her. I said, You know me better than anyone.

"This sounds so fake, but for the first time I felt that I was honest with someone, told her everything, and she was fine with it. I'm not uncomfortable with lying, but I didn't lie to her. I didn't feel I had to; I didn't have to pretend. I didn't want to, and believe me, this was something completely new for me.

"She explained that she was still legally married and I had three kids to think about and, again, it wasn't a good idea.

"A couple of weeks passed with me writing and writing, but I didn't hear from her. I started to panic, wrote and said, Forget the visit. Then I got an e-mail saying she ran into her husband at a party and they got to talking and were going to try it again. She thanked me for everything. She said without me she wouldn't have gotten out of her shell and applied for school—or even gone to the party where she saw her husband.

"Then I tried to talk her out of her husband and practically begged her to let me come see her with no strings attached. As friends. Or, at the very least, let's just stay friends anyway. She said she didn't think that would do anyone any good, especially if she went back to her husband.

"I didn't hear from her again, though I still e-mailed. Until one day the e-mail address was canceled.

"I was so depressed I couldn't get out of bed. Seriously. I didn't care about anything, and S. thought I had the flu because my eyes were red and I couldn't eat. Then I did get a cold, and still I was depressed. It took me two weeks to get dressed and another week to get back to work on the theater, which only reminded me of her. And I couldn't tell anyone what was wrong. I didn't care about anything.

"This went on for almost two months, where I felt I was just sort of sleepwalking. Losing her killed me.

"One day I came across her old fax phone number—we had stopped using it months ago once we got into a pattern of being online at the same time, and I thought I had lost it. Just finding it again made me happier.

"I called using our old signal. Nothing. So I wrote her a fax, and instead of a machine, a man answered. I hung up. I called again. Same thing. I hung up.

"Two more days passed. I called again. Again a man answered and this time I asked for the woman. Wrong number, he said and he hung up.

"The number was right—I checked—so I called again. When the guy answered I asked for the girl. He told me there was no one there by that name. This is an auto parts store and he was the owner, he said. In Morristown? I asked. New Jersey? he said. Nah, he was in Philadelphia.

"Something was wrong, I knew, but I didn't want to know because I was so wrecked over her. I called again. I asked if there was a young woman working there, someone in a wheelchair? (No.) Or did he have a daughter, maybe, and she was in a wheelchair? (No.) A friend of the family? (no), a client? (no), an employee's girlfriend? No, no, no, he said. I wanted to ask about a wife but didn't.

"Then, how did I get this number? I asked. And how did that girl know to contact me when I called?

"How the hell should I know? I'm a sixty-eight-year-old auto parts store owner in Philly. Maybe somebody was fucking with you.

"No. Not this girl. She wasn't like that. Not at all.

"Okay, he said. You seem like a nice guy so I'm gonna tell you nicely to stop bothering me."

▼　▼　▼

At this point two of the kids were being reprimanded for horsing around with their épées. The one kid was particularly aggressive and gleeful in his lunging technique. You could see the other kids were trying to pair up with anyone but him, but the class being as limited as it was meant there was no real escape. So what was supposed to be a rather genteel engagement was turned into one kid menacing another with a sharp object as the other kid tried desperately to protect himself. This kind of sparring naturally drew the instructor's attention and a lecture about sportsmanship and safety.

"So," I said finally, as the kids were lined up for their final lunge and parry, "did you ever hear from her again?"

"Yes and no. I convinced myself that I needed to know what happened to her, or that maybe she needed me—no one had ever gotten to me like this, and I thought if I could just talk to her I'd be all right.

"When I called the number for the last time, the man said, Just so you'll stop bugging me—it was me.

"I was confused. I said, What was you? And he said, The girl is me. I'm the girl. Happy now?

"You mean, she's someone you know and you pretended to be her?

"Nah, I made her up.

"It was shocking because I still loved her, I was still depressed over her. I said, You don't understand, I was going to leave my family for you! How could you do this to me? Why would you do this to me? How can you go around making people fall in love with you? You broke my heart!

"Tough luck, he said."

♥ ♥ ♥

The husband's voice went plaintive and whiny as he re-created his part of the conversation ("I was going to leave my family for you!"). All these months later you could still hear the sense of injustice the husband felt when he finally understood he had given his love—himself, really—to a dream girl and her heartless creator. What's more, he had felt affection in return, he was certain of it, he said, even though everything inside him knew it wasn't possible to receive something from nothing.

♥ ♥ ♥

Now the kids were removing their fencing gear, stacking shirts and masks and foils. I gathered up my crossword and purse. I asked if the guy ever told him why he went online at a construction website, pretended to be shy and disabled and female, and didn't ask for money or sex or anything, why he did it.

"Oh, I asked all right. I insisted because I was so angry—my whole life all screwed up—and he said, I did it to make you aware of handicap rights."

♥ ♥ ♥

As a writer I like this story because it functions as a good story should, with suspense, conflict, desire, a nice narrative arc, the sort of details that make it seem "real," finding love, losing love, and a tragic truth that is almost like a death. As a novelist, someone who is no stranger to the strange scenario, I would not have come up with "I did it to make you aware of handicap rights" as a rationale for hurting someone. The phantom girl that the married man fell for doesn't resemble a character—she *is* a character, a construct of someone's imagination.

The story also indirectly asks the question of what it means when we fall in love. What or whom do we love? Certainly, the married man loves the girl, but the girl is actually a sixty-eight-year-old auto parts store owner in Philadelphia, not a young disabled girl in New Jersey. It is important to recall that the married man wasn't looking for love; he was searching for building codes.

Which is exactly how the wrong man happens to you: the chance encounter, the conversational connection, the sense of finding someone who understands you, the eventual tumble into love. And knowing that the girl was imaginary hasn't mended the heartbreak of the married man; it's as if he's lost her twice.

Losing love twice frequently belongs in the realm of myths and fairy tales. Fairy tales offer many lessons: the value of goodness, bravery, honesty. They tell us to be nimble of mind because sometimes cleverness can do what brute strength cannot. They can serve as cautionary tales where the things you do to others may one day end up being done to you. For example, you might go through life, wooing women only to make them cry, until the day when you stumble upon your own worst self, waiting for you in Philadelphia.

Of Romance and Revolution

Diana Abu-Jaber

My grandmother, who'd come of age during the Great Depression, was dying for me to marry a rich man. Truly, she was without shame. On buses and airplanes, she would immediately ascertain the employment of the stranger beside her. If he happened to be anywhere on the scale between a Saudi prince and a Brooklyn podiatrist, she would smile winningly and say, "Well, I have the most darling granddaughter," then whip out my high school yearbook picture, and add, "She's *single*, too, just like *you*."

It was my grandmother's opinion that she had married "a wastrel," and my mother had also apparently fallen short of the mark. So Gram pinned her hopes on moi. I was raised with her injunction to "Marry rich! Why not?" ringing in my ears. Unfortunately, though, I always seemed to go for paupers—artsy turtlenecked boys in grad school, all of whom aspired to genteel pseudo-poverty, the tattered life-of-the-mind as college professors, or, even worse, "writers."

I was pretty sure I wanted true love and romance. And whenever I said so, Gram would roll her eyes and mutter, "You'll see."

Sure enough, by the time graduate school ended I still hadn't hooked up with anyone who owned his own jet. Instead, I went trudging off to teach innumerable sections of freshman comp at a big midwestern university. One day in late fall, I got roped into an English department party featuring turtlenecked grad students and junior faculty cradling cocktails, all of them arguing about postmodernism or something. And in the midst of all this chatter was a stranger, standing by the pretzel bowl, staring bullets at me.

He had long gray hair pulled back in a ponytail and there was a certain manic intensity to his face. I was twenty-six and easily annoyed: I rolled my eyes, smirked as scornfully as I could, and sauntered away.

The truth is, after growing up around my rich-husband-mad grandmother, I'd become suspicious of all forms of men. I was of the Jane Austen school of skepticism that held that if you glanced into a stranger's eyes across a crowded dance floor and felt fire, you should immediately turn and run into another drawing room.

I didn't feel any flames kindling when I looked at the guy by the pretzels, but he got my attention. I retreated to the other side of the room, turned, and looked: yep, still staring.

I sidled over to my friend Belinda, another freshman comp faculty slave. "Psycho alert," I said. "Behind you. Next to the pretzel bowl."

She looked over, then back at me. "Ah yes, but he's a famous psycho. That's Jerry Squatch. He stars in his own private cable access show, *Revolution Right Now.* It's like a Marxist version of *Wayne's World.*"

Now if she had said he managed his own hedge fund and vacationed on a private yacht off Martha's Vineyard, I would've yawned and gone off in search of the cheese puffs. But a famous local lunatic with his own cable access show? This warranted further investigation.

♥   ♥   ♥

I blame television for what happened next. Because when a girl's face-to-face with a potential date, she stands at least half a chance. She picks up on his energy, his smells, his tics. She gets seventy-three different sources of information telling her, *Don't date this guy, he's crazeeeeee.*

But a day or two later, I turned on the tube, hunted around, and there he was. Jerry Squatch's big, wild face filled the screen, along with a few glimpses of a dilapidated couch in the background. I couldn't help but note his strong jaw and nice dimples, a touch of Gregory Peck about the brow bone. Oh sure, he was babbling on about something political or other: the revolution will not be televised, blah blah blah. And oh sure, he flashed his phone number incessantly across the bottom of the screen and begged the local neoconservatives to call in and abuse him. But he also had a very becoming smile and a moustache reminiscent of Magnum P.I.'s.

It was a little like the way people are seduced by words—whether it's by a book or through e-mail. Words are idealized expressions of thought and feeling—clear, carefully selected, earnest. Much more manageable than actual, fussy, difficult humans. In a similar way, TV is the idealized person—packaged for public consumption.

I spontaneously began entertaining tiny fantasies of me and Jerry lolling around on his awful couch. Nothing serious—like a George Clooney fantasy. I like to think some residual, rational part of my brain realized that he was not promising boyfriend material. I'm always disappointed when I meet the authors of my favorite books (my friends excepted), who always turn out not to be Greek gods. Certainly the same was true of wacky TV people.

But one day, just a week after scoping out the show, I was ditching my office hours and hanging around the university bookstore when suddenly I felt the warmth of an overheated stare. I glanced up and there he was, my own private gawker. He still looked crazy, but this time I knew he was quote-unquote famous.

I strolled over, feeling sassy, and it was clear that right up to the last second he didn't expect me to actually talk to him. When I did, he jumped and looked over both shoulders before tuning in.

"I love your TV show," I gushed. "It's very . . . very . . . unique."

He pulled his ponytail forward over one shoulder and started stroking it like a pet ferret. "Thank you. I write and produce it myself."

"Do you really?" I tried to look astounded.

We went for coffee at a campus hangout where about thirty-seven of my freshman comp students got an eyeful of their teacher chatting with a scary guy with a gray ponytail.

At the café, Jerry and I proceeded to have the first of many nearly identical conversations, which went sort of like this:

Me: (cracking up) But you don't really believe all that crazy stuff you say?

Jerry: (offended) Why yes, as a matter of fact, I do.

Me: The part about anarchy in the streets? And tearing down the banks? Come awwwwwn.

Jerry: (offended stare)

Jerry was actually a lot like my grandmother that way—she didn't believe in banks, either, nosiree, and she didn't believe in "The Bankers." She believed in hidden panels in your underwear drawer and coffee cans brimming with loose change. Her brother talked her into some T-bills back in the forties, but aside from that, it was all about hiding money and marrying rich. Stuff like "interest" and "dividends" were just what The Bankers used to bamboozle you into handing over your paycheck.

What can I say? Jerry reminded me of my grandmother. I downgraded him from "lunatic" to "kook."

I admitted to my co-slave Belinda that I had a little crush on Jerry Squatch. But the problem with trying to date a famous loon is that there's no hopeful maybe-he's-just-shy grace period: everyone already knows the truth.

"Jerry Squatch!" she bleated. "You can't. I forbid it. He's *old*. He's *bizarre*. How did this happen? You bring disgrace on us all."

I shrugged. "We talked. I liked him. We went out for coffee."

She looked at me with incredulity. "You 'liked him'? You 'went out for coffee'? Oh my God."

The thing is, though, it turned out that when Jerry wasn't fomenting riots and advocating seizing the means of production, he was actually a really nice guy. Yes, he knew all the words to "The Internationale," but he also loved Abba. When it was time to go, he left a big tip (of course). But more to the point, he paid for both our coffees, which, in my experience, was a dating first.

So our courtship began.

I would trudge into work, teach back-to-back sections of bored-stiff freshman comp victims, holler at the guys in the back of the room to shutthehellupalready. Or else submit and ignore the mayhem while I wrote things on the board like *Thesis Statement* and *Conclusion*. Around noon, Jerry would come rumbling up in his rattletrap (foreign-made) pickup truck and save me. He'd be toting sack lunches—turkey and Swiss sandwiches, juice boxes, and oatmeal cookies. We'd drive to a nearby pond or park, eat lunch, I'd complain and complain and complain about freshman comp, and Jerry would stare at me crazily-adoringly. Then he'd drive me back to school, where I'd finish teaching myself into a stupor. After a few weeks of lunch, we started to smooch.

The thing is, in addition to being an on-air "personality," Jerry was also a janitor. At the university. Where I taught. Yes, that's right. With the great big jangling key ring and the baggy pants and the mop with a bucket on wheels. Night classes finished at nine, and an hour later, Jerry came to work. He wore headphones while he swabbed, tuned, of course, to political talk radio and NPR.

Jerry told me all about his pseudo-underground community of fellow custodians, guys who stockpiled booze behind the Dumpsters, or the one who had a broom closet full of pornography and panties he stole from the girls' dorms. It was a hard, labor-intensive job, tainted by social stigma and low-level wages (though better than freshman comp adjuncts made). Jerry gnashed his teeth whenever he talked about the ineffectual workers' union or his condescending boss, Marvin. "Marvin told us we're supposed to leave no traces when we clean. He said we're supposed to be like invisible fairies who sweep over campus, clean in the night, and then vanish." Jerry sneered and added, "Typical petit bourgeois."

Oh, and one more thing—since, not surprisingly, Jerry was the sort of guy who never frittered away money—by working nonstop day in and day out for more than thirty years and saving nearly every penny of it, he had more than a million dollars in his savings account by the time I met him.

♥　♥　♥

I think our fling actually took off because of Jerry's job. I used to write to Gram and regale her with all sorts of tidbits about my boyfriends (I'd never tell my parents—my dating life was strictly don't-ask-don't-tell with those two) and Gram would analyze their quirks, affectations, and future earnings-to-income potential.

At forty-eight, however, Jerry was a confirmed Marxist janitor: Gram would've had a heart attack. She didn't just want wealth for me—she wanted prestige. And she wasn't the only one. My friend Belinda was so horrified by our flirtation that she refused to even let me speak Jerry's name. I'd grown up in a working-class/professional family and I thought I was impervious to the vagaries of social castes, but I still found that I avoided mentioning him to any of my other colleagues, and I never invited him to any school functions. The situation was uncomfortable but exciting—his unacceptability gave our whole affair a touch of the illicit. I liked the nerve-wracking feel of keeping something secret. No one approved of him. How sexy is *that*?

Jerry moonlighted during holidays and weekends swabbing down a local restaurant. If I was still awake, I'd sometimes walk the four blocks from my apartment to the nearby bistro, which, at 1 A.M., would be empty as a crypt, chairs upended on the tables, a fresh mop-trail glistening on the floor. Jerry's mop in the corner, casting a film noir–style shadow over the scene. Jerry would come out to meet me, his ponytail flipped insouciantly over one shoulder, put his arms around me, and dance me into a corner.

Jerry saved his political agitation for the show; with me he transformed into a swain. On New Year's Eve, I trailed snow in the door of the bistro. I'd gone to a party with some friends and snuck out with a bottle of champagne, fluttery with excitement. Jerry took down some chairs, lit a candle at one of the tables, and put Coltrane's "Naima" on the stereo. We sat at our private table, smooching and drinking champers and sharing a bowl of strawberries from the walk-in refrigerator.

There was a forties-era quality to our fling: it was dreamy but chaste. We necked like teenagers but somehow I couldn't get interested enough in Jerry to actually sleep with him. Maybe it was because he'd smoothed down all his crazy Trotskyite edges for me. But I doubt it. For one thing, there was his bedroom to consider—it was like his response to the world for turning him into a janitor. The room was rancid with old laundry, jungly with unwashed sheets, dirty socks, and cartons of abandoned take-out food. The one time he lured me to his house, I stood in the bedroom door and said, "I'm not going in there."

But the problem wasn't just the clothes in the bedroom—I'm not *that* shallow—it was also the clothes he was wearing. Even though academics are notoriously informal, Jerry's wardrobe was downright skanky. His jeans were all in various proletarian states of rot—these he would pair with a matching reeking proletarian sweatshirt—and in the place between the bottom of his sweatshirt and the waistband of his jeans several anarchic rolls of undershirts and gray athletic shorts bubbled up. I later saw much this very same look peddled in the windows of Abercrombie & Fitch—but years too late for Jerry.

And that wasn't all. There was also my compulsion—growing ever more Dracula-like in its dimensions—to keep the light of day from falling on our affair. I just didn't want to be seen with a local nut/ kooky guy anymore. Not to sound too junior high about it or anything, but it was *embarrassing.* Yes, I know, the irony—the thing that attracted me turned out to be the very thing that . . . yadda, yadda. But having belligerent eight-year-old thugs bicycle up to your boyfriend and say, "My dad says you're a red Commie bastard and he's gonna tar and feather you," well, that sort of thing gets stale after a short while. People recognized Jerry everywhere in town—you can't believe how many people tune into cable access—and not all of them were being hip and ironical about it. Plus there was no telling what these viewers might take into their heads to say or do at any given moment. Once, in a restaurant, the waitress walked over with a bill and told us that another of her customers, upon finishing his dinner, had pointed at Jerry and said, "Karl Marx over there will be glad to pay my bill."

So despite my already waning affections, a few months into our romance, and with only the dimmest idea of what I was getting into, I agreed to go on Jerry's show as a "guest star." Jerry broadcast his rants three days a week and was, understandably enough, delighted to get a little filler material. Propping me on the famously ugly couch in front of a single camera on a tripod, Jerry introduced me as the "daughter of the prime minister of Jordan" (well, my uncle *was* once a minister in the king's cabinet) and asked me to speak on American foreign policy. I threw out a few ill-prepared platitudes about "world peace," which seemed to delight and enthrall Jerry. Then he sort of nudged into the frame beside me on the couch in order to add a few more classics of his own choosing ("Workers must seize the means of production," "Down with the banks," and "Religion is the opiate of the masses").

The day after my debut, the department chair tapped on my classroom door while I was in the midst of a lecture on induction and deduction. The whole class fell silent in an unprecedented way, as if they had all conferred about this moment in advance. No one looked at me.

The chairman—a midwestern, regular-guy sort of guy named Buck—informed me that one of my students was going to drop my freshman comp class because the student's mother had caught my "little act" on what Buck referred to as the "Jerry Squatch Variety Hour" and wouldn't have her son learning things from some godless drug-taking hippie.

Well.

I sat, hands folded in my lap, perched on the hot seat, and Buck drawled at me. "Diana, I don't know how you all take your religion and politics in *New York*, but here we take them *very seriously*."

That was probably the real beginning of the end for me and ol' Jerr. Astounding how quickly the charm wears off a relationship if it's made up of little more than charm.

♥ ♥ ♥

For Jerry, however, there was apparently more to it than that. While he might've been a Marxist anarchist, he was also a goony-headed romantic. He bought me a string of Barbara Bush–length pearls for my twenty-seventh birthday. He opened and closed car doors for me, brought me pink roses, and even, in a grandly optimistic gesture, cleaned up his bedroom.

But after my fateful meeting with Buck, I could see the writing on the wall. It had been fun, for a little while, to live in Jerry's alterna-vision—plotting schemes of utopian societies and playing at l'amour. But once it started making my already unfun job even less fun, well, very quickly, I didn't want any more of it at all.

Plus I was tired and broke and never had any time to work on my writing. I'd failed at my grandmother's directive to marry wealth, and it was crystal clear to me that I'd have to take care of myself. Period. I applied for a job at an even bigger midwestern university, a position requiring slightly less teaching and yielding somewhat more pay. When they offered me the job, I jumped at it. And then I realized I'd have to tell Jerry.

I came to see him in the abandoned corridor outside the English department office just before sunrise. It was the end of the spring semester and the sun was coming up early. I leaned against the wall, stared directly at the floor, and confessed to Jerry I'd be moving away to a new job in a matter of weeks. He turned pale and twisted the end of his mop in both hands. "You—you want to leave here?" he stammered. "You want to *move away*?" That gleam came into his eye. "You can't leave! Your life is here now—with me—don't you know that?"

"I'm sorry, Jerr," I said. "I've just really got to focus on my career now."

"But you hate your career!" he said, rather astutely. "You're an artist, not a teacher. Stay here. Let me support you. I'll free you from the taskmasters and you can focus on your writing."

"It won't work. It's just not . . ."

"What?"

"Well, it's not . . . *practical*," I said lamely. I kept staring at the floor, inwardly kicking myself up and down the hallway. Why couldn't I just say yes? I'd finally found the financial support my grandmother had wanted for me—not in a doctor or lawyer, but in a generous custodian. A sweet, good-natured guy. But it seemed that, for some reason, I didn't want it. "I've already accepted the job, Jerry," I told him. "It's too late."

For days, Jerry tried everything he could think of to convince me not to go. He wept. He told me we were soul mates. He bought new clothes. He asked me to marry him.

I said, no, no, no.

It was just that sad old song—one of us had only been goofing around while the other one was dead serious. And somehow neither of us had managed to consult with the other on this point.

After a week of fretful pleading, Jerry came forth with a new offer— he was thinking about dropping everything, quitting his job, and moving to the new city with me. "Maybe I should just do it," he said dolefully. "If this 'job' means that much to you, then I should put your needs first. I don't want to lose you."

I was flabbergasted. I couldn't believe he would be willing to uproot his entire life for our flimsy liaison. Plus I didn't remember inviting him to move with me in the first place. And being the coward that I am, I didn't have the gumption to keep saying no. Instead, I hemmed and hawed and finally said that he could come but that he would have to get his own place—on the other side of town—and that, even then, I couldn't guarantee I'd have any time to see him, as I'd be so consumed with my big career job.

To my horror, he actually considered this counteroffer. Several more days of fretful soul searching went by. In the end, in a moment of surprising clear-sightedness for Jerry, he conceded that perhaps it wasn't the greatest plan in the world. He would be dismantling his entire life in exchange for a bachelor pad in an unfamiliar town. And there were all his viewers to consider. His people.

I nodded, eyes once again stuck to the floor, inwardly whipping myself with a cat-o'-nine-tails for being such a big fat faker. "They'd be lost without you, Jerry," I said.

❦   ❦   ❦

A few weeks after I moved, Jerry drove the six hours to see me. Shooting for as impersonal a tone as possible, I arranged to meet him on campus. With the move to a new city, I'd lost every last shred of interest in Jerry. I planned to finally tell him, once and for all, that it was over, Bub. Instead, of course, once he was there in the flesh, I turned lily-livered. We drove around town for a while, and somehow we ended up at a U-pick orchard, filling a basket with apples. That had to have been Jerry's idea. It sounds idyllic, but it wasn't. Jerry kept sighing and staring at me. He was wearing a silk shirt and tan chinos that he'd bought from Chess King especially for this visit, but he had sweated completely through them. He kept trying to start conversations about things like "our future." But I couldn't even look at him; he set my teeth on edge. Before he went back to his motel, he gazed at me mournfully before climbing back in his car and driving away.

I waved and said out loud (to myself): please, don't come back.

I've always been hopeless at drawing lines, closing up shop, saying *hasta la vista*—no matter how badly I want to. And perhaps I sensed that if I said a clean good-bye to Jerry, it might also mean having to look back on our relationship and see what I'd wrought—which was that I'd hooked up with someone pretty much just to amuse myself. Just like I did when I was eight and the kid next door got himself a sweet red scooter (eventually dropping the kid like a hot potato when the scooter thrills wore off).

Jerry headed home, but, relentless and warrior-like to the bitter end, he began writing me letters. Ten-, eleven-, twelve-page, hand-printed letters, written in red pen on ruled notebook paper. Each one said essentially the same thing:

"Oh, my dearest, my loveliest, oh what sweetness! What infinite sweet, sweet, sweetness! To think of being with you, always and eternally, my darling beloved . . ."

Yes, it's true. Mr. Anarchy-Now wrote letters purpler than a baboon's butt.

This was the last straw. After months of teaching frosh to write clear thesis statements and starched prose, this sort of excess was intolerable. I read each new "missive" with a vague queasiness. A cohort once told me she'd had a boyfriend who was so obsessed with her that she'd regularly wake with his lips clinging to her mouth, his body draped over hers like a 180-pound crocheted afghan. We referred to him as The Breath Sucker.

After a very, very short time, as you might imagine, I began skimming Jerry's letters. They were all about longing, loving, craving, yearning, blah, blah, blah. Not a single line of gossip or even a mention of the weather. A good object lesson for anyone who might think she wants true romance: after a steady diet of quail's eggs and truffles, one quickly wishes for toast and water.

I just stopped opening the letters altogether.

The thick legal-size envelopes still appeared in my mailbox, every day, for an entire year. I carried them to the garbage with the credit card ads and pizza delivery flyers.

When that year was up, I moved to yet another academic post in another city and left no forwarding address.

At times, I marveled at the sheer faith, resilience, and fortitude that those letters represented: to be able to go on like that, writing page after page, with no answer or encouragement, to go on believing without a glimmer of hope. It was a bit like being a novelist. Or maybe it was a form of mental illness.

Are the people who keep the faith—whatever that faith might be in—our last true heroes, or are they just crackpots? Is it virtuous to believe in pure truths like Justice and Love, or is it just stupid? I wanted to admire Jerry, but in the end, I simply felt impatient and even a little grossed out by it all. The thing is, it finally dawned on me that Jerry didn't really care all that much about how I felt—he was carrying on the romance just fine all by himself. I was an excuse to get the ball rolling. Like many relationships, where everything works better over long distances, our relationship improved considerably for Jerry once I left.

After I moved away, I never heard from Jerry Squatch again. He'd become my past. For his sake, I hope he finally stopped pounding out those letters and found himself a nice Leninist comrade. But when I do think of him—which is rarely—I can't help but visualize him still bent over his kitchen table, not eating but writing, longing and dreaming and writing, pouring out his heart's desires to his absent ghost lover, pleading for their perfect love. Later, after he seals the letter in a legal-size envelope, he turns on his camera and begins the latest installment of *Revolution Right Now*. He speaks to his true heart's companions—his loyal viewers. He beseeches these invisible people, once again, to see the light. He tells them that he has the answer, follow him, that happiness and freedom and joy lie before them, if they will just do what he says: lay down their chains, overthrow the banks, and seize the means of production!

That Thing He Didn't Do

Jacquelyn Mitchard

*H*e was only perfect. Smart, talented, tall, athletic, handsome, and, as my boss delicately put it once, "absolutely redolent of sex." I wasn't the only one who thought so, not the first time I fell in love with him.

And not the second time.

"You've got *Patrick?*" moaned my girlfriends, all fellow cub reporters at my first job, a city magazine of the kind every good-size town seemed to sprout in the early 1980s. "How did you manage that?" they asked. And it was a valid question. There were hotter women in the newsroom. I was quiet and bookish, diffident, not very put together fashionista-wise, and stunned that Patrick had turned his eye on me. It started with a note on paper that unrolled when I turned the knob on my typewriter carriage (computers were just coming in) that said, "I know a great Mexican place, but I'd rather eat with you than with a book. Even a good book. P." Obligingly, enjoying the intrigue, I rolled a similar sheet into *his* typewriter when he was out on assignment. When he called, I hesitated so long that he asked if he was out of line.

"No," I told him with complete honesty, "I just can't imagine why. I'm not much of a live wire. I like horseracing, but not betting, you know?" He laughed. He had the best laugh in the galaxy.

Things progressed rapidly. Soon Pat and I had a daily date for lunch at his nearby apartment, where he'd become accustomed to watching his favorite soap opera. It cracked me up that he never missed it. "I got addicted when my mother was in the hospital," he explained. "She recovered, but I never did."

When Pat and I would come casually strolling back to work (separately, of course), both looking as though we'd run a five-minute mile, the women in my cubicle, including my boss, who had thirty years on both of us, would sigh. I was twenty; he was twenty-three. We made love in his old MG; we made love on his kitchen table, at the beach, in Parrish Park, on my father's porch, on a tennis court—but most often, and more often than most, at his apartment in the little bed he'd stuffed under the eaves. In life, I was a shy girl, too early out of college, a little backward in the world, a bit too much like Bambi, right down to the looks. And I was modest. I remain a modest woman, in most settings, who's never, for example, used the bathroom in front of anyone over the age of six.

But with Patrick, I was a vixen. Once, on a drive home, I removed one article of clothing every time we stopped at a stoplight. We ran out of stoplights before I ran out of garments. And when we weren't having at each other's bodies, we were canoodling in each other's minds. Patrick's and my conversations were some of the most challenging, comic, and inspiring I've ever had with anyone. He quoted Yeats; I quoted Shakespeare. He quoted Mencken; I quoted Samuel Johnson.

In sum, I adored Patrick, and he adored me. On those nights when he came back spent from a game of hockey (he played semipro) to find me waiting, and I climbed him like a tree to no avail ("I just don't have that much to give," he'd say with sweet exhaustion), I never found it strange. Our time together, even when we simply talked, discussing our lives' frustrations and elations, was electric.

Then came a great and irreparable error.

Life, in the form of my stupidity, separated us.

Much as he downplayed it, Patrick came from privilege. I came from the wrong side of the tracks, and I was too bullheaded to believe

I could fit into his world. He pleaded, and then, justifiably mistrusting my slew of lame excuses, hardened against me. I could never explain the shame and reluctance that drove me away; its sources remained, for a long time, mysterious even to me. But after Patrick was gone, I was devastated. Even when I married a good man, I often dreamed of Patrick. When money was scarce, when I had difficulty having a child, I dreamed of Patrick. I dreamed we'd married, and those long, long, long-unto-dawn summer nights were once again real. On mornings after such a dream, caught between sleep-reality and daylight, I washed Baby Rob's face and considered the wistful truth that everyone gets one chance in her life to love like that. I supposed Patrick had been mine. I was happy, but I imagined that I'd lost the man in my life who was my utter other half.

And one day, by chance, I opened a *Town & Country* sort of magazine and saw lavish wedding photos of Patrick and sweetheart-before-me—a perky blonde who was, like Patrick, to the manner born. Unwonted agony squeezed my heart. I felt like the female Jay Gatsby.

But at least it was over. Patrick would no longer be out there, dancing out of reach, at the edge of my consciousness. My life was my life was my life.

In my thirties, my life sucker punched me.

My husband, in his early forties, died of cancer, and the next two years were a delirium of fear and grief. But during that time I gritted my teeth and, more to hang on to some hope of a future than for any hope of its success, I wrote my first novel. That novel was a hit, and suddenly I wasn't the little girl from the wrong side of the tracks anymore, but a writer of, well, some small consequence.

One night, along with a group of well-known journalists and authors (among whom I certainly didn't belong), I was on a dais receiving an award when I met an old colleague. We talked of our younger years back in the city from which both of us had come, and he mentioned, of all people, Patrick Callahan. I smiled and said, "I should have married Patrick Callahan."

Looking perplexed, my pal said, "Well, you might not be too late.

His first marriage ended fast, and I think his second is on the way out, too."

I drove home with my stomach clenched. Even if I could find him, would he remember me? But how could he have forgotten me? Was he really divorced? Who could be fool enough ever to divorce Patrick? Was he changed? Of course he was changed. That would never matter. If Patrick were in a wheelchair, I would love him.

Months passed while I worked on my second novel. But the thought of trying to track Patrick down was never far from my mind. The day I wrote the last page, I picked up the phone. I had no idea where Patrick lived, only that he now was a contributing editor for a well-known political magazine. I knew such contributors often worked off-site, so I tried his old hometown.

When I heard his one-of-a-kind voice, I was too dazzled and choked up, for long seconds, to speak. But when I did speak, the thrill in his response was unmistakable. We talked that day for three hours—of my husband's death, my daughter and sons, my book and the way I lived now. We talked that month for thirty hours, about everything—his first wife's roving eye, his second wife's insecurity, his job, and his inability ever to forget me. By dint of increasingly touching and sizzling e-mails, by the time we'd arranged a rendezvous, we had de facto fallen in love without benefit of second sight, twenty years after the first time we'd set eyes on each other.

So shy and overcome with emotion was I that when I saw Patrick again, I could barely look into his eyes. But I melted into our first kiss, and so did the years. I'd been sick and was a bit peaky, but once a friend took the children out for the night, we sat on my porch for about fifteen minutes before heading upstairs. And I removed my clothing one article at a time, feeling like the filly I had once been. I forgot the little throwaway line Patrick had tossed off one night on the phone, as we imagined the first time we'd be together again, and how he hoped it would work out.

It didn't work out.

Patrick was impotent. He got close, but we got no closer.

My shock and guilt, emotions I successfully concealed, were overwhelming. Such things happened. No cause for alarm. He assured me this had nothing to do with me—he was simply looking forward to this, far too much, and his body was not cooperating. It had happened to him only once before, in graduate school, and for the same reasons. And so I chalked it up as a glitch and slept joyously beside my Patrick, waking to marvel at his face beside me again, a sight I'd never imagined seeing in this life. In the morning, we eagerly fell on each other again, but still to no avail.

There was no question of blame. I simply felt horrible, and later that day, to my embarrassment, I had the first and only panic attack of my life. Pat wasn't the only one who'd set too many hopes on this summer day. Though he'd planned to stay until the following morning, the night had been such a debacle that he left early. But before he did, we arranged a long weekend in Minnesota for a month hence—in a cottage I'd borrow from a friend—and I was absolutely sure everything would "work out" beautifully. I put it down to the pressure of twenty years' absence. After all, this was Patrick and me!

Not once in our month of conversations before the trip did we speak of our sad, mutual loneliness in my huge bed. But I noticed, and tried to ignore, that he didn't seem to be looking forward to our weekend as much as I was.

And indeed, on the morning before we were to leave, Patrick wrote me a terse e-mail.

He couldn't go at this time. He was, possibly, reconciling with his second ex-wife. Or not. At any rate, he was confused. He was sorry. He would always love me. Please, would I call so he could explain?

I wouldn't call so that he could explain. For three nights, I barely slept. My assistant, a beloved friend, finally and literally taught me the cathartic benefits of crying myself to sleep. I'd assumed that our new life together would be like the ending of a Nicholas Sparks novel, that we'd meld as if we'd never parted, make great love and literature and even a baby. We'd be one of the great writer couples of all time, and we'd never be apart again—just as we'd once hoped.

Hopeless and hurting, I grew gaunt. Even my children noticed my mourning. When, finally, I'd almost resumed my usual rhythm, Patrick called. We spoke on the phone for three hours, and at the end of that conversation, I agreed to meet him in California, where both of us had business on the same weekend a few weeks hence. The lake trip was forgiven, and he assured me that his second ex was out of the picture and the picture was filled, from frame to frame, with me. I wanted so badly to believe him, I did. As many have said, when the gods wish to torment you, they answer your prayers.

As I waited for him in the hotel, I was so racked with anticipation and, well, fear, that I went downstairs and bummed a cigarette from the night bellman, though I hadn't smoked in years. I washed my hair twice. I put on fetching but not seductive lounging clothes. When Patrick arrived, I held out my arms, sweetly, and we touched and held each other tenderly. We dressed for dinner; he looked like a prince and I felt like a movie star. I thought that even in Beverly Hills, people were staring at this couple who were so obviously and radiantly in love.

Once home, and giddy with champagne, we fell onto the bed. And he fell asleep, promising to make it up to me in the morning. But morning came, and Patrick didn't.

I was desperate. We took a long walk by the ocean. Shy people faced with an enormously difficult matter, we tried to talk it out.

"We love each other, right?" Patrick said. "And we have a door that we can't walk through. And so I think we should see someone, to-gether, and talk it out, because this is what both of us want more than we want anything else." We agreed to make time for this as soon as both our schedules permitted.

But something about these aborted attempts at a great love affair had affected Patrick, in a nasty way.

He became snippy when he called, criticizing everything from my new short haircut to my syntax. "You're *finished* with a project," he snapped, "you're *done* if you're a biscuit in the oven." When I told him I'd worked hard that day and thought I'd written a few good pages, he advised me to let others be the judge of that. He sent me a series he'd written, and when I commented on the nice dialogue in it, he snapped, "There was no dialogue. I only quoted one person!" He spoke of a young Asian woman to whom he was attracted, though he'd never asked her out. And he spoke again of his ex-wife, intimating, yet denying, that they were still intimate. I was distraught. What about "talking to someone"? What about "walking through this door"? What about us?

To my regret, I unsheathed my not-inconsiderable claws. I told Patrick I never wanted to hear his criticism again. I never wanted to hear his ex-wife's name, either, and if he wanted to see her even for dinner, he need not call me, ever again. But a week later he did, contrite and ardent and comic, and I relented. We made and canceled plans to see each other. And I knew full well that this could go on for a lifetime, in fits and starts, and drive me mad.

There were other suitors by then, who were, if not Patrick, interesting guys, some drawn by my fifteen minutes of fame, others simply drawn to me. One in particular was a younger man, an artist and builder, whose honest and hopeful attraction, to my children as well as to me, was touching and genuine. We came from diverse planets, but we found hours of common territory to explore. I really, really liked him. If not for the invisible strings that bound me to Patrick, I might have been thoroughly smitten. I didn't, as I had with others, tell him about Patrick, the still-unfinished business in my life.

If I could be with Patrick, really be with him, I knew we could prosper. No one could replace him. Yet daily, that prospect seemed less likely. His e-mails had dwindled to witty one-liners, while I was writing pages of passion and frustration. He returned my phone calls late or not at all. This rendered me so distraught that I was all but physically ill. In my mirror, I saw a woman on the verge of a meltdown. I lost weight and, for the first time in my life, repeatedly cried myself to sleep. I knew that he had withdrawn from me because of "that thing" he couldn't do. I knew that he wanted to uncouple, as it were, our relationship as a couple. But I still thought that we could make it (and make out) with enough time and patience.

I stopped phoning and writing.

And I believed, even hoped, that it was over. I began the deliberate and excruciating process of forgetting.

There was no communication for weeks. And then—the oldest story in the book—he rallied in pursuit. He had to have me back. And I bloomed. We began to speak of the beauty of our collected e-mails, and joked that we could publish them one day.

Finally, a night before I was to leave for several weeks on the East Coast, where Patrick promised to visit me and bring the two teenage daughters he rarely saw, I went to stay with Patrick at his town house in the city where we'd met, those many, many years ago. This would either be the beginning, I had determined, or the end. After a tepid comment about my new black dress and the newly slender arms that went with it, he was . . . chilly. He took me out to a fast-food Chinese joint. We brought home carryout. When I tried to snuggle under his arm on the couch, he concentrated on TV. When I tried to play with his dark curly hair, he took my hand and gently if dismissively, patted it. When I put on my sexy nightgown, he gave me a robe, about a foot too long. And still, I hoped.

You might be wondering how that was possible.

You might be thinking, now this chick, a house had to fall on her.

You might ask, how could a person smart enough to write it down be such a fool when it comes to matters of the heart?

Have you ever heard a Smokey Robinson song? Or one by Tammy Wynette, or Eric Clapton, or Billie Holiday?

Don't all of us, at some point early or late, try to combine and recombine the same ingredients, hoping against hope that the formula will result in a fine vintage instead of vinegar?

Of course, it wasn't the Patrick of here and now I loved but the one who lived in a memory palace. The man-of-now, who wrote those delicious e-mails, who sent me peach-colored roses, who said over the phone that we owned real estate just a floor below infinity, was both relic and receptacle of hope.

Most women think, or like to think, that they would put up with the nonsense I endured for about as long as it takes to blow out a candle. But I suppose that would depend on the brightness and intensity of the flame, and on the strength and nature of the woman. The flame was powerful. And perhaps depleted by loneliness and the ineffable force of love recalled and rekindled, I was not.

That night in Patrick's house, again, I questioned myself. Too much pressure? Too many expectations? Was I just not sexy enough anymore? And what about this mythic ex-wife? Was he fearful of what would seem an act of infidelity? Perhaps *she* was causing all this. Mired in my miserable feelings of inadequacy, with Patrick in grim silence, I didn't consider that somewhere along the way, my bonny prince had developed a physical problem—or that he'd had one all along. More likely it was a psychological problem, one that had nothing to do with me, that had battered him in the long, intervening years between our first enchanted encounter and our most recent disenchanted caress. Even *Patrick* said I caught the fallout from the times he should have vented righteous anger at other women who'd hurt him.

I ought to have stopped beating myself up then, made sure I had a Joni Mitchell CD for the airplane and enough change to buy myself a gin and tonic or two. But I couldn't. How, I kept asking myself, had such a great beginning seen such a lousy final inning? Had I come off as too *available*, not giving the hunter time to stalk the game? Hadn't I been the one to seek Patrick out first? And hadn't I been just as energetic as he in my premature professions of love? Were the remarks I made when he didn't call or when he snapped at me simply bitchy, leaving him limp, literally, with hostility? Even the sexual compatibility now didn't seem that huge a deal, not set against losing Patrick forever.

That this problem was *not mine* but his—even if it *was* my inability to light up his board—didn't immediately spring to mind. That it was darned weird, the business of the second and recurrent Mrs. Callahan—to be hung up on a woman who'd left you, after five years, during two of which you were allegedly in love with someone else—didn't strike me as pathological, only poignant.

I tried to start a conversation. Pat tried to sleep.

The morning broke cloudy.

I hadn't slept for a single minute. Patrick and I had clung to opposite edges of his bed like a couple cursed a decade before with a badly arranged marriage.

As I dressed and brushed my teeth, I caught sight of myself in the mirror. My eyes were puffy. Weariness and grief seemed to have sculpted my entire face downward. If this be love, could hatred wreak worse changes? After two periods of two years, separated by two decades, I gave up. I had to admit that, since that first failure, Patrick had treated me with increasing passive-aggressive neglect and finally downright hostility. He loved me, but I was a witness to something he couldn't bear.

Patrick could not get over his failure to find the key to that door, and he could not ask himself what it was that made that impossible. Nothing would change that. And I had been foolish to try so hard for so long, opening all the wrong doors myself—the ones with cardboard caricatures of me fat and with fangs, a harridan with a razor tongue.

Later that morning, after a last kiss that I can still feel, we said good-bye, and Patrick assured me that I'd see him soon. I saw tears in his eyes. My own were masked by dark glasses.

I've never seen him again.

Five weeks later, after leaving Patrick a message on his answering machine, I married that young artist, and since then, we've had three children. Our life, despite its early roller-coaster quality, has generally been pretty wonderful. We've never had the depth of intellectual compatibility that Patrick and I shared. But so much has compensated for the ability to critique authors together. We take care of each other. We share a mutual vision for our life and our children. We have a whole lot of *fun*, in bed and out, and my husband tolerates, even celebrates, my eccentricities. He makes me feel like a woman anyone would love.

A year ago, I got a short e-mail from Patrick, asking me if he could call. When he did, we had a long, all-over-the-place chat about my new baby and his book idea, which ended in his telling me he was about to be married.

I was genuinely happy. And I also genuinely wanted to hurt myself. That sharp pain lasted until Patrick said, "We coulda been contenders, you and me. It wasn't you. It was the place you were in." Not a word about the place *he'd* been. Blame *me*, I wanted to cry in pure desperation—what about him, and the place *he'd* been? Patrick said not a word about his own part in the passion that wilted on the vine, not a word about why, no recognition that it had been a powerful factor in preventing anything else from flourishing. He was going to leave me with the responsibility for the abortive sequel to our first love. He was going to make me wonder, always, whether we never got off the ground because of the weight of my baggage, because my head was too big or my heart too small. But that was not true, and I knew it was not true. I also knew that had it been in his power to say what I needed to hear at that moment, he might also have been able to walk through that door with me, as he had once said, instead of slamming it shut and running away. Even realizing this might have undermined his sense of his own masculinity.

I would never know if Patrick's inability to make love to me had been caused by a physical challenge, or if he felt, despite all his protestations to the contrary, that whatever recognition I had received in the world made him feel somehow diminished. As we said our good-byes, what I felt was genuine sadness and a certain determination.

Patrick was right about one thing: I wasn't going to blame myself, either.

A few months later, another short e-mail.

Patrick's wedding day had come and gone. He just wanted me to know, and he hoped he wasn't out of line, that he would always love me. This time, I smiled gently, reaching out involuntarily to touch the screen with one finger. That he loved me, I never doubted. That he knew what love meant I did doubt. And yet I was touched that he had felt moved to say this.

But perhaps like my husband, who'd never been married before but who seemed to grow daily in his understanding of partnership, Patrick would, too. I hoped so. I wanted him to be happy.

For, from a distance and through memory's merciful veil, I would always love him, too.

Soul-Mating

Ethel Morgan Smith

*Y*ou opt not to place a photograph with your ad: *Attractive, edu-cated, well-traveled African-American female seeking friendly male com-panion between the ages of 40 and 55. He should also be a gentleman, confident, emotionally and financially stable. Race open. My interests are tennis, hiking, traveling, and reading.* You don't say you're a college pro-fessor, on sabbatical for a year, seeking love to take back to your mostly white, small college town.

During the first week your ad runs you're surprised and delighted at how many responses you receive. One from as far away as Australia and another from England who says, "I know I can't be a true con-tender but you appear interesting, and if you're ever in England I'll cook you a great meal." You're impressed. The e-mails continue to fly for a few weeks.

The Aussie is doing some kind of research in the outback for eight weeks. When you suggest meeting for a cup of coffee, he informs you that it would be the most expensive cup of coffee on earth, since he is actually in Australia.

At first you answer all of your e-mails without looking closely at the profiles, since you're so flattered. In three weeks you go out on ten dates, more than you've had in two years. You're exhausted, but not having a good time. Not a bad time, but just not good enough for the effort.

"You've got to get through the quantity before you get to the quality," your friend Lisa tells you. You believe her since she dated a lot before she was married two years ago. But she's also younger than you and has more energy. And you're so ready for a close-to-quality date.

Your first date is brunch with Steven, who doesn't post a photograph of himself, either—because of his daughters, he says. He wants to chat before you meet. He tells you this after he's told you five times his name is spelled with a "v" and not a "ph." He doesn't trust folks who can't understand the difference. You give him your cell phone number. He's a forty-six-year-old divorced father of two teenage daughters, whom he adores. Divorced men who cyberdate always adore their children. Steven is on the slow side and immature for his age, he tells you. He says he doesn't believe in planning; life should just happen.

After your brunch he e-mails you and says he thinks you're an intriguing woman, but can't see being romantically involved since you don't look anything like Halle Berry. But he wants to be friends. You tell him you have enough friends.

John is your next date, who does post a photograph with his profile. He is tall and good-looking. He says he's really looking for someone to play tennis with. You like that, and think it's a good way to get to know each other. He wants to know if your game is any good.

Finally a date for dinner is set with John at a place called Flying Burgers because he has coupons for 50 percent off the meal. The drive is out of your way on the rainy night you meet. Just as his photograph promised, he is good-looking with a head of dark hair. Usually when cyberdating men say they're gray around the temples, it means they're almost bald. He is recently divorced from an alcoholic wife. Their two children have suffered terribly from their irresponsible mother. He wants to know if you have ever lived with any alcoholics. When you say no, he continues talking about the evils of alcoholism.

John says because he is so good-looking he goes out on many first dates, but he is seeking something deeper. He says dating women under forty is a waste of his time since they only want babies. Some women have even offered to pay for the reversal of his vasectomy. You say that won't be an issue for you.

Your second week of dating you complain to your friend Lisa that you're not attracting a high enough quality of dates.

"You've got to screen them better."

"How?"

"For one thing, look at their education level. Come on, you're a college professor. You know what I mean."

You agree, but you don't want your potential dates to be put off because you're a college professor. It's not exactly perceived as a sexy profession. Your next date is with a never-married fifty-five-year-old dentist. A red light goes on, but you hope that he has at least lived with a woman or two for some time. He also says he looks like Michael Douglas. From his photograph all you can tell is that he is Jewish and has longish dark hair.

Michael Douglas Look-alike and you meet for drinks at a loud bar in a mall near where you live. You're fifteen minutes late, but he's later. When he finally arrives you can hardly hear each other talk. His longish hair is short and he doesn't look like Michael Douglas. You ask him why he never married; he says he spent a lot of years being gay. "I see," you say.

Your next date is with Tony. You meet him for lunch near your office. Tony is three times divorced and has three spoiled children whom he adores, he tells you. When you see all his gold jewelry, you order a glass of wine. Tony says he doesn't believe in e-mailing too much, it's just words, and he thinks *it* works or *it* don't.

You agree with Tony and order another glass of wine. He doesn't ask you anything about yourself other than what subjects you teach. Before you can answer he tells you that he was a bad student. He finishes his meal before you and is ready to leave for his next appointment. He asks, "Where do we go from here?" You tell him you're going back to your office.

Michael is your next date. Black women are his preference. You talk on the telephone three times for an hour before going out. When he tells you he is into black women, you tell him that makes you feel uncomfortable. He backs off some and apologizes for coming on so strong. You know you're not going out with him when one night on the phone he asks how many lovers you've had.

Your friend Lisa tells you she's sure you'll find a better match soon. You continue to receive responses to your profile. The men often describe themselves as laid-back, athletic, fun-loving, and could be passionate with the right woman.

You receive an e-mail from a man with the nickname Prince. He describes himself as Haitian-American, tall, dark, and not just handsome but "could make any woman fall on her knees." He wants to talk rather than e-mail. He says he can tell everything about a woman from her voice. He gives you his telephone number at work and asks you to call him. You do. He says he likes what he hears and thinks it's time to get together, but he wants to start off totally honest. You say you think that's a good idea. He informs you that he has been living with a woman for three years, but "the thrill is gone." He isn't going to give her up until he finds somethin' better. You tell him you're the wrong girl and hang up the telephone.

Allen e-mails you. He has just moved to the area and, like you, is interested in getting to know people. He's from New Mexico. You meet for lunch. He is fifty-four years old and moved to the area to be close to his six-year-old son. Allen is shy but pleasant. After the date, every Monday morning for three weeks you receive a long, detailed e-mail from him telling you what he did over the weekend with his son, including everything they ate. After the third e-mail you ask him if he wants to go out again. Three weeks later he e-mails back and says yes. He apologizes for taking so long to get back to you, but says he has a dating phobia.

The next day you receive an e-mail from an African-American man who says you have a nerve wanting to go out with white men. He wants to know what's wrong with the "brothers." You e-mail him back and say you're open to race, and would be interested in talking to him. You never hear from him again.

That night you telephone another girlfriend and ask if she wants to go on a holiday with you. She wants to know where. You say someplace where there are no men.

Your Friend Always

Joyce Maynard

I was thirty-nine years old. I was living with my three children in
a small New Hampshire town, writing a syndicated newspaper column about my life. But my life at the time was going badly. My mother
had died the year before, within days of my husband's announcement
that he didn't want to be married to me anymore, and now the two of
us no longer spoke, except to deliver some new and bitter accusation.
I was rapidly going into debt with my lawyer, and being evaluated by
a guardian ad litem whose assignment it was to assess the job I was
doing as a mother for the purpose of recommending to the court
which parent was the more fit to raise our three children.

The winter was cold. Christmas was coming. I was an orphan. And
then one day, a letter dropped through my mail slot.

I had been a writer long enough by this point to recognize the ori-
gin of this particular letter. The return address was written in pencil,
for starters, but more significantly, it was accompanied by a long string
of digits. I knew what that meant: its author was in prison.

The letter began with an unlikely salutation: *Dear Lady Joyce.* At
the facility where he was presently incarcerated, the author of this letter told me, most of the inmates favored publications along the lines
of *Penthouse* or *Biker Chick* for their reading matter. As for himself,
he waited all week for Saturday—the day my syndicated column appeared in the local paper, which was delivered to the prison library. He
loved reading my stories about life with my kids—baseball practices

and birthday parties, a misplaced hamster, a disastrous encounter between my son Willy and an eggbeater he'd thought to put on top of
his head while in the "on" position.

"It makes me feel like I'm part of a regular family, reading what you
write," he told me. "I like to pretend I'm there in the kitchen with
you, having some of your homemade biscuits." At the bottom of
the page, he explained to me that though his real name was Dennis,
he went by a nickname, which was how he signed his letter, with the
words "For real, your friend always, Lucky."

The letter touched me. As far removed as his circumstances were
from my own, something in the tone of loneliness and longing was
recognizable. And so I sent him back a note.

"Dear Lucky, thank you very much for your letter . . ." Because it
was Christmastime, I enclosed our annual family Christmas card photograph: me and my children, sitting under our tree. I wished him a
happy holiday, though truthfully, I didn't hold out a lot of hope he
had one of those in his future that December, any more than I did.

In record time, there was a new letter from Calipatria State Prison—
this time twice as long. He must have studied that photograph for a
long time, because he'd noticed every single thing about it: the mismatched socks my son Willy wore (just barely visible under the cuffs
of his pants). Audrey's earrings and braces. The fact that Charlie appeared to be left-handed. My golden dress, which my lawyer boyfriend, Don, would have called tacky; but to this man, I looked like a
princess. He signed off, "For real, Lucky."

♥   ♥   ♥

This was the moment, probably, when a more sensible woman would
have ended the correspondence. But his words—which had touched
me in the first letter—now brought tears to my eyes. In a handwriting
so tiny I had to strain to read it (an effort to conserve paper, probably),
he told me about his own family: his childhood in the orange groves
of southern California, his parents, Ava and Hank, his grandmother
Mamie, who used to tell him stories and bake anadama bread. His

family was poor, but his grandmother made him little figures out of orange peels to play with. He wrote about his dog and his first car and a certain stretch of Highway 1 he loved, around San Luis Obispo. He described a trip he wished he could take me on, along the Pacific Coast Highway, on the back of a motorcycle, writing with so much detail it was as if we had actually traveled every mile. I had never ridden on a motorcycle.

He talked about me and my children, too, in a way that confirmed, if there was any doubt, how devotedly he'd followed my columns, and for how long. He knew all my stories, knew about the farm in New Hampshire I'd left, when my marriage ended, about our dog Opie and how he pulled me up hills when I went Rollerblading and held his leash, and Willy's love of the Oakland A's, even though we lived in Red Sox country.

He had also read between the lines, to an amazing degree. Although I had said very little in my column about the divorce, he knew he had no use for my ex-husband, to put it mildly. How could any man let a treasure like me go? he wanted to know. And though I might have told him a few reasons why—and my former husband certainly could have expounded at length on the subject—I was in the mood to hear words of simple appreciation and unbridled praise, and that's what Lucky offered.

♥　♥　♥

I will tell you now one thing about men in prison: as much time as the rest of us spend going to jobs, taking care of our houses and meals, our children, our pets, carrying on relationships and breakups, paying bills—having sex perhaps, if we are lucky—that is time men in prison have for writing letters. Not surprisingly, they get good at it. Their letters are very long. They pack a lot into those letters.

So when I wrote a sentence to Lucky, as I did that first time, he wrote back five pages. When I wrote back a paragraph, he sent ten pages. When (barely ten days later, having received two more responses) I wrote back a full-page letter, the envelope that arrived back, in record time, contained fifty pencil-written pages, with writing on both sides.

He wrote now about what a brave woman I was, raising three kids on my own as I was doing, driving two hours to take them to a ball game in Boston, shoveling the snow to get them to school on time, working like a dog to put food on the table—and he knew I was a good cook, too, he could just tell from reading my columns.

"What I'd give for a slice of your pie," he wrote. *Just to smell those cookies in the oven.*

In all those fifty pages, there was nothing of romance or sex, only the deepest kind of respect and affection, and something else, too: I got the sense, from what Lucky wrote, that he understood me in some strange way, as nobody had for many years.

I was dating someone at the time, though admittedly the relationship had grown somewhat tepid. But immersed as I was in a bitter and scary divorce and custody battle, I took comfort in the fact that Don was a litigator with a major Boston law firm—a kind of lawyer who (as he himself explained to me) ate nails for breakfast, or acted as if he did, anyway, when any kind of legal battle came up.

Still, it had not escaped my notice that Don was lacking in a certain kind of courage on other fronts. A few months earlier, for instance, on a camping trip together to Oregon—a journey he had undertaken somewhat reluctantly—Don had refused to eat any of the wonderful plump marion berries surrounding our tent because they hadn't been washed.

Now I was hearing on a daily basis from a man in Calipatria, California, who didn't seem to have this kind of problem. His letters contained a kind of animal passion and fearlessness that made my heart beat faster when I read them. More than I wanted to admit, I found myself looking forward to Lucky's letters.

❦   ❦   ❦

A person might be thinking here—and I would not argue if he or she did—that I appear to be a woman lacking in a certain level of judgment. But I know a good writer when I see one, or read one. And over the years, I've encountered a few—virtually none of them the equal of the man who had now embarked on the practice of sending me daily missives from Calipatria.

Lucky never wrote about life in prison. He wrote to me about his life before he got there—wonderful, funny, tough, gritty, and authentic letters, with not a cliché in the whole hundred pages.

It was clear he had experienced a lot of loss in his life, too. His first wife had died in childbirth, so he had raised their daughter on his own. He had gotten married again—to the most beautiful woman in the state of California. But one day when she was riding on the back of his Harley, he'd had an accident. She was horribly burned, and so disfigured she refused to let him ever lay eyes on her again. She disappeared shortly after that. His parents had died, too. Like me, he considered himself an orphan, he wrote.

And then his daughter had died, of a rare fever. The letter he wrote about her death—accompanied by a photograph of a beautiful three-year-old lying in an open, flower-strewn coffin—was among the most wrenching I had ever received.

♥ ♥ ♥

I could have said I was just offering a little kindness to a man in prison, or maybe (less admirably) that I was curious about his story. But here was the truth: My desire to write back to Lucky came out of something more than the simple impulse to offer kindness, and it was about more, too, than fascination with his story. More and more, over the course of that long winter—as my court case dragged on, as the snow fell, and I watched my children riding off to their father's house on Friday nights, and I lay in bed wishing I could call my mother, only she was dead—it was Lucky who offered comfort.

I had friends. I had a boyfriend who called me on his car phone, driving home from work, before heading off to the gym—a man who took me out to expensive restaurants on weekends. But at the end of the day, more often than not, I found myself climbing into bed alone with a glass of less expensive wine and the latest of Lucky's letters. And there was always a new one; they arrived on a daily basis now.

On Valentine's Day, Don took me out to dinner, during which he received a call on his cell phone requiring immediate attention. Lucky made me a drawing. Unlike my ex-husband, he wasn't much of an artist, he wrote, but a guy on his cell block, who was more the artistic type, had made the outlines for him, and he'd colored it in: a picture of Mickey Mouse holding out a bouquet of flowers.

At some point over the course of that winter, Don and I took a trip to the Pacific Northwest again. Hiking with him on that trip (never his favorite activity), I had spotted a bug of such an extraordinary size and shape that I had taken it upon myself to locate a glass jar, and punched holes in the lid, for the purpose of bringing it home to show my sons.

On the plane home, Don had expressed extreme discomfort at sitting next to me, knowing that this bug was in my purse. And maybe partly to provoke him—maybe, even, with the image of Lucky in my head—I had said, "You know, for five hundred dollars, I'd eat this bug."

He'd been disgusted. "What am I talking about?" I'd said. "I'd eat this bug for a hundred." And when that got an even more horrified response, I'd held the bug up to my lips and told him, "I'd eat this bug for ten bucks." Our relationship ended soon after this.

But the relationship with Lucky—whatever it was—continued to develop, and with a kind of intensity and emotion I could no longer deny.

When I wrote back now—as I did, at greater length than before—I didn't simply respond to his stories. I told him mine. Not as long or as impassioned as his, but I told him about my life and about my children. I described a terrible argument with my son Willy, then age seven, that had started when I accused him of disrespect and he had walked out of the kitchen and gone up to his room, and put on a Guns N' Roses CD, top volume.

I had stormed into my son's room then. I had taken his CD player away, I told Lucky. My son called me a terrible name. I slapped him. He picked up the phone and called his father, who was now charging me with child abuse.

And here I was, at eleven o'clock on a Friday night in February, pouring out my story to a man I'd never met, in the Calipatria correctional facility. And reading, closely, what he wrote back by way of advice.

Lucky knew what it was to be an angry little boy, he wrote. He'd treated his mother badly, too, in the past. Now he looked back and felt terrible remorse.

"He's trying to be a man," Lucky wrote. "He wants to prove how tough he is. He wants to show no woman's going to push him around."

Of course, if my son's father were there where he belonged, Lucky wrote—or if *he* were Willy's dad—he'd be taking the boy aside and having a good hard talk with him. "It's too much for one woman to do all on her own," he wrote. "Even a strong woman like you needs a loving man at her side."

That man would be him, of course.

As for me: I wasn't sending Lucky any words of love, but if I looked deep in my heart, I would have had to say, love was what I had begun to feel for him. It was love that had nothing to do with dinners in good restaurants or vacations to the Caribbean. This kind of love was about nothing more or less than the purity of a true heart. And maybe, too, there was an element of relief in there, that this man was not going to show up on my doorstep tomorrow to disappoint me. He was locked up in California, three thousand miles away. I could just know that somewhere on the planet was a man who, as he reminded me in every pencil-written letter, would cut out his own heart and hand it to me, if that's what I wanted.

♥   ♥   ♥

I know how this sounds. So I will say, in my defense, what any woman who has been single for a while probably knows already. I had been out in the world of dating long enough by this point to understand that just because a man you may be dating is a cardiac surgeon, say, or a tenured professor at some Ivy League university, or a partner in a major Boston law firm, is no guarantee that he won't be a sociopath. Now I was receiving daily expressions of undying love and passion from a man who had been labeled by society as a complete outcast. It probably said something about the previous thirty-eight years of my life, but I had begun to consider the possibility that maybe I had actually located the one truly good, honest man on the planet. Someone who was—as he himself reminded me every time he signed off—"for real." And everything about him (including his grammar and spelling, not to mention his address) suggested this was so.

He sent me a photograph of himself—and in case a person might suppose he was a handsome man, I will say simply, he was not. But I had been married to a handsome man. I knew how far that got you. In this photograph, which he'd gotten someone to take expressly for me, Lucky stood in front of a cinder-block wall that appeared to be outside, in some kind of prison exercise yard. In the picture, he had a long and scraggly beard, and some kind of bandage over his head. He was wearing what he had told me, in the letter that came with the picture, was his best shirt. Misbuttoned.

And still, it didn't matter. I was moved by this man. As unwise as I told myself it was, at the end of the day, the thoughts that most comforted me were of his fierce and wild willingness to protect me. My lawyer ex-boyfriend, hearing of my ex-husband's various legal efforts in our divorce, had talked of filing motions, interrogatories, taking depositions. But I liked better what Lucky said when he heard what was going on. If he were there, he wrote, he'd make the man eat his underwear.

Friends to whom I cautiously disclosed news of the correspondence (though not its full significance in my life) were expressing concern. Invariably, they asked what crime he was in prison for. I didn't know, I explained. Unfamiliar with the etiquette of these things, it struck me as a little rude, asking, and Lucky hadn't volunteered the information.

It was almost spring now. Lucky's letters had begun to include tips to pass on to Willy, a pitcher, about ways to improve his motion, and jokes for Charlie, reminders to me not to let any boy mess with Audrey or there'd be hell to pay from you know who. (It was definitely a challenge, conveying pitching know-how on paper, but he tried, though upon reflection I opted not to share Lucky's pointers with my younger son.)

▼   ▼   ▼

Meanwhile, the battle over custody of my three children was getting worse, with a court date set for summer and legal bills so high I didn't even open them sometimes. When Lucky started talking about my coming out to California to visit him—and in fact, you could get an apartment, very cheap, not far from Calipatria—I realized I was in too deep. I sent him a letter to say there was no future for us. "I think we should discontinue this correspondence," I wrote.

Within a week came the news: Lucky was getting out on parole soon. First thing he planned to do once he was out: come see me. With luck, he'd be in New Hampshire for the start of Little League season.

For the first time in the six months of the relationship (there it was, that word), I registered fear. I didn't want Lucky to visit. A man on paper, a man who came in once a day through the mail slot, was as much of a man as I could deal with right about then.

Now, though, his letters took on a new excitement and passion, if such a thing was possible, as he described to me how it would be when he got to my house. How he pictured me opening the door to him. How he would put his arms around me. And more.

I did, then, the thing I'd resisted before. I called the prison. It took a while to work through the channels, but finally I got a woman on the phone who was the counselor assigned to prisoner number D076952—Lucky.

▼   ▼   ▼

I tried, as I laid out my story, to do so in the most businesslike and unemotional fashion possible, but the facts spoke for themselves. "I've been corresponding with this inmate for a while," I told the woman. "Now that he's getting out on parole, he's been talking about coming to visit my children and me. So I thought I should just find out . . . what he was in for."

Long silence on the other end of the phone. "I must tell you," she said, "we are prohibited from divulging this information over the telephone. I could lose my job."

"I understand," I said. Already, I was feeling like a fool, and worse, a woman of faint heart. I had betrayed the trust of this good man.

"But you seem like a nice person," she said, and her voice was grave. "So I'm going to do it anyway.

"First tell me," she said. "Are you alone where you are? Do you have someone nearby that you could talk with if you needed to?"

I was okay, I told her. I wasn't but I pretended otherwise.

"To begin with," the voice on the other end of the line told me, "your friend will not be released on parole anytime soon. Considering the fact that he is serving two consecutive eighty-year sentences, he will not be eligible for parole until sometime after the year 2150.

"Dennis, or Lucky, as he calls himself," she said, "killed his parents. Killed and then decapitated them."

She said more, but I took in only part of it. He had been on the loose for a couple of years before the police in southern California had found him, she said. He was hiding out on a ranch, picking oranges. In the course of the arrest, he shot a deputy, left him brain damaged. This was fifteen years ago. He remained in maximum security, considered to be the most dangerous kind of prisoner.

"I'd be grateful," she said, "if you would not let this inmate know you have spoken to me. He is a highly explosive individual."

What she recommended, she said to me, was that I take a gradual approach to breaking off the relationship (there was that word again; suddenly it left me nauseous). Assuming breaking it off was what I wished to do, she added.

Yes.

But I couldn't do what the counselor suggested, and simply, slowly, begin to disconnect myself from this man. The next day, when the latest letter from Lucky dropped through the mail slot, I left it lying on the floor of my front hall where it landed. I did not open the next one, or any that continued to show up, daily, for many, many weeks after that.

At some point, a long time after I'd gotten the news about Lucky and ceased writing to him, I opened one of the letters that continued to arrive. The words I read hit me like a blast of some noxious gas—toxic and putrid as decaying flesh. The handwriting was familiar, but the same hand that once filled the pages with words of loyalty, compassion, and understanding—and undying love—now formed accusations of wrath and contempt beyond any I had encountered in my life. I used to say, of Lucky, that he was a man who—unable to make love to a woman in flesh—had developed the ability to make love solely with words, more powerfully than I would have known to be possible. Now I discovered the power of words on paper—his—as a force of unspeakable violence. His words did everything but draw blood.

After that, I didn't open any more of his letters, though they continued to arrive—no longer daily, but now and then—for close to a year.

That summer, I spent four days in court in the trial over custody of the children my ex-husband and I still shared, though the two of us could no longer speak to each other. The judge ruled that our children could continue to live with me and visit their father on weekends. I was ruled to be a fit mother, after all. The thought did not escape me that had the court known about my correspondence with Lucky, the judge might have concluded otherwise.

♥ ♥ ♥

I did not look again at the letters in the box in the back of my closet, but I couldn't throw them out. Maybe because they contained a part of my history that—troubling as it was—I needed to document. Maybe it was simply my abiding belief that you don't throw out good writing.

So I kept Lucky's letters, the reminder of a person I was once, and hoped I wasn't anymore. It was many years before I could bear to take them out and look at them again:

Now listen up baby. I don't have much to give you in the way of trinkets and such. I'm betting there's guys out there lining up to take you out to fancy restaurants and put a ring on your finger—24 karat, who knows? Guys that'll buy you a car, buy you a house, fly you to gay Paree. Me I can't even plant a kiss on those sweet lips of yours, not that I wouldn't chew off my right arm to do it.

All I can give you when the day is done is one goddamn thing, and that's my heart. I see who you are. I know you like I know my blood. I read what you wrote and I read between the lines too, baby.

I'd die for you. I'd kill for you. There isn't words to say it, but if you close your eyes and take a breath, you'll feel it. Someplace in California, there's a man locked up in a concrete box that's got you in his brain right now. Put your hand on your heart, baby, and feel it beating, imagine me inside you.

I'm with you now. I'll be with you forever.

Thirteen years have passed since that long and lonely winter—the hardest of my life, or one of them anyway—when I found my comfort in the letters of a double murderer who called me Lady Joyce. The part about loving me forever proved untrue, no doubt, but the other part—about remaining in my brain—has a certain truth.

I do still think about him sometimes. Perhaps he thinks about me, too. It is an odd thing to know that in a cell in southern California, even now, all these years later, there may still be a photograph of me and my children taped to a cinder-block wall: my son Willy in his Oakland A's jersey, my daughter wearing braces, my son Charlie holding a Boston terrier who is dead now. Myself at age thirty-nine, in my golden Christmas dress.

Swoon

Ann Hood

*W*hen I was a little girl, maybe four or five, I fell in love with a little boy with the unlikely name of James Stewart. He had already been kicked out of kindergarten, and that combined with his cowlick and freckles, his swagger when he played a cartoon for me on his Kenner Give-A-Show projector, his confidence as he handed me a raw potato and said in France they were called omelets, all of it began my lifelong path toward the handsome guy, the troubled guy, the bad guy. My mother stormed into his room that day as we watched Daffy Duck and chomped on that "omelet," flicked on the lights, and dragged me home. "Ann," she said, "why don't you play with Chuckie Stewart? He's a good boy. Not like that brother of his."

My fate was sealed years later, in the summer of 1973. I was sixteen years old, and all I wanted was to see George Carlin at the Warwick Musical Theatre, an outdoor tent where everyone from Robert Goulet to Creedence Clearwater Revival performed. George Carlin, with his routines about the hippie-dippie weatherman and the seven words you cannot say on television, would do only one show, and that show was sold out.

I worked, that summer, at Jordan Marsh at the Warwick Mall, as a floater. That meant I worked in whatever department was short-handed: I drifted from Linens to Typewriters to Records, flirting with stock boys and salesmen along the way. My friend Beth and I spent every morning lying in the sun at Scarborough Beach. At noon, we rushed home to change into work clothes, then drove to Jordan Marsh together to float.

Beth had a serious long-term boyfriend named Tommy. They had already picked out names for their children. I had a crush on Bob, a stock boy with a deep tan, dazzling white teeth, and blond hair tinged green from chlorine; by day, he was a lifeguard. Bob would find me in Men's Wear or Gift Wrap. He'd lean against the large rack of suits he was wheeling. He'd flex his biceps and say, "So, what have you been up to?"

"Nothing," I'd say. "You know, the beach." I would toss my long blond hair. I would act uninterested.

"Did you hear?" I'd say. "George Carlin is coming to the Tent."

He'd nod, looking vague. Bob always looked vague, but who cared?

"It's sold out, though," I'd say.

"Huh," he'd say, then he'd roll off.

One day Jerome from school appeared at my house on his bike. Too tall, too skinny, class salutatorian Jerome was my buddy. We were in Advanced Placement classes together. He ran cross-country. He liked to climb mountains. He could recite all of George Carlin's routines from memory.

"Guess what?" he said.

I didn't guess.

"I got tickets to George Carlin. Want to go?"

"Yes!" I said. My hinting had paid off, even if it meant going with Jerome.

"How nice," my mother said as we watched Jerome pedal home. My mother liked Jerome; he wanted to be a doctor.

A week later, standing bored in the Children's Department, splitting the ends of my hair, I heard the rattle of a cart. Bob appeared with a rack of coats.

"So," he said, "I got those tickets you wanted. George Carlin? Wanna go?"

My first thought was that I finally had a date with Bob. My second thought was that I was already going to George Carlin with Jerome.

"Sure," I said.

He grinned. I grinned. He and the coats walked off.

"Here's what I need you to do," I told my mother when I got home that night. "You need to call Jerome and tell him I'm really sick. With mono!" I said, impressed with my own ingenuity. "Tell him there is no way I can go Friday night."

My mother stared at me hard. "I'm not doing that," she said.

"But you have to!"

"No, you have to do the right thing."

This was one of the many times when I longed for parents who didn't leave difficult decisions up to me.

"Fine," I said, and I went to the phone and called Jerome and told him I was too sick to go with him.

On Friday night, I put on my cute white halter dress that showed off my tan and wore all my silver bangle bracelets from Mexico, and rode off with Bob, guilt-free. Until we got to the Tent and slid into our seats, which were right next to Jerome and his brother. Jerome looked at me, but didn't say anything. In fact, he never spoke to me again. He did, however, become a doctor. Bob never even went to college. The last time I saw him, he and his beer belly were sitting outside of the local fire station giving cat calls to teenage girls.

But that night, after George Carlin, when Bob and I walked into Friendly's and other girls whispered about how cute he was, when he leaned across those baby-blue bucket seats and kissed me good night, Jerome disappeared. That was it. I was on a path to finding Mr. Wrong, falling for the boy with the best smile, the widest shoulders, the one who made other girls swoon.

In some strange cosmic alliance, every time my Mr. Wrong swaggered into my life, he was shadowed by another guy who my mother knew would be perfect for me. My mother had married young, and stayed married to my father, who was a tall, handsome blond. But, she warned me, looks fly out the window when you're broke or fighting. "Uh-huh," I said, knowing how ridiculous her point really was. Wouldn't I rather be poor with a dashing man than with someone with bad teeth, someone shorter than me, someone bald?

"There needs to be substance," my mother said. "Something underneath all that gloss." She listed my father's wonderful attributes: he was a good listener, a hard worker, a kind man. He had a good sense of humor.

I didn't disagree. But I also knew that the first thing she noticed about him were those blue eyes of his.

My next stock boy drove a Mustang convertible and made All-American in hockey.

"I don't like that boy," my mother said after my first date with Sean. "He's too cocky."

My head was still fuzzy from slow dancing with him the night before at a place on the beach. Clearly my mother had never kissed a boy to the sounds of waves crashing against the rocks, with the top of his car down and the sky shot full of stars.

Two years had passed since George Carlin, and I was about to go off to college. I imagined watching hockey games all winter, the girlfriend of the star player.

"Full of himself," my mother said.

I rolled my eyes, even though it was true that when we weren't kissing or dancing he was giving me excruciatingly detailed reports of his hockey games.

After three dates, my mother started asking me what had ever happened to Brad, the nice boy who wanted to go to law school. The one who always brought her flowers or candy, who always sat and talked with my parents before we went out.

"Mom," I explained, "he is so boring."

"Boring!" she said. "He's intelligent. And funny."

"Then you go out with him," I said, catching sight of that Mustang rounding our corner. And I was off.

When Sean stood me up a week later and disappeared from my life, leaving me with a lifetime hatred of ice hockey, Brad appeared to hold my hand and tell me what a jerk Sean was. For years, Brad kept that role, buying me dinners and counseling me after yet another Mr. Wrong broke my heart.

Away at college, I could keep my bad boyfriends to myself without hearing my mother sigh and ask what had ever happened to the *nice* guys she'd liked so much. I dated the bartender with the moustache, the deep voice, and the girlfriend back home; the tortured premed student who still mooned over the girl who had broken his heart; the aloof rich boy who couldn't commit. All of them too good-looking, tall, and brawny, heartbreakers.

When the John Denver look-alike confessed his crush on me or the nerdy science guy who drove a Gremlin asked me out, I could almost hear my mother urging me to go, to forget my bartender, my premed student, my rich boy and give these other guys a try. Sometimes, tired of awful boyfriends, I would go, only to find my mind drifting away from the earnest smiles and pleasant conversations. I wanted my heart to beat too fast. I wanted to be kissed hard. I wanted to swoon.

By the time I moved to New York City and fell in love with an un-employed actor with a drinking problem, my mother had given up on me. Two hundred miles from home and ten years older, on a flight from San Francisco to New York, I met my actor and an airline pilot; I was the flight attendant. The airline pilot, in his uniform, had an easy smile and a kind face. My actor wore cowboy boots. He was tall and curly haired, with cheekbones to die for.

My mother would pick the pilot. I knew that. But I was smiling up at the actor, handing him my phone number, and falling once again. The actor loved my cats as much as I did and cooked me my favorite Mexican dishes. He brought me flowers and rubbed my feet. And he drank. Too much. At first, I pretended he didn't. But after a while I couldn't pretend anymore. So I left him, as heartbroken as ever.

That was when my mother asked me why I didn't want to find Mr. Right. "That's ridiculous," I told her. "Everyone wants to find the right person."

"Well," she said, "then why don't you?"

Even though I argued with her that my type of guy was different from hers, that she wanted me to spend my life with some boring guy in some boring place, I wondered if maybe she was, just a teeny bit, right.

A few months later, when a six-foot-two-inch man with the dark good looks and brilliant smile of a movie star sidled up to me one night after I gave a lecture, I decided to listen to my mother. So what if he made me tremble? So what if he drove the cutest car I'd seen in a long time? I was not falling for another Mr. Wrong.

He called and sent me flowers. He came all the way from Providence to New York City just to take me to lunch. He listened to me when I talked, and held my hand with such tenderness I thought I might faint. All this plus he'd gone to an Ivy League school, had grown up in the town right next to mine, and was kind to his mother. Was he the guy for me? Or the one my mother wanted for me? I was more confused than I'd ever been.

In the past, the choice had always been simple, the men one way or another. Every one was either a Jerome or a Bob, and I fell for Bobs, again and again. But Lorne was a Jerome in Bob's clothing. Steady and successful, he could still jitterbug in my kitchen in the middle of the night. Kind and thoughtful, he was so cute I could hardly think when I was around him.

"I met someone," I told my mother.

"Oh, boy," she said, already shaking her head.

Then she met him, and as we walked out the door hand in hand, she whispered to me, "Finally."

Well, Reader, I married him, thirteen happy years ago. Not too long ago, my mother read me an obituary in the local paper. When she was finished, she sighed and shook her head.

"Who is that?" I asked her.

"Pinky," she said. "My first love." She waved her hands dismissively. "Oh, he was a good dancer," she said, "but he had a wandering eye. That man broke my heart, over and over." She caught my smirk. "How do you think I recognized all your bad boyfriends?" she said.

I can't help but think of my own daughter, Annabelle, all grown up, giving her heart to the boy who is a good dancer, a star ice hockey player, the cutest guy in school. Can I reach across the years and keep her from their charms? Will my stories serve as warnings, or will they simply reveal the chasm in our ages? Even if I had known about Pinky and his irresistibly suave self, I am certain I would have still boldly stepped forward, ditched Jerome for the handsomer Bob, and continued on my own crooked path.

When Annabelle is old enough to ask how you know when you find Mr. Right, I will tell her that when my mother met my father, she fell for his big blue eyes first, and the rest of him later. I will tell her that the first thing I noticed about her father was how good-looking he was, but how that wouldn't matter if it wasn't for all of the other wonderful things he is.

And despite this, I suppose she will—she must—go off with too many Mr. Wrongs before she's ready, at last, for Mr. Right.

My Hades History

Dana Kinstler

I *had a dream about you.* That was his opening line. In a diner, on Second Avenue and Second Street, on a bitter evening. November 1988. Over a plate of crispy french fries and a Diet Coke—his with two limes. I ate a Greek salad. *Please,* I thought. We were dining with mutual friends; I'd seen him once or twice, but we'd never spoken before.

You were in a beautiful house, and beneath the porch, he continued, as if telling a near stranger a dream, about her, in a first conversation, was casual, *there was steam rising. It was your pie!* His dark eyes flashed with excitement. *Smoke was rising, all around you! This was your steaming apple pie.*

—Watch out for those floorboard cracks, I joked, salting my fries. I didn't want him to see into my eyes. *Are you nuts with that pie dream already?*

In the summer, this man, whom I'm calling Harry here, invited everyone to his loft for a screening of one of his films. I attended with my boyfriend—he was going to break up with me in approximately nineteen days, which would take me by surprise. In Harry's bathroom, I delighted in all the details: antique bronze spigots on the sink, seashells in an iridescent sea-green dish, black-and-white photos of Old New York, including of this neighborhood, Tribeca, when it was the site of the Hudson River ferry. His loft sat on the edge of the river, but had views only of neighboring warehouses. Above the sink, on a shelf, was an ebony chopstick inlaid with mother-of-pearl, one I still keep on my desk.

I stared at the photo of the ferry: my grandmother rode this ferry upstate to work in a Catskills hotel when her father died suddenly, a child laborer; later, she became a garment worker, hat model, and seamstress. These were stories thrice-told, in my grandmother's uptown apartment. Sometimes I wondered how events were altered by the retelling. My grandmother's voice and demeanor intensified as she delivered the stories again, as if, this time, she would recapture what was lost and hand it over to me to preserve and reissue, a tale worth keeping alongside the trimmings and notions, snaps, velvet ribbons, and buttons that filled up her bedroom drawers.

Harry's father was in the hosiery business; my grandfather had produced girdles, bras, corsets, and hospital kits during World War II. Harry's parents and my grandparents had all lived side by side, we'd find out, in the formerly Jewish neighborhood now known as Harlem.

Harry would deem them "garmentos."

Behind the only closed door in Harry's apartment, I wondered if I'd been in his bathroom before, in another life, in a dream. His wedding rings were in a dish next to the sink. Anyone could put them on was the presentation. There were three, one inlaid with a braid of gold. This one twirled endlessly on my finger. Men's wedding rings always looked strange. My father had never worn one. My father's hands I'd studied, and he'd done many studies of mine. He'd used my hands to finish portraits of society people—corporate executives, astronauts, politicians, and always, nude women.

I had never finished college, dropping out with a half-dozen incompletes, and now I was an office assistant for a think tank, which made me feel intelligent by association.

In Harry's bathroom, above the ring dish, was a photo of teen Harry, leaning over his electric bass. Harry, twenty-five years earlier, at sixteen, resembled Mick Jagger. Now he had the humble smile and apologetic voice of a man thrice-married without a child. There was something I could do for him.

When I emerged from the bathroom, I looked into Harry's brown eyes, saw excitement and vulnerability; not unlike my father's, they emitted boyhood wonder and century-old sorrow.

He was offering me food—guacamole, chips, and fire-roasted tomato salsa from the Mexican restaurant around the corner. He served them on a gold-leaf platter that I suddenly knew had been a wedding present.

—It's only been a few months, my then-boyfriend told me, as we walked up Greenwich Street. —He's still heartbroken.

What was it about his brokenness that made me want to see more photos and unveil the bathroom mystery?

♥ ♥ ♥

November 1989. Harry waited in a taxi downstairs from my East Village home. He was holding two tickets for Marianne Faithfull at St. Ann's Cathedral in Brooklyn Heights, tickets I could tell he'd bought for me. I'd been dodging him ever since last summer's breakup. *He's too old*, I told my friends. Forty-one to my twenty-seven—not quite a May-December couple. But we both grew up in Manhattan; my father still lived in the studio, my childhood home, and Harry's parents were still uptown. Old New York, something to talk about.

Harry took me for Japanese, out of the chilly November air. I ordered sashimi and soup.

—*Wow*, he said. No rice?

I was never comfortable being admired; I asked him his story. He told me he'd traveled all over the world, even been to the South Seas, on film shoots. He'd been in the industry since he was a teenager; like my father, he'd never been to college, but started working young. He'd been a gofer, cameraman, and then director and producer, starting his own film company, Harry's Sound. Also like my father, he read a lot—literature, history, and *The New York Times*. We both loved the Frick museum. *Only a native New Yorker*, he murmured, paying the check, tipping generously, hailing another cab to Brooklyn.

En route, he said he'd once been a radical. Well, he'd tried to get to Woodstock, hadn't he? To dodge Vietnam, he'd feigned crazy. "Feigned" crazy; feigned "crazy." In the dark, I couldn't see where the finger wiggles went.

Snuggled into the church pew, Harry's hand was on my back—this could be affection, it could be a pass. This was exactly as far as I would let him go. Marianne Faithfull appeared, candles and stage light illuminating her silhouette. In tight black pants and stiletto heels, blond hair around her face, she bent over the microphone, crooning to her former lover, "Why'd Ya Have to Do It?" She spat, punk siren, enraged, near-sobbing, *Did she swallow?*

Harry grinned with the rage of the recently divorced. The lighting made her chiaroscuro, glow and shadow, and the room, in heartbreak unison, pulsed in a giant exhalation of smoke and fire, as if we were all going down on a chariot into the bowels of the earth. Harry pushed closer to me, but his touch felt familiar, almost parental, as if he were entitled to some affection, and I, childlike, carried on as I always had—ignoring the one who craves you.

After, we waited on the subway platform. I did not want to be kissed. A rat scurried across the tracks, and someone whistled, another shouted. Here was Manhattan's underworld at night: this entry also the land of the unseen, spirits and beggars, rogues and their captors; subways slid in and out of stations, carrying us into the tunnel under the water and back to the island, our home.

Under a streetlamp, on East Tenth Street, I grumbled my good night. I didn't answer his calls for several months.

♥   ♥   ♥

But I wasn't snatched up by Hades, to live in his underworld; I jumped from the yellow taxi, told his intercom I had arrived, entered his building, pressed the elevator button, tumbled out of the elevator into his living room. There was no hallway. Nothing separate: from street to shaft to living room; this immediacy was narcotic, like gazing into a whale's eye at the Coney Island aquarium, like the rising steam off a shrimp dumpling in Chinatown, it was my city heritage, it was home. It was my here and it was my then; not a new story, but an old story retold.

Summer 1990. The living room was full of sunlight, a butterscotch hue that covered the velvet couches and bounced off the soup ladles hanging from the racks in the center of the kitchen; where the cooking started, where the sleeping ended, on the long wooden table, on a wide queen bed overlooking Greenwich Street. Lying on this bed made me feel perched on top of a ship going around the skinny end of the island; sunlight dribbled in splotchy haphazard bliss all over the room. The bedspread was pale gold, the color of moth wings; I would wrap myself in this and gaze out into the reflection of the industrial windows across the street. The endless variety of light. Light for different moods.

I was home from college; I'd returned to Rhode Island, to finish off the incompletes, and this distance had made it possible for me to let him in. I was a two-year-old emotionally, needing to say *no* for months until I could reverse my stance.

I was studying *Ulysses*, and as I lay in Harry's bed, listening to the foghorns on the Hudson, I read the final sentence to him, Molly Bloom's soliloquy: ". . . and drew him down to me so he could feel my breasts all perfume yes and his heart was going like mad and yes I said yes I will Yes."

Harry's eyes were glowing.

—You might direct a film yourself, he told me with admiration in his gaze. With my editing eyes, he said, I could direct the players and tech men and create a scene of artifice and replica, emotion and light. Filtering the feelings would be the challenge, of course, because I wasn't well versed in controlling mine, except when I was around those more out of control; Harry called me "the calm one."

My father had said I had a good eye; I could use it as a pointer in his studio. Harry showed me early cuts of his films and asked me to tell him what not to keep.

—Time is not your enemy, he said. Harry was using black kalamata olives to doll up his sauce—*puttanesca*, or harlot's sauce, his specialty; he worked its unctuous pulp into a perfection he might have marketed if he'd wanted, and he threw a jar of capers in at the last, amid hunks of fresh-grilled tuna swirling in the red mass. His hair was blue in the light, speckled with cut diamonds and distorted oblongs, scattered from the tin Mexican kitchen lamp hanging over the stove, hair blue as the 1940s models in my father's early inked illustrations. He looked like a sushi chef from behind, bending, bowing to his creation.

It sounded as if he were talking to the room at large, although I was the only person there, but I was used to his noblesse oblige. Harry said to beckon to time, put it into my art; at my age, I did not yet understand the backward glance of regret and missed possibilities.

He would hold my hand at my grandmother's funeral; later, at my sister's wedding in France; and again, standing over her firstborn daughter in her Paris apartment. I did not see time as my friend; there were seconds folding into the hour and these blocks were the countdown. When college was over, I'd have to find a career; also, I had to make it until my thirtieth birthday, beat the odds. Harry's odds: that he only went out with twenty-seven-year-old women, and, at exactly four years, all relationships fell apart.

I could not find a photo of any of his wives, but I didn't believe all cuts went to the same place; I hoped he'd save my photo forever.

♥   ♥   ♥

Greek myths always made sense—my father's studio had electric flames in the fireplace, and also a hat model's Styrofoam head, a severed plaster hand with painted-on veins, and a pair of alabaster breasts that pointed toward the Chrysler Building.

My mother, earthy and gentle, left my father while I was in college; she forgot her silk blouse, velvet cape, and pearls. She returned to the country, where she worked in a plant nursery and grew vegetables, wearing a sweatshirt and jeans.

My older sister and I had an enormous book of Greek myths, which I devoured, studying the illustrations. I was especially captivated by Apollo's deft escape via chariot, which reached to heights and depths unseen. These stories haunted, with their replaying of heartbreak and wandering amid the manipulations of deities with their amplified human traits. I was in love with huge, sweeping, raging, lusting Zeus, who always ensured that events turned out his way. Once, my sister dressed as Demeter for a school play, white sheet wrapped around her Greek goddess–style, garland of ivy leaves, and plastic purple grapes in her hair. I recited Persephone's lines while she screeched her vow to retrieve me, her stolen daughter, from the underworld where Hades still kept me. My sister, always my savior, so full of passion and loyalty and pluck, always my heroine.

She moved to France at age twenty, leaving me alone in the apartment with my father, in a place of exile and profound mystery—one I still seek, oftentimes with a motive even I can't decipher.

▼ ▼ ▼

Despite our age difference—Harry listened to sixties R&B, I craved seventies disco and punk—Harry and I had this in common: a family with lots of fighting, violence in the air. My parents had maintained a level of societal acceptability, chaos hidden beneath. Harry's stories made me secretly vow to protect him from anyone who might hurt him again. Our traumas, it was understood, were not to be repeated, one reason Harry gave for never having children; there was a litany of things we'd never do or say to each other.

As if a Ouija board spirit were moving my hand, I heard myself say things at the worst possible moment, chief among them the ultimate provocation: *Are you ever going to marry me?*

Never say never, his classic response, only urged me to win, without resorting to that age-old method—lying about birth control, a trick I swore I'd never use. I told him I'd just flushed it down the toilet, and we played a kind of Russian roulette, which, thankfully, never bore fruit.

He kept me on a weekend tether, a schedule of Saturday nights only, with an occasional Friday. It was as if I'd been granted visitation rights; I kept a few items in the bathroom, as I'd learned to do in each of my parents' homes: body lotion, toothbrush, a set of clean clothes. His hair conditioner I borrowed, in secret.

Harry let me use his hairbrush, his bathrobe, and one drawer in the bathroom of his loft. Just not his conditioner. This he bought from the hairdresser in my childhood neighborhood, which made me feel entitled.

It wouldn't work on my hair, he told me.

This exclusivity made me want in all the more. There were film wrap parties, screenings and dinners, none of which included me. My attempts made him crazy. Only he could decide when to reach a hand out to cup my ass and coax me back inside.

He used rice paper screens to separate me from his work, or to separate sex from his life.

I was always on the wrong side of the screen, is how I saw it.

His glasses, his camera, his laptop—all screens led to his interior. His creative source, places I needed access to. Pairing his socks made me feel complete. So did bringing up his mail or sorting through the snap peas and discarding any with rotten ends.

I just wasn't supposed to want routine. Random domesticity. Or else I'd ruin it, he said. All three of his marriages had ruined it.

In the summer, Harry found rentals in the Hamptons. *Acabonic, Sagaponack, Amagansett, Montauk.* These Indian names were like the harvest at the end of the summer, when soft fruits started to ripple and mold, and the hard produce of winter appeared: squash, gourds, pumpkins, apples; when I told him I loved him, I waited and listened. The breeze was in my hair, and bike wheels were spinning fast, the beach windy and rough. The money was almost gone.

—No one to plant with. There's no garden anymore, my mother reported when I called.

I peeled apples on the porch on Acabonic; while Harry was inside making fish soup, I was baking my first apple pie.

In November, en route to Paris, Harry used his mileage to bump us to first class; we received warmed cashews and almonds, wider seats, and leg room. I'd never traveled first class; while we flew, he told me about his last trip to Paris, on a film shoot with wife *numéro deux.*

—We were at the George Cinq, this vicious hotel, he told me. *Vicious* meant beyond rating. They ate at the top of the Eiffel Tower. I'd heard about the hangovers and shopping; I'd formed a relationship to this tale, complete with inner monologue to accompany it. This wife was "hysterical" although beautiful; once, she'd thrown the blender out the window onto Greenwich Street. I was the calm one. Harry's memory world was so alive, I was the guide through his dark history, my listening illuminating his past loves, biggest mistakes, most exciting adventures and calamities.

I was sure they made love all over Paris, in the halls of the George Cinq; "hysterical" equals lots of sex.

As a teenager, I'd been in Paris, staying in a hostel and eating cheap Vietnamese noodles. I'd never stayed at a four-star hotel. Harry and I were staying in my father's friend's apartment, since "drip, drip, drip"—we were spending what was left from the last film. He'd heard about a restaurant from a producer in L.A.; this woman's voice was often on his machine—a voice unctuous, facile, and suggestive of much more than lunch, I was sure. But I placed a reservation for us in my near-forgotten high school French. When I hung up, he made love to me with such intensity and absorption that when he looked into my eyes, I was sure he would devour me.

In the apartment, at night, the shadows loomed; the strangeness of this foreign dark and the unknown within French closets kept me awake. Harry escorted me through each room, checking under every bed, even opening the cabinets beneath the French sinks until I could see there were no interlopers waiting to find me.

At the Rodin Museum, Harry's eyes welled up; he was having a mystical experience. We stood in front of *The Lovers,* Rodin's signature piece; the bodies were twisted in an embrace, locked in the marble. I couldn't get Camille Claudel out of my mind, the muse and student whom Rodin wooed and abandoned, who eventually went mad, giving up her own work forever. Harry took pictures of me in front of this statue.

Then he took me to the Lolita annex of the Agnes B. boutique. He chose a navy wool schoolgirl jumper, which didn't reach my knees.

—This is good-quality wool, Harry said approvingly.

In the parochial frock, I felt shame of familiar dimensions. There has never been a time I've liked being admired, but particularly not when my body was developing.

The decision not to buy it haunted me for months; if only I had purchased the Lolita jumper, I'd have kept Harry in love forever.

That night, in front of the restaurant in the *Marais*, I wore a blue velvet cape.

—But, mademoiselle! You did not come last night! You and your father cannot eat here, do you understand? Never. The maître d' was pushing us out the door.

—But, monsieur—

—*Non non non non non non non!* He slammed the door behind us. It was my French. I had said tomorrow, when I meant in two days. Harry was furious.

This, too, I will never forget; when I imagined myself wearing the unbought jumper, I pretended we'd eaten foie gras, boeuf au poivre, tarte tatin, instead of burgers and fries at the McDonald's on the Champs-Elysées, where we ended up after fighting our way there. Shouting, cursing up the boulevard, Harry marched ahead, only turning his head to cry:

—You never take care of me! You never do!

♥   ♥   ♥

Harry took photos of me in Paris, naked, as if I were his model and muse. I wanted to pose for his pictures, have a purpose to my life, one that inspired art—this was the adhesion I knew. He took them in black and white, just as my father had photographed my mother back in the 1950s, when my parents were in love. They stood in front of the gargoyles of Notre Dame, and I've kept these photos in my drawer. The look in my mother's eyes, beneath the winged monkey, says she's just been asked to undress.

In her Paris kitchen, my sister pulled me aside.

—He looks just like Dad!

When I showed my mother Harry's Parisian photos—I'm in clothes, of course—she fell silent, biting her lip.

—This could be me, she finally said without looking up.

In between films, Harry came to me, cleaved and stuck to me, in grouchy, irascible fits; he hated being without a film crew. No money coming in.

We ordered in, still, as if he were not out of work, as if I were earning more than an entry-level publishing check. I would say, *Order me Thai*, and that made him angry. I had become more like a hungry daughter, craving sustenance, greedy and selfish, wondering when it had gone bad.

♥ ♥ ♥

July 1992: the summer of bare breasts. We were legalized to nurse in public, which, in New York, translated as sunbathing topless on the beach. Harry couldn't take his eyes off the tits, mine and everyone else's; neither could I. There were brown nipples, pointy nipples, café au lait breasts pointing to the cloudless sky; some were sunburned, marking their defiant, exuberant, first exposure to ultraviolet—I thought "ultra violent"—rays.

Harry was gazing and musing.

—This would make a vicious documentary.

He munched on a potato chip.

—The hardest part about breaking up is imagining someone with another body. Then, after a while, even that fades, he added.

I was covering his toes with sand, I was burying him down into the beach. He was eating from a container of take-out lobster salad, to the tune of $8.23 a bite. His eyes, behind the Ray Bans, were still on the breasts; I saw cartoon exclamation marks and stars all over the lenses.

—I want you to propose to me like that. I pointed as a small plane dragged a banner across the clear sky. Harry crunched on a potato chip and groaned.

—That is just torture. He shook his head.

At the moment, I wished I could disappear down into his Diet Coke bottle and become his genie.

My time was running out. Two years—we were halfway done.

My father's nudes had gone up and down the hallway in our apartment, and as a girl I'd always wondered how my breasts would turn out. I wanted to know: Had he painted these women while we were all sleeping? Or while I was at kindergarten? I knew his models used our bathroom to change, soaping their hands with the bar of Ivory soap, drying them on the paisley towel. Did they walk from bathroom to studio in the buff? Or borrow my mother's bathrobe? All halls led back to his studio. It was a large cavernous lair, where he waited for his sitter, whom he referred to as his "next victim."

♥   ♥   ♥

November 1993. Harry did not show up for couples' therapy; the therapist told me that it could take a few weeks to work it out, it could take a lifetime. I knew what he meant. That week, I'd received my first credit card; as I ambled down Madison Avenue, I found myself in Harry's favorite Italian shoe store. I emerged carrying three pairs. Intoxicated with the purchases, I switched trains; in the tunnel, with Andean pipes echoing all around, I slipped down the longest flight of stairs I know, and my shoes went tumbling, one after another, past the homeless and professionals, until they landed on various steps, or at the bottom.

Harry had told me that a good pair of shoes made the difference.

I spent my last token to get to Harry's loft. This had become a habit—arriving with only loose change. A dependency habit, my childlike stance, a bond Harry resisted. It was one thing to take me to dinner or shopping when he was flush, but now I'd worn him threadbare. I was defiant about four years of traipsing to him, and although he sometimes offered cab fare, he refused to stay at my village studio—not since our first night.

I said I wanted commitment, but did I? In hindsight, weekends only with Harry were easy; this freedom enabled me to avoid any constant domesticity, one that would deprive me of liberties and replace them with household responsibilities. I was thirty-one, but emotionally a teenager. I'd purchased a pale-blue flowered baby blanket at an Amagansett yard sale, but this was for me.

Harry ranted about my immaturity, pointing out I added nothing to his social life: my friends were so young and insubstantial.

That night he was livid.

I don't remember what I said; as the youngest in a volatile family, I am facile at igniting the incendiary scene. In the 1970s, as a dieting teenager, I'd carried a box of raisins with me from room to room, dropping them everywhere, including my father's studio. I wasn't allowed to enter this space uninvited, but I just couldn't resist sneaking in. Did I mean to leave the betraying raisins that led my father to accuse me of trespassing? In high school, I invited my dad to argue about involvement in Latin America while he painted the secretary of state. Did I mention that his government portraits were evidence of his support for our oppressive regime, and therefore he was an oppressor?

Now, with Harry, I directed the reality television show—I staged the scene without study. Although I have no idea what words I used because, after a fight, I can't recall what I've said: this is my darkness, my Hades within.

Why aren't we married? Why don't you spend the night at my house? Why can't my cats live here?

It might have been a comment about all the other people I knew who were getting married or having babies, never mind that I was barely paying my own rent.

That night, Harry shoved me up against the wall, his hands around my throat. As I felt my breath tighten, I heard, for the first time since we'd been together—coming up on four years now—*maybe this man would not be a good father for my children.* When he pushed me out the front door with my empty wallet, refusing to let me back in, I wandered up Hudson Street to my apartment, and knew, for the first time, at 2:30 A.M. in the bitter cold, that I was done.

Maybe I fought like that to replicate my parents and see what could be overcome. I came to understand and forgive them. It was Harry who'd suggested I start eating out with my father, after keeping him at arm's length, and we'd had him down to Harry's loft for supper and a film. I'd been out of touch, and after the breakup, I invited each of my parents back in.

♥ ♥ ♥

July 1994. On Hudson Street, leaving work, I bumped into an old friend. Some of these were coming back into my life, ones who had been abandoned for four years. Some never returned. But this man gave me a big hug.

—You've got your *duende* back! *Duende*—he meant my soul.

I recalled the three pieces of Harry he left me with.

—You have to fall in love with yourself, Harry had once said.

—Pay your credit card just above the credit line, he'd recommended.

—See you in your dreams, was how he said good night on the phone, a closing line straight from his underworld, a place with neither schedule nor permanence, all mystery and make-believe. And I would trap his words inside a moon-shaped pie, crimp the edges, then pierce it, see the steam rise, freeing angels and demons alike.

Setting My Hair on Fire

Raphael Kadushin

Everyone, at nineteen, is dumb and beautiful in equal parts, though they won't realize it until years later. For me, at nineteen, the operative word was *dumb,* because I was incessantly focused on the vague intimation of my own perceived beauty, and I was so busy scrutinizing my face in mirrors—actually mirrors, toasters, spoons, shop windows, car bumpers, polished apples, shot glasses, and anything that threw back a reflection—that I didn't see much beyond my own image. And so I inevitably missed the signs of impending doom that were so overt, when I got to London at the end of my nineteenth year, that they didn't really qualify as mere foreshadowing.

These signs were more like a big banging drumroll, the prelude to disaster. It was as if a contemporary, groaning Greek chorus had assembled to warn me: the *Deliverance* fiddlers, the voice from the crawl space, the madwoman in the attic, and the B-movie Main Street stranger who goes bug-eyed and begs the protagonist, aka first corpse— also full of stupidity and beauty, in equal measure—not to proceed with her whimsical plans to camp overnight in that big Gothic mansion. And still I was oblivious. I'll go to London, I thought at nineteen, gazing in the mirror, and some man will fall in love with me and I will be saved. Someone else, I figured, could pick up the slack and take over the task of examining my ethereal face.

That's what I thought. The first intimation of doom was the way I wound up coming to London. I didn't fly into Heathrow unattached. No, I was trailing behind the Beaver girls, who could suck the romance out of a twilight dinner for two in a Tuscan trattoria. The reasons I chose this particular program—the Beaver College junior year in London—elude me now. I was enrolled at the more boho Sarah Lawrence College at the time and there wasn't, from what I remember, any kind of sisterly alliance. On the contrary. The Beaver girls, I'd quickly discover, thought of the Sarah Lawrence girls as die-hard dykes, the kind of gals who consider arm-wrestling a first date, and they looked on Sarah Lawrence boys like myself as something even worse: hopelessly fey fags.

Which in my case, of course, was true, and which immediately damned me, along with my sole friend in the London program—an arty, unkempt girl named Heidi from Austin, Texas, who also had no memory of why or how she'd fallen in with the Beavers. Heidi and I, gossip had it, were well-known junkies escaping American authorities, and by the first week of class some kind of emergency drill seemed to have been established and thoroughly rehearsed; when we entered rooms they quickly emptied.

But it didn't really matter. The Beaver girls were only an emblem of my own displacement, and after that first week they simply evaporated from my view (along with any actual classes; all I remember from the year academically was one frantic week of writing term papers that bore absolutely no relationship to any assigned topic). While our classmates were busy stampeding through Laura Ashley boutiques or maybe actually attending classes, Heidi and I did what any two pretentious American college kids would do. We wrapped long scarves around our necks and circled Bloomsbury, hunting for Virginia Woolf sites, and mostly we set out looking for a distinctive kind of Englishman. We wanted the ones wearing tweed coats, the ones who pushed their long flopster bangs off their big foreheads with bigger hands in a feckless, masculine way. We were hunting for men who were sarcastic and literate.

The question, of course, was where to find them, and that's when the second sign of certain doom materialized. My puny room in a South Kensington apartment was the kind of classic bed-sit that constitutes an archetype in the great British tradition of Jean Rhys and Sylvia Plath, the kind designed to induce suicide in even the mildly depressive. The room looked out on a dead garden, and it lacked any warmth, in a very literal sense, because the only source of heat was a tiny space heater mounted in the wall, which stayed cold to the touch except for the arbitrary thirty seconds each day when it would inexplicably burst into flames. "It's what they call a death trap," Heidi noted happily. Because there were also no electrical outlets in the room, my well-used hair blower—probably my most intimate friend at the time—lay useless in the suitcase I never bothered to unpack, and I had to dry my long hair by hanging my head over the side of my lumpy bed and willing the space heater to flame up. So it took me half the day to dry my hair and then I had only a good five to ten minutes outside, in the world beyond my bed-sit, before my own floppy bangs reverted to their Jewish roots and started their slow, insidious, demented curl, even though I would move my head very slowly, like a geisha, or a Las Vegas showgirl, when I inched my way through the British drizzle.

One afternoon, exhausted by my attempts at cosmetology, I fell asleep. My wet head, as usual, was hanging over the side of my bed, and when I woke up I smelled something crisping, like a bad British breakfast. What was that? I thought, putting my hand to my head, where my fingers suddenly cupped a crusty thing, like a dust-bowl tumbleweed.

This, as it turned out, was a charred, blackened chunk of my hair, burnt as ruthlessly as English toast by the fire of my suddenly flaming heater. In an instant I was half bald, and for the next month I had to scrape together the kind of lavish comb-over you don't usually see on nineteen-year-old boys.

The crisped hair was another intimation of doom, but my youthful stupidity reasserted pride of place. Most people, I convinced myself, wouldn't notice the deep side-part or the stumps of blackened wildfire crazy hair poking out under my sweeping bangs. No, no one would sense anything amiss.

But of course people did—drunks were always itching for a fight, especially drunk beauticians—and this was only the start of the insults. Setting out to meet men in London in the eighties wasn't easy. The city, which is always getting caught in the act of swinging again, was supposed to be especially swingy at the time—something to do with neo-punk or retro-glam—but it was swinging in a cautious way. While there were plenty of gay bars in town, the British homos hadn't yet learned how to give up their tweedy approach to things. Since none of them were ready to fully surrender their dignity yet—it's an American gift—the stately English gays would gather in their clubs and then shyly dance alone, or, worse yet, dance with their own reflections, in the mirrors that for some reason circled every dance floor.

"You'll have to find another way to meet men," Heidi said—she was dating a jumpy, coked-up Spanish busboy by then, confirming the Beavers' worst fears—and surprisingly I did. My salvation came in the form of a weekly gay lib meeting that had devolved into a straightforward dating night at London University. By the first meeting I was hooked, partly because I had never been so popular with the gays. There was a simple explanation for this. Americans, I found out much later, were considered easy prey and pea-brained bum boys by the Brits, because of our said lack of dignity. But of course I thought my sudden popularity at that first meeting, in a book-lined parlor of the student union, was due to my mysterious allure—the well-practiced Mona Lisa half smile, the otherworldly air, and my by-then especially deft way with a comb-over. Oddly, there was no attempt at even perfunctory academic discourse or queer theorizing that night.

Getting right down to the business of speed petting, the group played a game they clearly knew well. Someone would turn off the lights and then you had about five minutes, in total darkness, to snog whichever fellow gay libber—finally released from all that tiring dignity and British etiquette by the mere flick of a light switch—would pounce first and start feeling you up. The initial melee was a disappointment. When the lights came up the person extracting his thick tongue from my mouth was one of those pink-skinned English lads who run to fat in their early twenties after a childhood of too many sticky toffee puddings. But on the second round of rutting in the dark I actually, for the first time that year, got lucky. When the lights came up I found myself pressing against nothing short of my English dream. He was older than I, maybe in his mid-twenties. He was tall, and he had the long brown eyes and olive skin that somehow surface in certain pockets of England. His body was fine-knit and muscular, not the kind of bunched muscle that slides into middle-aged paunch but the sort of elegant, long-torsoed, fluid muscle that seems like an honest birthright. His dark brown hair fell in unstudied bangs across his forehead and he had an air of calm that was a blend of assured intelligence, grace, and quiet, knowing charm. He was the master, the kind who doesn't have to strap on those goofy Halloween black leather chaps because he is so clearly in control, and I was something else: his boy, his student, his American.

And unlike the pink-skinned student, this one knew how to kiss in the dark. His long tongue licked my lips and then swirled lazily, deftly, around my own tongue. And this is what happened: I was in love the instant his tongue slid into my mouth, even before the lights came up, the way you can fall in love in a minute. People dismiss that kind of infatuated feeling as something primal and therefore shallow, but the primal is primal because it runs so deep. I think that immediate sort of love is, in its own way, as real as the loves that start slow and last for years. Or at least I did at the time.

His name was Adan and I still remember things about him: the way the soft hair on the strong tendons of his very long forearms (not bushy jungle hair but spare and downy, so you could just see it in certain lights) framed the black leather of his wristwatch band, and how he smelled peppery and smoky, like a mix of Tabac and musky underarms.

The smell matched his manner: masculine but not in any self-conscious, cocky way. He was oddly tender.

But after that groping first meeting I didn't hear from him. Instead, of course, I heard from the porcine boy—Jerry—who went to college in East Anglia. And because I'd sleep with anyone then, I went up to visit him one weekend, which we spent in his disheveled dorm room, the rain dropping listless outside like an echo of our anticlimactic romp. The only thing heated about the weekend was our mutual betrayal. I dismissed him, and his tongue, by drumming my finger on the gray sheets, after the bumping around in his bunk bed. And he was ready with his own genteel switchblade. "You know," he said as we lay in bed, "Adan is something of a slag," and as proof he produced a porn magazine.

The centerfold was my lover-to-be, spread out on his own snowy white sheets, his olive skin wearing a kind of halo. "So there you have it," Jerry said, happy to dash my hopes, to ruin everything for me, to prove that the man he knew I really wanted was just a louche slut, as shameless as any American. And for a moment I was surprised. This was before it was considered stylish for college boys to turn occasional tricks between classes and spend a few weeks on rentboy.com, to prove you weren't just another egghead. But even then I wasn't easily shocked. Mostly I thought Adan was brave and his sexual availability—which struck me as a form of generosity—didn't resonate as sluttish with me. If it came coupled with emotional distance, promiscuity seemed alluring to me; the man who is glibly open with his body but otherwise a cipher was my erotic model.

Plus there was something else: Adan's penis, in the picture, wasn't just long but thick, actually meaty, and it was the first uncut penis I had ever seen, which made it seem even more potent and also slightly frightening. In fact, I thought the hooded oddity was some mysterious deformity.

So when he finally called, weeks after I returned from East Anglia, more than a month after our first kiss, I already felt we had formed some sort of bond. He clearly didn't, though, and I went dead at our dinner at a Soho pizzeria. That year, when I never really knew who to be, I didn't talk when I was nervous, so I maintained my chilly madonna smile, as if I was peering out of some other, more rarified realm. He was slightly teasing, and easy, and it didn't matter what we said. What mattered was the way his Adam's apple bobbed in his long throat, and the light fur of his sideburns, and his thick lower lip.

What mattered was the way he pulled off his pants, with one strong tug, in my narrow bed, by the space heater that was plotting to scorch me for good.

And then he didn't call again. "You know I didn't want to tell you," Jerry informed me during one of our occasional, desultory phone calls, "but he's actually something of a whore. He lives with a sugar daddy and that's why he doesn't have to work at all. He's sort of like a geisha."

Silly, I thought; at least the sugar daddy wouldn't be any competition. I pictured a big bald man in cashmere sweater sets, singing along to some opera tape, swishing all over the place. Pure comic relief and a fat wallet. I was nineteen and I was so skinny I could play my hip bones like a drum. My hair had grown in and I could fling it from side to side. My face, in my mirror, looked soft and hard at the same time, and my pupils were dilated all the time.

But it didn't matter. All that spring in London it rained and I lay on my bed, by my homicidal heater, and even Jerry stopped calling. "We'll go to all the museums," Heidi said, standing by my bed, alone again after her boyfriend went back to Spain. "We could go to Paris for the weekend." But Paris, I thought, wasn't as romantic as London, where you come to die, and all I could do was wait on the bed, still catching a whiff of him sometimes in the sheets.

And then I decided to do something brave. I had to call. I don't know why I did it in public; maybe because I thought the British would politely ignore any melodramatic scene, or maybe so I'd have witnesses. But I went to the Russell Street tube station and I picked up the grimy public phone and I called him, my fingers stopping for a minute at each number.

The phone rang twice and then his voice, a small miracle, picked up. "It's me," I said, as if that would explain everything, and because he was smart, it did. "You're the sweetest boy," he said to me. "You're a precious boy. But I am with this man and I can't see you; I can't afford to see you."

He said this very quietly and tenderly, and my heart split straight down the middle, the way people say it does—it split the way a dry log splits cleanly in half when a lumberjack takes an ax to it—and I knew this was all I'd remember from that year and I dropped the phone so his voice seemed muffled, very far away. The receiver dangled and knocked against my knees and I started keening, in the entrance to the tube station, in front of all the English people who pretended they didn't see me, and I couldn't tell if I was looking through my own tears or that scrim of rain that followed Jean Rhys everywhere she went as she fled from bed-sit to bed-sit.

A decade later I went back to the tube stop. The phone was still there in the entrance of the tube station and it was still raining, and I wondered what had happened to Adan. Was he still alive? Was he still paying penance, for his own loves, with the fat man? People say there is a Mr. Wrong, but there isn't really. There is only someone who teaches you what you need to know, when you need to know it. And Adan, who disappeared in all that liquid rain, taught me an essential lesson before I turned twenty. Because when I heard his voice for the last time, as the phone fell down to my knees, something happened; at that moment my beauty suddenly lost all its romance. It just, in an instant, became a flimsy, mundane gift, the one I wanted to leave behind.

Ardor and Its Discontents

Alicia Erian

At the end of June 2005, a relatively successful director whom I will call Trent Vetter wrote to me. He said flattering things about my first book, a collection of stories called *The Brutal Language of Love*, and asked if he could talk to me about a writing project. I was with my friend Beth at the time, at her parents' house in Northampton, Massachusetts. I had just done a reading at Odyssey Books in Mount Holyoke. We came back, and I checked my e-mail on her little brother's computer. We screeched over Trent's message, then immediately looked him up on the Internet to ascertain whether he was gay, married, taken, or single.

This had been my life for the past three years, since my husband and I separated. I was trying to find someone to marry and have a baby with. It wasn't really working out. Not only that, but I was very bad at managing the pain of it not working out. As a dater, I was not light on my feet. I was heavy and lumbering, like an elephant. Or a caveman. I would meet someone, then beat my chest as if to say: ME WANT HUSBAND! ME WANT BABY! If I had met me, I would've found me hilarious. Most men weren't me, though.

Trent was single. Furthermore, we had a great talk on the phone and decided to write a script together. Beyond that, he began calling me and saying things like "Are you sad?" to which I would respond, "No. Are you?" To which he would respond, "Yes, I am sad about my ex-girlfriend, who I broke up with nine months ago." I would report these conversations to my literary agent, Peter, who was suspicious. "What's he telling you that for? To let you know he's single?" I would say that I didn't know, though secretly I was thinking the same thing, and was glad for the confirmation from an outside source.

Trent pushed the deal through with his production company very quickly, and by mid-July I was living in Los Angeles. The plan was that in the six weeks before I had to return to Massachusetts and my teaching gig at Wellesley College, Trent and I would pound out a draft of the script he had outlined.

I continued to believe that Trent was flirting with me. He was attentive, we talked about personal things, he removed a leaf from my hair. Then one night, as research for our script, he sent me to a parenting meeting where I had to pretend I was pregnant. The whole thing turned out to be kind of upsetting, since I ended up worrying that this would be the only time in my life I'd get to say I was pregnant, and it was a lie. I cried all the way home, then wrote about it in my e-mail diary, which I was sending to friends back in New York. Then I removed all the parts where I cursed Trent and sent him my report of the evening. He wrote back right away, filled with apologies for having put me through that trauma. He cared that I was in pain. That sealed the deal for me.

The next day, I told Trent I had a crush on him, and he was taken aback. It turned out that I had misread everything, and the feeling wasn't mutual. I cried and he was nice. He hugged me and said, "Don't think I haven't thought about it, because I have." He suggested we take a walk or go to the movies, but I couldn't imagine doing either of those romantic things with someone who wasn't in love with me. I suggested we just get busy writing.

I can't remember if we got any decent work done that afternoon. Probably not. I was too distracted by the shame of having fallen for someone who hadn't fallen for me.

I rallied that night, however, and the next day took a more aggressive approach. Over lunch, I informed Trent that I still had a thing for him, even though he didn't feel the same way. He told me that was unhealthy. Then he got mad and said I was trying to say that if he didn't love me, I wouldn't write him a good script. I became offended. We were both very offended. We drove home in silence. I said something like, "How can you say for sure that you'd never be interested?" and he yelled, "Look! All I want from you is a good script!" He was making it seem like I had been insane to think he had liked me.

It was a humiliating mess. We tried to work that afternoon, but of course it was tense and weird. Finally, Trent announced that he had to go and exercise. "Right now?" I said. "Yes," he said, and he left. He later e-mailed and said that he didn't think we should work together anymore, and that I should work on my own. He said that he felt he was getting in my way. I wasn't thrilled about this, since he was getting half the money and was officially my co-screenwriter, and also because writing a script would go a lot slower with just me on the job. But that was what we did.

I became extremely depressed and lonely. I began to look forward to the first week in August, when another one of my literary agents, Joe, was going to be in town. He was very good at taking care of people, and I knew that spending time with him would go some way in curing me. I was right. The first night I saw him was at a dinner with my film agents. They were pushing me to do something I didn't really want to do, and finally Joe stepped in and said, "I don't think Alicia is interested in that," and the subject was dropped.

The next day, I spoke to Joe on the phone. We thought about possibly getting together that night for dinner. I wanted to. I wanted more cure. But a man named Steve, who had hand-sold nearly two hundred copies of *The Brutal Language of Love* at his bookstore, was giving a reading, and I had promised to attend. I explained this to Joe, who said it was the right thing to do, and that he respected me for not canceling. Even that was a little bit of cure.

I didn't put on a fresh face of makeup that night, or even a clean T-shirt. I only changed my shoes. I had bought a glitzy pair of green slides at Calleen Cordero on Beverly Boulevard and wanted to try them out. The other part of my cure was spending large amounts of the option money for my first novel, *Towelhead*, which had just come through after a year of contract negotiations.

I drove to the gallery where the reading was to take place and toddled in on my heels. I said hello to Steve, then set my bag down in the seat behind his and went to get a drink. When I returned, a man was sitting in the seat beside mine. I thought: Why does he have to sit there when there are a million empty seats in this place? "Excuse me," I said, and he moved his very long legs so that I could get by. Steve was turned around in his seat, talking to this man, and I waited for him to introduce us. He never did. Instead, he finished the conversation and turned back around. After a moment, the man beside me held out his hand. "I'm Robert," he said. "Alicia," I said, and we shook.

There was still some time before the reading, and Robert and I started talking. I bragged about *Towelhead* and he told me that he was about to return to school to get his M.F.A. in fine art. He was a photographer, and he was in a band, and he had come to the reading because a friend of his had pictures hanging in the gallery. He pointed to the pictures and said, "Those are hers, if you want to take a look."

At some point I remarked on his returning to school, and he said, "You know when you were in college, and there was an older student there, and they were always so much smarter than everyone else? That's what I'm going to be." Then he stretched his arms and clasped his hands behind his head, as if he were lying back in a hammock. I thought: Who is this madman?

The reading began. Steve was first, and he would turn out to be the best of the evening. He was followed by a man who read a story about a serial killer who wrote letters to the families of his victims, explaining how he had raped, tortured, and killed their daughters. There were an endless number of these letters in the piece. I started to get irritated and glanced repeatedly at Robert's hands, which seemed to be pretty large, if I was seeing clearly. He rubbed them on the thighs of his pants occasionally, and I imagined that his palms were sweating because he had a crush on me. I began to panic about how I would get to see him

again. I knew he wouldn't make a move after I had done all that bragging about *Towelhead*, but I thought if I made a move on him, he
might take it and run with it.

When I left, he was outside in the street, smoking a cigarette with
a chubby woman who turned out to be the artist whose work he had
come to see. I said, "It was nice to meet you, Robert. I'm giving a reading in a couple of weeks, if you'd like to come," and I handed him my
card. He stuck his cigarette in his mouth, took the card, then shook
my hand too hard. It hurt, and I liked that.

He e-mailed the next day and invited me to go to the beach. I wrote
back saying I'd love to. This was on a Friday. We planned the beach for
the following Wednesday.

In the meantime we didn't stop writing. We started making more
specific beach plans, and I became anxious over the fact that he had
described the beach as remote. I was thinking about the serial killer
story from the reading. I was also thinking about François Ozon's film,
See the Sea, which is bloody, and also set on a remote beach. I wrote to
Robert and asked him if he was a serial killer.

He didn't write back right away, and I was pretty sure I had lost my
date. Then a message appeared later in the day. It opened with: "Oh
Alicia, I am not a serial killer, but that is a fair question when something like that story we heard is stuck in your head." *Oh Alicia.* It was
with great pride that I informed my journal readers that I had exasperated him after only three days.

There was more e-mailing. We talked about how we couldn't remember what the other person looked like. In my head, Robert had
morphed into a kind of toad. Short, fat, bald, and four-eyed. I didn't
tell him this, and I didn't much mind if it was true. I was happy
enough with a toad who could write letters the way he did. Not just
the quality, but the frequency. I'd zap him, and he'd zap me back. It
was sheer joy. As a writer, you come to understand that not many people will be as inclined toward words as you. To discover that Robert
was was to discover that I had a new need.

I had dinner with Joe on Monday night. He gave me good advice about men. After dinner, I got lost driving home. I decided to call Robert and ask him for help. I could've used my map, but I'd been nervous for the last couple of days, thinking about how we'd only been writing and not actually talking, and thought this would be a good excuse to take that step.

I vaguely remembered his voice when he answered the phone. It was murky, as if he were speaking through fabric. I said, "Robert? This is Alicia. I'm lost in my car. Can you help me?" He said yes and asked me where I was. I told him Brentwood. He said, "Whatever you do, don't get out of the car." I laughed. In the end, he told me to go back the way I had come. He said there were no shortcuts. I said okay. He said to call him if I had any more problems, and we hung up.

A few minutes later, he called me. He said, "Is everything all right?" I said, "Yes, I'm almost home." He said good. Then we started talking. Soon, I pulled into the driveway of my rented house and turned off the car. I started to tell him I was home, assuming we would end our conversation, but somehow it never happened. I stayed sitting in the car, talking. At one point I said, "Robert? You might as well know. I'm getting divorced." He started laughing. He said, "Alicia, I'm getting divorced, too. This morning I wept, thinking about telling you. I was sure you would run away." We couldn't believe we were both getting divorced. Privately, I couldn't believe he had cried over it. And admitted to having cried over it. I thought he seemed like a weirdo in the best possible way.

My phone died and I went inside to plug it into the charger. Robert had already left a message by the time it was up and running again. I called him back. We continued talking. There were long silences. I said, "Are you there?" He said, "Yes. I'm just . . . overwhelmed. Alicia, I like you so much." I told him that I liked him, too. At one point, he said, "We have to have dinner tomorrow night. I can't wait until Wednesday to see you." We spent some time reminding each other what we looked like. Robert claimed that he had been getting clear pictures of me each morning when he woke up. I could still only picture him as a toad. Then he told me he was six feet six inches tall.

We kept talking, and soon Robert became panicky. He appeared to have frightened himself with all his emotions. My sense was that he was terrified of getting off the phone because he thought this would make me think he didn't like me. "Why don't you just hang up?" I said. "We're going to see each other tomorrow. I'm tired, too." He became overwhelmed again. I could literally feel the phone lines shivering with his relief.

I knew how Robert was feeling because I was beginning to figure out that he had a lot in common with my soon-to-be ex. Simply put, these were men who had grown up with mothers who made them take care of them emotionally. Then, as adults, they hooked up with women who were equally needy. They can't help it, these men. It's all they know of love.

What seemed different with Robert was that he was letting me help. He was letting me participate. My husband never seemed to need me, which made me feel kind of useless. Ever since our breakup, I had been in the mood for someone high-maintenance. I had energy to spare.

A lot of people knew about my date the next day. I had friends in L.A., and several of them called to make sure I had been able to get a pedicure appointment. Other friends wrote to warn me not to have sex on the first date. My friend Nelson joked that I would show up with one leg raised in the air. It's not that I'm particularly easy or anything. I hardly ever go on dates. It's just that when I do find someone I like, I don't like to wait around. ME WANT PENIS! NOW!

I was nervous and sweating as I got ready that night, and stuck a paper towel under my white sundress. Then I took a picture of myself for the journal. Robert called to say that he would be fifteen minutes late due to a parking snafu in his lot. I didn't answer, just listened to the message.

He was exactly fifteen minutes late. He drove a silver Nissan Sentra station wagon, which he parked on the street in front of my house. He knocked, and I opened the door. He was standing with his shoulder to me, holding a bowl of tomatoes. He was definitely six-six, and dressed very well. I was mortified that I had ever thought of him as a toad. He had a beard and brown eyes and sun in his skin.

I invited him in and he gave me the tomatoes. They were from his mother's garden. He had visited her earlier in the day to get his cooler for our beach trip the next morning. On the tomatoes, which were yellow, he had written my initials in red: AFE. There were a couple of tiny flowers stuck in there, too.

He wouldn't stop staring at me. I asked him if he wanted a tour of my house, and he said sure. I showed him the kitchen, then my bedroom. He looked around, then said, "May I kiss your hand?" I said, "You can kiss my cheek."

We drove to the restaurant where Robert had made reservations. I informed him that I was sweating, but did not tell him about the paper towel. I told him that I was aware of the fact that I was acting like a robot, and that I would probably calm down eventually. He said, "Would it help if I told you I didn't care about sweating?" and I said no.

At the restaurant, I understood that I was sweating because he was the most handsome man I had ever gone out with, and this was making me nervous since I wanted to keep going out with a handsome man. Also, he wasn't boring, and his hands were giant. I commented on them, and he reached one across the table so I could touch it. I wondered how it was that he could perform simple tasks like typing or untying a knot.

We had a hard time not talking about our marriages, so we talked about them. In a way, it was a relief. Not so much what was said, but just to be with someone who understood the concept that discussing spouses didn't mean you wanted to be with them. Even gone, they're a huge part of your life. You can't just erase them.

A couple of times I tried to get him to elaborate on different things, but he wouldn't. He said he was worried about being boring. He said his wife had told him he was boring. I had told my husband he was boring, but didn't mention this. One woman's trash is another woman's treasure.

After dinner, we went outside to get the car. It was parked right in front of us on the street, but the valet had the keys, and he wasn't around. Robert had put his arm around me as we walked out of the restaurant, and now he had both arms around me, and was pulling me to him. He said, "I really want to kiss you now, but I'm going to wait until we get home." I said okay. Then he kissed me. He had a big tongue and he was sloppy and a licker. But he was slow, too, and bossy, and his giant hands were all over me. This was ardor. This was something I had never once known.

We went to the beach the next day. Robert had packed a picnic. He had an umbrella. He had a blanket. I wore my bathing suit under a pair of white sweat pants. I was nervous about the cellulite on the back of my legs. I wondered how much cellulite Robert's wife had had.

It was hard for Robert not to touch me as we drove. He was quickly developing a habit of hurling himself into my lap at every red light. He seemed to want to be stroked and petted. We stopped at a Mc-Donald's so I could pee, and when we were walking back to the car, he lifted up his shirt and held it there. I said, "Why are you holding your shirt up?" and he said, "Because I want you to rub my tummy." I said, "I'm not rubbing your tummy in public," and he said, "IT'S THE BEACH!" We laughed. He was the type to laugh heartily about something, then stop, then start up again. I wasn't that type, but I pretended to be so I could join in.

At the beach I offered to carry the umbrella down to the water. I didn't really want to, but I was trying to prove that I was independent. Robert had mentioned that he'd had to do everything for his wife.

On the beach, we set up camp and lay down. We started talking and making out. Things got the way they did when you're soaking someone up and you can't get enough of them and time slips by as if there were only twelve hours in a day. The front of Robert's shorts became dotted with semen. I tried to feel the size of him as he pressed against me. I was fearful in the most exciting of ways because of his hands and feet and height.

We went in the water since I had to pee, but nothing came out. It was too cold. Robert suggested I hop on his back and try to pee that way, but it didn't work. I wished it had. I wished I had managed to mark my territory. In the end, he went back to the blanket, while I peed alone in the surf.

On the drive home, we listened to music. Robert was very much into sixties stuff, and played me a song called "All I Need Is You." He got excited about the second verse and said, "Listen, this part is about animals." We then discovered that we both liked the band Guided By Voices. (I've given Robert the fake name of Robert in this essay after Robert Pollard, the singer of that band.) We listened to their seminal CD, *Bee Thousand*, then felt even further kinship when we both wanted to turn it off after the fourth song. He dropped me off at my house on his way to see his therapist.

The next night, Thursday, he told me he loved me. We were facing each other in my bed. We had our clothes on. He said, "Alicia, I'm falling in love with you." I told him that I was falling in love with him, too. A moment later, he said, "Alicia, I love you." I said, "What?" I wasn't sure I'd heard him right. He repeated himself, and I said, "I love you, too."

I wasn't actually sure if I did or not, but I have a policy that if someone tells you they love you, you say it back. I think it's brave to tell someone you love them and you shouldn't be left hanging. Perhaps more important, I don't find love as sacred as most people. I think it often comes quickly and easily. For me to say I loved Robert—or for him to say he loved me—was not so much a revelation as a summation. If we couldn't call the previous week love, then what else would we have called it? Infatuation? A crush? Perhaps. But what an insult. True or not, neither of us was in the mood to think in such low terms.

Later, we made love for the first time. I unzipped his pants and discovered that I was right to have been both fearful and excited.

On Sunday, we had dinner with my friends Josh and Tina and a friend of theirs. At the table, Robert whispered in my ear that he was so glad to be there with me, that he'd never been so proud to be with a woman. When we got back to my place (which he had begun to call the Treehouse, since trees were what you saw outside the windows of my bedroom), he carried me upstairs, dumped me on the bed, then informed me that he wanted to be my boyfriend. He asked if I would be his girlfriend, and I laughed. I wasn't so much drunk as happy. I loved his velocity. I felt I had finally met my match.

On Monday morning, we played Scrabble. I won. I took a picture of the board for posterity.

On Tuesday, we went to the beach again. This beach was more secluded than the first. We were the only ones there for most of the day. We took a long walk at the beginning, talking about how great it would be to own a beach house. I thought he might've been slightly irritated with me for whining about all the rocks I had to climb over. He held my hand whenever necessary, but maybe he was wishing I wasn't such a baby.

We got back to the blanket and lay down, wrapping our arms around each other. This was how we spent most of our time. Occasionally he fretted that I would find him too needy, too clingy. I said nothing. I was in the market for needy and clingy. I couldn't conceive of my good fortune.

We talked all afternoon. He told me about how when he was a kid, he would always interfere with his much older brother Curt's makeout sessions on the couch. Eventually Curt took him on a picnic, where he explained, "You might not believe this, Robert, but one day you're going to want to be alone with a girl."

Robert also said he'd had a terrible time adjusting to college. It had taken him a couple of years to really make the transition. He said, "You know how everyone always says they hated high school but loved college? Well, I loved high school. I never wanted to leave."

I understood then that Robert and I were very different people— that his looks had not only allowed him to charm Curt's dates but had let him coast through a period that was the worst of my life.

We went swimming, and I sat in Robert's lap in the water, facing away from him and looking out to sea. He put his hands on my hips and murmured, "You were built for sex."

We watched a woman in the surf nearby getting photographed. The waves kept jerking her top around, and finally she just took it off. When we got out of the water, I took mine off, too. It occurred to me that I could've gone topless all day and it wouldn't have mattered. I stayed topless for a short while, then changed into dry clothes. Robert said he could watch me walk around in a T-shirt and no bra for hours.

We stopped and had some cheap Mexican food on the way home. As we sat outside at the plastic table, I said, "You know what I like?" Robert said what, and I said, "I like how when I'm with you, I don't have the feeling of needing to keep my options open." I thought Robert would agree. We were always in agreement about how much we liked each other. But he didn't say anything. I felt instantly ashamed for liking him more than he liked me.

In the car on the way home, I tried desperately to sing some songs. Robert was musical and I wanted to impress him. My husband had always said I had a nice voice. I knew what I was really thinking: if I can sing perfectly, Robert won't want to keep his options open, either.

But I kept going off-key. Robert was sympathetic. He said, "Now you know how I feel when I can't stay hard. I know I'm capable of it, but it just isn't happening."

It was true. He was having problems during sex. I didn't think much of it because I didn't care. There was too much else going on to enjoy. I figured his problem would iron itself out. And it wasn't that he always had it. Sometimes he had it, sometimes he didn't. When he had it, though, he became obsessed with the idea that I would think he didn't find me attractive. This would've been impossible, and I told him so. I'd never felt so attractive in my life.

He spent the next day, Wednesday, cleaning his studio apartment in preparation for my first visit that evening. I walked in to find his paintings covering the walls. Most of them were pretty good, and I told him so. I would've said this even if they hadn't been, but it was nice to feel like I didn't have to lie.

He took me out to eat at his favorite local restaurant, a place with a seafaring theme. The food wasn't too good, but Robert said we were there for the atmosphere.

At one point when I was trying to tell him something, he rubbed my back and said, "Little baby." We were filled with endearments for each other. I often forgot his name, which was not nearly as meaningful as baby, honey, dearest, or sweetie. Whatever I was to him was always prefaced with "little." Little Person, Little Squirrel, Little Baby. I am not little. I am five feet ten inches in heels, and I'm almost always in heels. But Robert's height rendered everyone tiny. An airplane looking at ants. There was something incredibly precious to me about getting to be small again at thirty-eight.

We went back to his apartment, and I read him a short story I'd written that had just come out in *Penthouse*. I'd meant to impress him, but my sense was that he didn't really like it. Even so, we started to have sex afterward. It was all wonderful until he went soft. Then he became exhausted. He brought out his futon, which he kept in a cardboard box in the corner of the room, and we lay down on it. He began a discussion about how we needed to slow down. He said he wanted what we had to last longer than three weeks, and that he felt like he was burning the candle at both ends. He wanted us to pace ourselves. None of this sounded right to me, and I started to cry.

He said, "You think I'm saying let's go from ninety to zero. But I'm saying let's go from ninety to sixty." I understood his point, but those thirty miles terrified me. They were filled with a loss of momentum, whirlwind, passion. It was like dousing a fire with water, as opposed to letting it burn down to embers.

Robert continued to reassure me, but I was off in my own world of panic now. No matter what he said, I knew I was getting dumped.

When I couldn't stop crying, he suggested we get some sleep. I lay down with him, stiff as a board. I rolled partway off the skimpy mattress and onto the floor, and he didn't do anything about it. I wanted to go home and start getting over the breakup. When I told Robert I was thinking of leaving, he said he didn't understand. He had bought fruit for breakfast. Why was I going?

240 ♥ Alicia Erian

I didn't understand how I would ever manage to remain in a situation where someone else would be in charge of the pace. I saw my future as one in which I would be making constant requests for love, and these would be fulfilled or denied as Robert saw fit. I saw my heart breaking with every denial.

Robert took me home. I didn't talk. He insisted on walking me in when we got there, and I fantasized that he would take it all back and stay because he was afraid of losing me. But the power had shifted. He'd tested me and I'd failed. Instead of staying at his house and having breakfast and ignoring his boring proclamation, I had opted to reveal that I would die if he left me. Whoops.

I tried a bunch of different things before he left. I got angry and told him I really resented how fast he had made the whole thing go. I cried. I dried my eyes and acted resigned. I was trying to find the one way that would change all of this.

He left, and I cried some more. I went in the bathroom and started hitting myself in the head and telling myself that no one would ever love me. Then I got it together and went down to the kitchen table to write Robert an e-mail. I apologized for not handling things well and said I'd try to do better. I called my friend Ben in Boston, who was an early riser, and asked him to call me back. He did. I knew he would help because he had an ex-wife who was sort of like me in terms of her pathology. Ben had a high tolerance for pathology. So he listened to me cry and told me he couldn't say whether Robert would be able to handle this or not. That wasn't particularly comforting, but what was comforting was to have him not be disgusted by me.

In the morning there was an e-mail from Robert saying nice things about how he would hang in there while I had my reaction. He thanked me for writing and telling him I was upset, which was the opposite of his ex-wife's approach, which was not to speak to him for two weeks. I felt a little better. I felt that since he was praising my honesty, it would be a good idea to give him more. I wrote and told him about hitting myself in the head. I added a nice bit about a recurring fantasy I have about being whacked in the head with a baseball bat. He wrote back and said he didn't know what to do to help me. His tone was cold. I was instantly ashamed. I had only wanted more praise.

I tried to call him but he wouldn't pick up. I left a message. He called back and said he hadn't picked up because he'd thought I was going to yell at him, like his ex-wife would've. I said, "Why would I yell at you?" After that was settled, he turned mean. I asked him if he was angry, and he said a little. I asked him why, and he was quiet for a moment, then said, "You made me responsible for your physical safety. I worried that you would hurt yourself." I apologized profusely. I was desperate. I had been in the throes of desperation since the night before, and it wasn't helping me in the least, but I was still answering to it, still in its hold. Not only did I apologize for that, I threw in some extra bonus apologies for anything I could think of, since apologies not only seemed to calm him down but also made him cry. For example, I apologized for saying that he had set the pace for the relationship, and admitted that I had been a full participant. He wept as he said, "You and I have this in common, Alicia: integrity." I thought, no we don't, because I really do think you set the pace for the relationship. But that didn't matter since now we had integrity in common, and maybe that would bring him back.

I had a reading that night, the one I'd invited him to on the evening we met. We had planned that he would drive me there, but now he was so upset, he said he didn't know if he could come. I didn't want to force him, but Trent was going to be there, and Robert was much taller and more handsome, and I wanted to show off that I'd moved on. It wasn't just that. I thought that if he saw me read and do my charming Q&A, he'd fall back in love with me. I was resorting to my tiny bit of celebrity.

In the end, we decided I would drive myself and he would drive himself; afterward, he could go home with the friends he'd invited, and his gay Uncle Rex, who was also coming.

I got lost on the way to the reading and sweated like a fool. When I finally arrived, the first person I saw was Trent. I felt more warmly toward him than I had anticipated, and dumped my camera in his lap, telling him it was his job to take pictures. Then I went over to say hello to Robert. "Hi, sweetie," he said, smiling, and I imagined we were doing better already. I met Uncle Rex, who was sitting beside him, and made a mental note to win him over later. He seemed like someone who might advocate for me with his nephew. I was out of my mind with cockamamie schemes.

The bookstore was Armenian, and it was the biggest audience I'd ever had outside of a bar. I read well, conducted a lively Q&A, then had twenty-five individual conversations with twenty-five sweet Armenians who had all bought books and wanted them signed. This took a while, and as I did my thing, I could hear Robert milling about, collecting people to go out to a bar afterward. He wasn't going to head home after all. Again, more relief.

In the bar, it was me, three of Robert's friends, and a few of the Armenians. I knew Robert wanted me to talk to his friends, so I did, but it was difficult because two of them were under twenty-five. They were the same age as my students at Wellesley. I ended up career counseling one of them.

At one point I got up and played pool with Robert's oldest friend, who was Japanese, and an Armenian woman. Robert's friend told me that he knew he was breaking "best friend etiquette" but that he hoped he would get to see me again. Later he leaned into me and said, "You're everything he said you were." I was over the moon. Maybe it was ridiculous to think that Uncle Rex might advocate for me, but here was someone who clearly would.

The evening wrapped up, and I couldn't find my car. Someone else had parked it. So Robert drove me around looking for it. We found it, and had a boring kiss good-bye. I knew we wouldn't stay together that night. I knew it was part of the plan to pull back. Only I had no idea how to pull back after so much tumbling forward. I got in my car and drove too quickly away from Robert. I knew he would read this as being angry like his ex-wife, but I couldn't help it.

The next morning, I had a meeting on the production lot. It went well. I told hilarious jokes about me and Trent, leaving out the part about how we weren't working together anymore because I had misread him, made a pass, and now he was nervous to be around me. In the middle of the meeting there was a call, and when I checked my messages afterward, it was Robert. He said nice things about the reading the night before, then wanted to know if I would meet with him and his niece sometime that day. I was enraged. I didn't understand how any of this was pulling back. Seeing each other two days in a row? Meeting more family members? It made no sense. I went shopping and tried to calm down.

After dropping $700 on two pairs of shoes, I called him back. He warned me that he couldn't talk for very long because his niece would be arriving at any moment, and I warned him that I couldn't talk for very long because I was in the middle of buying exercise pants with a gusseted crotch. We made plans to meet for dinner, and when he hung up, he called me "kiddo."

That night, he and his niece picked me up. He kept trying to get us to tell each other things about ourselves. It seemed important to him. Then he took us to a Polish restaurant. I sat in the backseat so his niece could sit up front. I have a beloved young uncle, and when I was younger, I hated every one of his girlfriends.

On the way home, when it became clear that Robert was going to drop me off first, I got depressed. Then, at my place, he parked and he and his niece came inside. I hadn't invited them and didn't know what to do when they were there. I asked if they wanted to play Scrabble, and they both said yes. Robert said, "Are you sure we won't be cramping your style if we stay?" I said no, and wished he would stop flip-flopping on the pulling back.

While we played, Robert spent a lot of time gazing meaningfully into my eyes and squeezing my hand under the table. I knew he was trying to convey his commitment to me, and I wished I could tell him that the best way to do this would be to stop making trouble where there wasn't any.

I lost the game. After we packed it up, Robert instructed his niece to wait for him in the car. Then he told me he was worried about me, which made me feel sick. It was bad news when a man worried about you. They wouldn't fuck anyone they thought was pathetic. The worst part was, in my own stupid way, I felt like I was starting to get a little stronger. I had made plans to go shopping with my friend Andrea the next day, and thought this indicated some sort of independence. Robert asked if we could talk when I got home from shopping, and I said I'd call him.

I felt okay when I woke up the next morning. Not great, but like I might be able to make my way over this hurdle. I might've even sung in the car on the way to Orange County.

At the mall, I bought Robert: a Sensa pen, a Deluxe Scrabble board (he only had the plain kind, with no grooves), a pale green shirt, a box of chocolates, a box of Australian apricots, and two personalized bike license plates reading *Robert* and *Alicia*. I knew I was going overboard, but with each purchase, I had a sense that I was making an investment, that I would see some returns.

Andrea was skeptical. She didn't criticize me for the gifts, but I could tell she also didn't like the sound of Robert. I have very protective friends, and none of them like the sound of anyone who doesn't know how lucky he is to be with me. I told Andrea that he did know, but that he was just scared. She said something like "Uh-huh."

I called Robert on the way home, as promised. There was no answer. When I walked in my house at around 11 P.M., I found an e-mail from him. He said that I was a wonderful woman, then listed my various attributes. He then said that he could see from my intense response to his simple request for space that we would not be in a position to have a healthy relationship. Then he dumped me.

This was Saturday night. I had come home thinking we would talk things out, and I would offer my more sensible, centered self as a kind of gift. I would maybe even go over to his place and give him his presents. Now I could see that none of this was going to happen.

I wrote him an e-mail asking didn't I have a say in any of this, and couldn't we talk it over? I pointed out the fact that he was always saying we were in this together. When I woke the next morning, there was no reply. I was very depressed. It was terrible to have gotten my bearings only to find I was too late. I called my friend Laura and bawled. In the middle of our talk, Robert wrote. He said yes, that I could have a say in this, that we could talk things over.

A half hour later he was on my front steps. I invited him in, and we hugged. He went and sat in a chair, and I sat in his lap until he told me I was too heavy and to get off. I took the chair next to him, and he put his head in my lap. He sat up after a while and said he didn't have anything to say. He said he would just stare at me if I didn't mind.

Later, we went upstairs to lie down. We wrapped our arms around each other, which was something that still felt right. He said, "I'm not going to do more because I don't know how things are going to turn out." I nodded. Then he tried to have sex with me. He couldn't stay hard. He flopped back on the bed, strangely satisfied. "Nope," he said. "It just isn't going to work."

Finally he told me that he couldn't be a boyfriend right now. Not just to me, but to anyone. I said okay. He said, "Aren't you going to yell at me?" I said, "For what?" Then he said that he didn't believe I existed.

We spent the rest of the afternoon together. We ate, we window-shopped, I bought a pair of cowboy boots. He draped himself over me the entire time. I paraded around in my boots, and he couldn't take his eyes off me. He seemed happy. I thought this was because we were getting back together. I thought that maybe all he had needed was to say things to me that would've crushed his ex-wife, and if I held up, I would get him back. I really and truly thought this.

He dropped me off that night, explaining what he would be doing for the rest of the evening. I knew he explained this because he wanted me to know why he couldn't spend more time with me. Then he said to call him tomorrow when I was done working on the script, so we could make plans to hang out.

The next day when I called him, we made plans to play Scrabble, then for him to go off to band practice and for me to do script work, then for the two of us to meet up again to go to a movie. "There's just one thing," he said.

"What?" I said.

"I really can't be your boyfriend. I mean, I want to do all this stuff with you. But I can't be your boyfriend."

I understood everything then. I opened my mouth and said the things I would need to say in order to respect myself at a later date. I began with, "Then, maybe we need to end it right now." I went on to tell Robert that I thought he had treated me poorly. That he had gone too fast, making me think it was safe to involve myself heavily, then pulled back and left me hanging. I said that I thought it was a shame to throw away what we had. I said there was only one reason to keep seeing each other that week, which was my final week in L.A. He jumped on this. "What?" he said excitedly. I said, "Well, if you think you might be able to be a boyfriend at some point in the future." He paused, then said, "No, I don't think I'd be interested in that." I said that he needed to come over and get his stuff.

We hung up, and I went around the apartment, putting things in a bag. There was the electric toothbrush I'd gotten him, two of the photographs he'd brought over for me to keep during my stay, his Scrabble board. I looked at all the wrapped presents I hadn't given him in my bedroom cupboard, then shut the door. The license plates were tucked in a card I'd written to him the day before in which I'd said that relationships were like art, and that you often had to make a mess before you made something beautiful. It didn't make sense to give him that now. He had quit at the mess.

He arrived, and I gave him the bag. I cried, and he hugged me. He cried, too. He said I was incredible, and I said, "Not incredible enough." I clung to him. He said he would love to be friends, if I ever felt up to it. I had no idea what to say to that. Even he seemed ashamed. Then he said, "I'd better go," and he left.

That was on a Monday. I cried almost all day, every day, for the rest of the week. Saturday was my birthday. I turned thirty-eight. Some friends held a beautiful party, and I went and did a good job of not being depressed. Then I went back to my rented house and packed to leave.

On the plane the next morning, I didn't know where I was. I didn't know why I was leaving one place and going to another. I knew I had to start teaching soon, but that didn't seem important enough to travel for.

At Logan Airport, my friend Beth picked me up. She was so happy to see me, and I told her that I hated Boston and that it was ugly and terrible and that I didn't want to be here. She fell silent and I apologized.

At home, I panicked. I still didn't understand what I was doing there. The panic was as strong as when my husband and I first broke up. I had no idea what to do. I became hysterical. Finally, I called my friend Laura. She said we would talk this thing through, and she would stay up all night with me, if I needed it.

I had known Robert for eighteen days. That was it. I wish I could say that those eighteen days didn't render me catatonic for a month afterward. I wish I could say that a terrible depression didn't set in after the catatonia. I wish I could say that at least I managed to give Trent an excellent script. But he hated what I gave him. It was about herpes, which I guess isn't very Hollywood. I wish I could say that I don't think about Robert anymore.

What I think about is picking him up at Logan Airport. I think about jumping into his arms and wrapping my legs around his waist. I think about being his baby again, and Robert calling me little, and Robert finally understanding that it's wrong to hurt people who are smaller than you.

The Composite Boyfriend

Audrey Niffenegger

I met him at the Isabella Gardner Museum in Boston, where he worked as a guard. I met him in a class I was taking. I met him at a school where we both taught. I met him at a party; we smiled at each other across a crowded room. We were introduced to each other by our mutual friend Paula, an Austrian immigrant who had escaped from the Nazis as a young girl.

I asked him a question about a painting; we chatted; we went out to a club that night; afterward I brought him to meet my best friend, who was ill and in the hospital. I was taking a trip to Amsterdam, he was Dutch, we went out for coffee so he could tell me what to see when I got to Holland. I ended up spending New Year's Eve with him at his mother's house in Arnhem. I gave him my phone number but accidentally transposed two digits because I had just changed it. He managed to call anyway. I saw him standing alone at a party, smiling at me. "Who's that?" I asked Sylvia, because he was handsome. It was her party. She sighed and told me I didn't want to know him, but she wouldn't tell me why not; I ended up driving him home. I don't remember how we began. Somehow we did.

It was 1985. It was 1997. It was 1992. It was 1996. It was 2001. It was spring, winter, summer, autumn, winter.

He was an artist, a neurobiologist, a writer, a legal secretary, a musician. He was writing his dissertation on Wittgenstein. He was tall and didn't drive; he always wore a blue windbreaker and went everywhere on his bicycle. He was shorter than me and had an accent. Until I got used to it I replied to many of his utterances with "What?" He was extremely good looking, movie-star handsome, but his hands were always quite red, as though he had been boiling them. He smiled a lot and was a good ballroom dancer. He loved the Cubs, barbecued ribs, and high-heeled shoes. He wasn't patient but he was very well-read. He hardly read at all and went to the movies a lot. When he was a child he was obsessed with *Star Wars.* He was obsessed with *A Clockwork Orange.* His parents were divorced, and had each married people he didn't like. His father had died the year before we met; one day I went over to his apartment and saw a *yahrzeit* candle burning for his dad.

I loved listening to him practice the flute. His apartment had almost no furnishings, and the sound filled the rooms and reverberated in my chest. I didn't think he was attractive except when he was absorbed in drawing or watching TV or concentrating on what someone else was saying. Then his face was transformed; it was wise. I liked driving him places, having aimless conversations, smoking sometimes despite his asthma. He always drove fast, as though we were late for a movie.

He made beautiful photographs. He was writing a novel about a man with eidetic memory. He had terrific hair. He was going bald. He didn't have any tattoos.

The sex was great, the sex was okay, the sex was a huge problem. The religious scruples, the foot fetish, the antidepressants, the porn addiction, the irrational fear of STDs, the lack of sleep, the boredom of monogamy, inexperience, mismatched expectations.

We talked about getting married. I was standing in a dirty phone booth in Penland, North Carolina, talking to him long-distance in Boston when he proposed. I waited eagerly for him to ask me to marry him, but he never did. He proposed when it was too late, after I'd left him. I knew it was going nowhere, we had no future. I kept hoping, even when it was obvious that he was going to dump me.

The obsessive-compulsive disorder he hid so brilliantly: he lived like a deranged squirrel, all his possessions wrapped in plastic and stored in Tupperware containers stacked up to the ceiling. He was recently divorced, but insisted he was over it. He mentioned his ex a lot. He lived across the country, and stopped calling. Three months later he called at 2 A.M., drunk, asking if he could borrow money. He placed a personals ad while we were still dating; a friend showed it to me; I called the number and left a message. We never spoke again. We were getting into bed one night when he said, "I think we should see other people." He was already dating someone else. He found me sexually boring and stopped touching me. I found him unattractive and refused to sleep with him.

It ended.

We are still friends. We go to the movies sometimes, or out for dinner. He called once years later. We don't speak. He and his wife sat next to me in a café; I ignored them and they asked for another table. We once considered getting back together, but thought better of it.

Next time he will be perfect. Next time.

Acknowledgments

Many people contributed to making this book a reality, and I thank them all, most especially Mary Stewart Hammond, who believed in this book from the second she heard about it, and who went to valiant lengths to help it see the light of the day. I owe you big-time, Mary Stewart.

My marvelous agent, Miriam Altshuler, has truly been there for me and for this book. I couldn't have done it without you, Miriam.

That goes double for my husband, Jamie Young. It took me a while, but I am finally learning the difference between Mr. Wrong and Mr. Right.

Thanks are also due my terrific editor, Nancy Miller, whose eagle eye and red pencil have made this a far, far better book than it otherwise would have been. I am also grateful for support and help of various kinds from Noelle Rydell, Janice Eidus, Yona Zeldis McDonough, Joan Laurion, Joan Fischer, Nancy Holyoke, Laura Kearney, Pamela Reilly, and Marilyn Annucci.

Finally, this book is for all the women (and men) who have shared their experiences with me. Telling our stories is what we do to feel less alone.

About the Authors

Diana Abu-Jaber's food memoir, *The Language of Baklava*, was a *Book-List* Editor's Choice pick. Her second novel, *Crescent*, won the PEN Center Award for literary fiction and the Before Columbus Foundation American Book Award, and was named a Notable Book of the Year by *The Christian Science Monitor*. Her first novel, *Arabian Jazz*, won the Oregon Book award. She is a professor at Portland State University and lives part-time in Miami.

Christiane Bird is the author of *Neither East Nor West: One Woman's Journey Through the Islamic Republic of Iran* and *A Thousand Sighs, A Thousand Revolts: Journeys in Kurdistan*. She is currently working on *Two Sultans and a Princess*, a story of romance, slavery, and geopolitics set in nineteenth-century Oman, Germany, and Zanzibar.

Harriet Brown is the author of *The Promised Land*, a chapbook of poems, and a number of nonfiction books, including *The Good-bye Window* and *Madison Walks*. Her work has appeared in *The New York Times, Poetry, Prairie Schooner, Vogue, Ms.*, and other magazines and newspapers. She lives in Madison, Wisconsin, with her husband and two daughters. Her website is www.harrietbrown.com.

Sara Ekks is the pseudonym for a writer who lives and works in Chicago. She would like to meet a guy who supports himself and puts out.

Alicia Erian's work has appeared in *Playboy, Zoetrope, Nerve, The Iowa Review, The New York Times Magazine,* and other publications. She is the author of *The Brutal Language of Love,* a short-story collection, and the novel *Towelhead.*

Susan Jane Gilman is the author of the bestselling memoir *Hypocrite in a Pouffy White Dress* and the humorous feminist tome *Kiss My Tiara: How to Rule the World as a SmartMouth Goddess.* She has written for *The New York Times,* the *Los Angeles Times, Ms., Real Simple,* and *Us,* among others, and has won awards for her short fiction. She currently resides in Geneva, Switzerland, as an opinionated lady in a neutral country—though she remains, eternally, a child of New York.

Ann Hood is the author of seven novels, including *The Knitting Circle* and *Somewhere Off the Coast of Maine*; a memoir, *Do Not Go Gentle*; and a collection of short stories, *An Ornithologist's Guide to Life.* She's the winner of two Pushcart Prizes for nonfiction, a Best American Spiritual Writing Award, and the Paul Bowles Prize for Short Fiction.

Michelle Huneven is the author of the novels *Round Rock* and *Jamesland.* Last year, at fifty-two, she married Mr. Right. So don't give up hope.

Raphael Kadushin is senior acquisitions editor at the University of Wisconsin Press and contributing editor at *Bon Appetit.* His award-winning travel journalism appears regularly in a range of magazines—among them *National Geographic Traveler, Condé Nast Traveler, Town & Country Travel,* and *Out Traveler*—and his books include the critically lauded anthology *Wonderlands: Good Gay Travel Writing.* He is currently completing a novel.

Dana Kinstler's fiction won *The Missouri Review*'s Editors' Prize in 2000, and has also appeared in *Mississippi Review*; she contributed to the anthology *My Father Married Your Mother.* She is working on a collection of linked stories and a novel, and lives with her husband and two daughters in the Hudson River Valley.

Caroline Leavitt is book columnist for *The Boston Globe* and the author of eight novels, most recently *Girls in Trouble*. The winner of a New York Foundation of the Arts Award in Fiction, she was also a National Magazine Award nominee and a finalist in the Nickelodeon Screenwriting Fellowship, and she won second prize in the 2005 Goldenberg Prize for Fiction. She lives in Hoboken, New Jersey, with her husband, the writer Jeff Tamarkin, and their young son, Max. Her website is www.caroline leavitt.com.

Marilyn Jaye Lewis is the award-winning author of *Neptune & Surf,* a trio of erotic novellas. Her short stories and novellas have been translated into French, Italian, and Japanese. Her popular erotic romance novels include *When Hearts Collide, In the Secret Hours,* and *When the Night Stood Still.* She is the founder of the Erotic Authors Association. Upcoming novels include *Freak Parade, A Killing on Mercy Road,* and *Twilight of the Immortal.*

Joyce Maynard has worked as a reporter with *The New York Times,* a syndicated columnist, a magazine journalist, a radio commentator for NPR's *All Things Considered,* and a novelist. Her novel *To Die For* was adapted into a film directed by Gus Van Sant, starring Nicole Kidman. She has published two volumes of memoir, including the bestselling *At Home in the World,* which was translated into nine languages. Her most recent work of nonfiction is *Internal Combustion: The True Story of a Marriage and a Murder in Motor City.* Her five novels include *The Usual Rules,* named one of the ten best young adult books of 2003. Maynard performs frequently with The Moth, a New York City–based group dedicated to the art of personal performance storytelling, and serves on the faculty of The Stonecoast Writers' Program, a low-residency M.F.A. writing program based in Maine. Her website is www.joycemaynard.com.

Jacquelyn Mitchard is the *New York Times* bestselling author of *The Deep End of the Ocean, A Theory of Relativity,* and *The Breakdown Lane,* along with seven other books for adults and children. She is a syndicated newspaper columnist and a contributing editor for *Wondertime* magazine. She lives with her husband and seven children near Madison, Wisconsin.

Audrey Niffenegger is the author of *The Time Traveler's Wife* and the illustrated novel *The Three Incestuous Sisters*. In addition to being a bestselling novelist, Niffenegger is a printmaker, painter, photographer, bookbinder, and collagist; she also makes drawings. Her work is in the collections of the Newberry Library, the National Museum of Women in the Arts, the Library of Congress, the Houghton Library at Harvard University, and Temple University, among others. She is a full-time professor in the Interdisciplinary Book Arts M.F.A. Program at the Columbia College Chicago Center for Book and Paper Arts, where she teaches writing, letterpress printing, and fine-edition book production.

Whitney Otto is the author of *How to Make an American Quilt, The Passion Dream Book,* and other novels. She was born and raised in southern California. She says, "A New Age friend recently told me that my husband and I have been together a very long time, since we were first married in rural Ireland in the fifteenth century, to which we replied, 'Yeah, tell us about it.' "

Marge Piercy is the author of seventeen novels, most recently *Sex Wars*. She has also published seventeen books of poetry; her most recent is *The Crooked Inheritance*. She is also the author of a memoir, *Sleeping with Cats*. Her work has been translated into sixteen languages. She gives a great many readings and workshops, and some lectures.

Roxana Robinson is the author of seven books, most recently *A Perfect Stranger*, a collection of stories. She has received fellowships from the NEA and the Guggenheim Foundation. Her work has appeared in *The New Yorker, The Atlantic, Harper's, The New York Times*, and elsewhere.

Ntozake Shange is the author of "for colored girls who have considered suicide/when the rainbow is enuf: a choreopoem," which won an Obie and was nominated for Tony, Grammy, and Emmy awards. She's published three novels: *Sassafras, Cypress and Indigo* (a PEN/Faulkner nominee), *Betsey Brown*, and *Liliane: Resurrection of the Daughter*. She has a new novel forthcoming entitled *How I Come by This Crying Song*, which she co-wrote with her sister, Ifa Byeza.

Jane Smiley's most recent book is *Thirteen Ways of Looking at the Novel*. She has written many novels and books of nonfiction, including *A Thousand Acres*, which won a Pulitzer Prize. She lives in California.

Ethel Morgan Smith is an associate professor of English at West Virginia University and the author of *From Whence Cometh My Help: The African American Community at Hollins College*. Smith is also the recipient of many fellowships and awards, including a Fulbright to the University of Tuebingen in Germany; a Rockefeller Foundation Fellowship in Bellagio, Italy; a grant from the National Endowment for the Humanities; and a research fellowship at the Women's Research Center at Brandeis University. Her writing has been published in national and international journals.

Catherine Texier is the author of four novels—*Chloé l'Atlantique, Panic Blood, Love Me Tender*, and *Victorine*—and a memoir, *Breakup*. She was coeditor of the literary magazine *Between C and D* and is the recipient of a National Endowment for the Arts Award and two New York Foundation for the Arts fellowships. Her work has been translated into ten languages. She lives in New York City.

Robin Westen is an Emmy Award–winning writer and the author of four books. She has been published in dozens of national magazines including *Glamour, More, Good Housekeeping*, and *Psychology Today*, and lives in Vermont with her husband and son.

NPR commentator **Marion Winik** is the author of *Above Us Only Sky, First Comes Love, The Lunchbox Chronicles*, and other books. She lives in Pennsylvania with Mr. Right, who is a miniature dachshund, as well as her anarchist troublemaker husband and their many children.

About the Type

This book was set in Garamond, a typeface originally designed by the Parisian typecutter Claude Garamond (1480–1561). This version of Garamond was modeled on a 1592 specimen sheet from the Egenolff-Berner foundry, which was produced from types assumed to have been brought to Frankfurt by the punchcutter Jacques Sabon.

Claude Garamond's distinguished romans and italics first appeared in *Opera Ciceronis* in 1543–44. The Garamond types are clear, open, and elegant.